SAVOY! CORSICA! TUNIS!

In the Oasis of Gabès

SAVOY! CORSICA! TUNIS!

Mussolini's Dream Lands

by

BERNARD NEWMAN

Author of
"*Baltic Roundabout*," "*Ride to Russia*,"
"*Spy*," *etc., etc.*

HERBERT JENKINS LIMITED
3 DUKE OF YORK STREET, ST. JAMES'S,
LONDON, S.W.1.

A
HERBERT
JENKINS'
BOOK

First Printing 1940

Printed in Great Britain by
Wyman & Sons, Ltd., London, Fakenham and Reading.

CONTENTS

ILLUSTRATIONS

ILLUSTRATIONS

INTRODUCTION

EVERY summer I look for trouble. Year after year
tragedy has descended on the countries through which
I have passed. Usually my choice has been deliberate—
it was not difficult, years ahead, to prophesy stormy days
for Spain, Albania, Poland, Czechoslovakia, Roumania,
and the Baltic States. Occasionally I ran into trouble
by accident, for I scarcely expected it to come so soon
to Finland.

In 1939 my choice was easy. "Savoy! Nice! Corsica!
Tunis!" had shouted the Italian deputies, setting a new
fashion in diplomatic usage. Already I had been looking
anxiously at the Western Mediterranean. The outburst
of the well-paid male voice chorus made strife inevitable:
the only unsettled question was the date.

So in the summer of 1939 I set off to glance at the
disputed territories. I had one anxiety—would my
journey be completed in time? Since the seizure of
Czechoslovakia war had become inevitable, only postponed from crisis to crisis. So much I could foresee.
I was even confident that Mussolini would not enter the
war until he was convinced that Hitler had won. Since
I did not think that Hitler would win, I considered that
the question of Savoy, Nice, Corsica, and Tunis might be
raised by Italy with a suggestion of buying off: that
France might even offer some concessions in Tunis in
return for Italian neutrality. What I could not foresee
was that France would collapse at a single blow.

On my way out to Savoy I passed through other
provinces which were quite certain to be included in the

scene of strife; and, in spite of the title of the book, out of sheer generosity I throw in a superficial sketch of Alsace-Lorraine.

*　　　*　　　*　　　*　　　*

I set off in unusual circumstances. The rape of Czechoslovakia and the certainty of war had suggested in the spring of 1939 that I should increase my life insurance. Yet, to my amazement, I was turned down flat. When I demanded reasons, the company quite properly referred me to my own doctor.

Unfortunately, I had no doctor. Except for war wounds, the last time I needed the services of a doctor was at the age of four, when I had measles. Since then I have been classed in the 'husky' category so far as health is concerned.

However, I nearly always do as I am told, so consulted a practitioner. To my surprise, he treated me very gravely: I had serious blood pressure, and a tired heart— had over-worked it severely. He gave me a strict diet, and this I promised to maintain. His further instructions were more difficult: I must take things very easily, must not do anything energetic, must not walk uphill, and should keep out of the sun: a nice lazy summer, in fact. When I suggested riding a bicycle he held up his hands in horror; then devoted another quarter of an hour to emphasis of the seriousness of the position. I gathered that I was liable to drop dead at any moment.

Maybe in his anxiety to persuade me to be careful he went a little too far; if I must drop dead, why not on George?

*　　　*　　　*　　　*　　　*

So I accepted the diet and dropped the rest of his instructions. The general route I had planned contradicted every one of the doctor's ideas. But how could a man sit down and rest in the summer of 1939, when Europe was rushing madly towards war? I set off to ride across those pleasant places which were so obviously doomed to be the scenes of strife.

My plans were indefinite as ever; my route varied at the slightest incident of the wayside. My companion was a bicycle, George: an old companion who is now a friend, and who has never let me down. I could almost believe that George would go on even if my heart failed.

By my contract with the publishers, my expenses must not exceed five shillings a day. It was a bit of a squeeze, for part of the journey passed across tourist country, where five shillings do not go very far. Inexpensive nights in Tunis squared up the average, however, and I came through without breaking my word.

This book is a superficial record of a ride through some of the fairest provinces of France: a last glimpse of the old France—whatever happens, France will never be the same again. As I write, France writhes under the heel of a conqueror, and some of the provinces are designated as the victor's spoils. But the war is not yet over: France has lost, but Hitler has not yet won. The fate of Alsace-Lorraine, Savoy, Nice, Corsica and Tunis will be settled by the British, not by Germans, Italians or French. That is why a glimpse of these debated lands ought to prove of some interest.

BERNARD NEWMAN.

Harrow,
    August, 1940.

CHAPTER ONE

ALSACE-LORRAINE

I

I HAD taken a ticket to Lille, where I had to make a business call. Unfortunately, when I got there I had forgotten the name and address of the man I was to visit, for in my usual casual fashion I had left his letter at home. I sat down in my room in the hotel, determined to use every form of reconstruction which memory training advocates. I found it difficult to concentrate, for there was a fair not a hundred yards away, and the musical accompaniments of French merry-go-rounds are even more discordant and individualistic than their British counterparts. Eventually my battle with memory triumphed, and I sallied forth to make my call. Again I was foiled. Not till I returned home weeks later did I discover that my recollections were only partially correct—I had transposed the name of the man and the street in which he lived.

It was Sunday next morning, and I was surprised therefore when seven priests ensconced themselves in a third class compartment into which I had made an early and somewhat illicit entry before the train actually drew up at the platform. On any other day I would have been prepared for an invasion of priests, but on a Sunday morning one would have imagined them at work curing their souls. However, priests are notoriously good company, and soon we were on friendly terms. In the early stages of the journey six of them dutifully produced religious books; the seventh quite frankly began to talk politics with me, a debate in which the outstanding sextet quickly joined. Soon the debate was more than lively; indeed, at one point I thought that they were going to forget that they were priests, so violently contrasted were their opinions. But they were Frenchmen. No other race can be so furiously indignant over a trifle one minute and so charming the next.

My only complaint about their company concerned their size. I am myself euphemistically described as of generous proportions, but many of the priests were bulky. It was quite impossible to wriggle: I was hemmed in a corner as securely as a sheep between the knees of a shearer. The hard wooden seat began to get very uncomfortable. During a lull in the conversation, therefore, I began to consider where my journey proper should commence.

Savoy, Nice, Corsica and Tunis I had undertaken to explore: yet Savoy, I knew, was mountainous and would demand the hardest labour of George and myself. Of George I entertained no doubts, but my own physical fitness was not of the first grade. During the winter I eat too much and exercise too little. Spring is usually a period of rectification, but it so happened in 1939 I was continuously occupied. Thus it seemed to me to be essential that I should ride for a week to get into condition before tackling the mountain passes of Savoy: I had to harden my heart as well as my muscles.

A glance at the map had settled that difficulty. Alsace was the training ground I needed. An old favourite of mine, I had tramped its valleys more than once in 1919 and 1930.

A few days along the level, a few days toiling among the mountains of the Vosges, then not even Alpine passes need dismay me. But where should I begin?

The growing heat of the day gradually affected the conversation. We ate solid sandwiches, then leaned back silently. The atmosphere was oppressive; when the window was closed the stuffiness was impossible, when it was open we had to endure a continuous bombardment by those particularly vicious black smuts which are a feature of French railway engines. Further, the vivaciousness of the conversation declined under the combined influence of the heat and the soporific effect of food. My original interlocutor still continued to talk, but the others gradually subsided and unashamedly went to sleep. One of them, the fattest of them all, began to snore. That settled it. I can stand nearly everything in the world, but snoring worries me.

"Where are we?" I asked as the train halted. I was looking out of the window, but French station-masters have a knack of disguising the identity of their stations; it is all part of a huge conspiracy to tempt the traveller to go right beyond his intended destination, and then charge him excess fare both ways when he gets back.

"Sedan," announced the priests who were awake.

"Sedan!" I cried. "I get out here."

It was a sudden decision, for I had never intended to get out there. Yet when I considered it, what better place to start my ride than Sedan? I was deliberately following a trail of potential trouble. Why not begin at an ancient scene of battle?

Such was my reasoning. Now I know that my sudden descent from the train was prompted by that evil genius which sends me to places and countries just before trouble afflicts them. I did not know that Sedan was to be the scene of the German break-through in May, 1940. Yet I ought not to have been surprised when it happened. One day countries will pay me heavily to keep out.

II

It was ten years since I had visited Sedan, but I did not find it any more interesting. Historical places seldom are. If you wish to get thrills at Sedan, you must wander far from the town itself to the scene of the battle which raged along a great arc about it. Best viewpoint of all is Bazeilles. I can always thrill at the Inn of the Last Cartridge.

The battle was going badly for the French, hopelessly out-manœuvred and out-weaponed, yet their spirit was unconquerable—had that of their leaders been half as high, disaster might have been avoided. In a little cottage on the outskirts of Bazeilles there gathered a number of stragglers from many units, mostly of the Marine Corps. About seventy men were there, most of them officers or N.C.O.s. There they determined to fight it out to the last.

They did—to the last cartridge. Attacked by overwhelming masses of Germans, they repelled wave after wave of assault. But the moment approached when further resistance was impossible: ammunition was almost exhausted. A fresh attack was launched, and a last thin stream of bullets punctured its ranks. A Marine officer at the window fired the last cartridge, and the heroic episode was over. De Neuville's famous picture is one of the most striking in military annals. Survivors of the fight posed for him: the atmosphere is that of furious battle, but the faces of the men reflect their heroic despair now that they have realized that they have fought '*à la dernière cartouche*'.

The inn is now a little museum. The last time I went there, its curator was actually one of the non-commissioned officers who fought so valiantly within its walls. Now, alas, he is dead. In its way the museum is one of the most interesting in the world. If you want to know why the French were beaten, you have only to examine the samples of armaments used by both sides: the German of surprisingly modern pattern, while the French are more like archaic relics from museums. Among the exhibits was a tattered Union Jack, for a British ambulance rendered magnificent service throughout the battle.

I moved on to the Ossuary in the heart of the village. We in Britain prefer to bury our dead, but in many continental countries, France particularly, the people seem to like looking at skeletons, and almost any church can show you a remarkable array of bones. Nearly three thousand French and German soldiers were killed in the combat about Bazeilles. Instead of burying them, the French built an ossuary—a darkened chapel where the skeletons now lie in full view. At least, half of them do. After the battle the French were ranged on one side of the chapel, the Germans on the other, but during the war of 1914–1918, when the Germans occupied Sedan, the sight of so many German skeletons obsessed the nerves of imaginative German soldiers, and three of them committed suicide in the ossuary; the German half was therefore covered over.

I could not quite see the sense of that, for the French skeletons could still be seen; and, if you have a fear of death, a skeleton of one nationality is just as frightening as that of another. To me there was no fear, but only pathetic horror in the rows of bones which had once carried the flesh and supported the brains of men. Of women, too, for among them is the skeleton of a woman, a *cantonnière*, who paid the penalty of her calling. By her side lie the miniature bones of her child.

With thoughts of war dominating my mind, I rode out of Bazeilles, to dismiss them abruptly as I saw

B

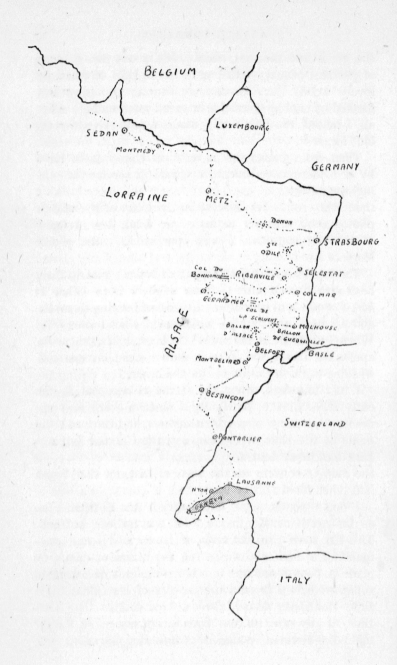

BELGIUM

LUXEMBOURG

GERMANY

SEDAN

MONTMÉDY

LORRAINE

METZ

DONON

Ste
ODILE

STRASBOURG

COL DU
BONHOMME

RIBEAUVILLE

SÉLESTAT

GÉRARDMER

COLMAR

COL DE
LA SCHLUCHT

BALLON
D'ALSACE

BALLON
DE GUEBWILLER

MULHOUSE

MONTBELIARD

BELFORT

BASLE

ALSACE

BESANÇON

SWITZERLAND

PONTARLIER

NYON

LAUSANNE

GENEVA

ITALY

the green and pleasant countryside about me, a scene of pastoral beauty. Here were gentle hills crowned by lovely woods; lazy brooks trickled along the valley, flanked by smiling cornfields or green pastureland. After all, I mused, the Battle of Sedan is nearly seventy years old: forget it.

Then, from among the maze of directive signs erected by a modern government to direct passengers on the highway, I noticed one board larger and more striking than the rest. Its inscription peremptorily forbade photography within a radius of ten kilometres, because of the fortifications. I was now in the zone of the Maginot Line.

The inn where I halted for a late lunch could scarcely be described as expensive. I was served with a substantial *hors-d'œuvre*, a mushroom omelette, veal with vegetables, and a sweet; and my bill amounted to six francs fifty. When I regarded it with wide open eyes, the proprietor apologized for the extra fifty centimes—this, he explained, was due to the inclusion of the mushrooms.

I had forgotten the name of the village, but in the early days of the Battle for France a German communiqué struck a chord of memories: it mentioned the name of the place where the extension of the Maginot Line had been broken. I scarcely needed to turn up the map to confirm that it was at Carignan that I had had lunch for six-fifty francs.

I don't wonder that they carried the Maginot Line as far north as Montmédy. It is a fortress in itself. The old town rises abruptly on a wooded spur, commanding a modern town in the valley below. True, it made a poor resistance in 1870, and in 1914 its forts collapsed before the German howitzers; yet for a third time Montmédy found itself a centre of battle. This time, at any rate, its resistance was strong. For a fortnight the Germans pounded at its outer defences; they captured one concrete pill-box—at a cost of several hundred casualties. Not until France's spirit weakened did Montmédy fall.

From the roadside I saw ample traces of the strength of the fortifications. Broad belts of wire running haphazardly across cornfields: narrower yet more vicious rows of steel rails embedded in concrete, intended to stop any charging tank. Sometimes from the crest of neighbouring hills I remarked a tiny pimple which was not quite natural. Then I knew that for every casemate I saw there must be a dozen unseen. To-day it is fashionable to decry the Maginot Line. I saw it in its strength and was impressed. Yet no fortifications in the world are impregnable unless they are firmly held.

George climbed painfully up to the walled town, with its commanding citadel. The hill is so well wooded that only the walls and the towers of a dilapidated church show through the trees. The walls are of colossal strength, with an ancient drawbridge and dry moat. To-day, I suppose, the fortifications of the town itself are no more than a curiosity, but it was amazing that they could not put up a show in 1870. The citadel was still in military occupation, and parts of it might not be visited.

As I was refreshing myself after the stiff climb, I remarked to a local ancient on the number of half-caste children running about, with those rather pathetic skins beloved neither by the white nor the black races.

"Yes, there are dozens of them," he agreed.

"Why?" I asked.

"Ah, you see, some years ago there were a lot of Colonial troops billeted here."

"Ah!" I said, expressively, suggesting the worst.

"Poor little beggars," he commented. "It's a strange thing: I suppose it's natural that white people look down on them, but black people look down on them, too. They have a hell of a time."

"I can understand that. And then, of course, the peculiar circumstances——"

"What circumstances?"

"Why—er—their illegitimacy——"

"Who talked about illegitimacy?" he asked, sharply.

"Why, I understood you to say that these were the children of Colonial soldiers and local girls."

"So they are," he declared. "But the soldiers married the girls first. No, sir, we don't do things like that in Montmédy!"

III

The road was picturesque as I turned southwards towards Stenay. I had been invited to see something of the Maginot Line, and the headquarters of this region were there.

When I arrived, it was gently pointed out by the Orderly Room sergeant that this was Sunday, and that even staff officers appreciate occasional recreation.

"But I can tell you where you will find Captain Dupont," he went on. "He always goes swimming on Sunday evening. You'll find the place about a mile up the river."

I trundled George along the tow-path: the bathing place was evidently frequented by the *élite* of Stenay, for the costumes would not have shamed a Riviera resort. I donned my mundane shorts and plunged in. In the middle of the river I collided with a good-looking man who was swimming strongly.

"Excuse me," I said, after mutual apologies. "Can you tell me which man out of this crowd is Captain Dupont?"

"I am Captain Dupont!"

My luck is like that. I have come to depend on it, and am annoyed when infrequently it lets me down.

So I went back with Dupont to his substantial flat, where we dined, argued politics and told funny stories about Hitler. His only failing was excessive hospitality.

"That is one thing I like about the Englishman," he said. "When the Frenchman has had two glasses he is drunk, but the Englishman is never drunk—at least, when he is he never shows it. It is a magnificent national trait!"

With such a high standard of performance expected, I judged it best to remain teetotal.

I was in the very heart of the Maginot Line zone as I rode from Stenay back to Montmédy and on to Longuyon. Low clouds and showers could not disguise the beauty of the scene. This is picturesque country with wooded hills, rising to a thousand feet. Down in the valley are scores of grey villages, prosperous but unkempt. The Frenchman has not a tidy mind. Many a peasant farmer whose bank-book (or, more likely, his stocking) would make me envious, is content with a litter about his farmstead. In this morning's riding I saw a remarkable succession of scrap-heaps in the main streets of the villages. They included enough old iron to make Hitler envious.

At Longuyon I saw them making the famous enamelled pottery, and wanted some. Yet I could scarcely carry it about on George for weeks to come.

"I will pack it carefully, and send it by post," said the man.

"Yes, but then I shall have to pay customs dues!" I protested.

"In this case, about two shillings," he smiled.

He did not realize that we were not discussing a matter of two shillings, but a question of human pride. I have never yet met the man who paid customs dues with grace.

The clouds descended from the hills and encased one. Yet I sensed that I was still passing through pleasant country as I plodded to the south-east. Then, however, the immediate environs became purely utilitarian, for I was moving across the great ironfields of Briey. Iron is useful, even essential, but its natal places are seldom picturesque. Briey itself was a surprise, standing abruptly on a hill, but I was not sorry that the enveloping clouds hid from view the maze of chimneys belching grey or yellow smoke, or the undistinguished medley of dwellings alleged to be human habitations, which lay beside my route as I pedalled into Metz.

IV

For a good many generations Metz has been trying to make up its mind whether it is French or German. When I was there soon after the last war the German element was very pronounced: there was an unsettled atmosphere about the place, indicative of confused thinking. A single generation has made a vast difference: there is nothing hesitant about Metz to-day. Although, as might be expected in a frontier city, there is a pro- portion of people of German blood among the population, the majority are of French stock. I do not know the official figures; it would be very difficult to get an exact idea. I applied my own rough and ready tests. I asked the way of casual passers-by in German: only two of the first ten understood German—or, at least, admitted to a knowledge of German.

A better test was provided by a local newspaper. The French newspapers go to extraordinary limits to save their patrons the expense of buying a paper. In England we put out intriguing posters; in France the newspaper has a salon where it posts up the most important news of the day. In stirring times there are always crowds having a free read. Now in a bi-lingual city like Metz many papers publish two editions, in French and German. I watched carefully: the people reading the news in French always outnumbered the German readers by four to one.

Metz comprises two cities: the maze of irregular streets about the cathedral is provincial France: the suburbs of solid houses are very German—the railway station exclusively German: it even includes a tower designed by the Kaiser himself. Like Hitler, he had artistic ideas: both would have been happier if they had stuck to architecture.

The city is well sited at the confluence of the Moselle and the Seille: branches of the rivers pop up everywhere, and part of the central city is built on islands. The western flanks are picturesque, with long views over the hills which were the scene of disastrous battle in 1870.

I revisited the sights of Metz—there is a lot to see. The cathedral is famous: I grinned again at the statue of the prophet Daniel, who bears an uncanny likeness to the Kaiser. The height of the cathedral is surprising, and its delicate stonework encloses a maze of beautiful glass. The atmosphere was easy and unstrained: indeed, pigeons flew about inside the cathedral as well as without, to the occasional discomfort of the worshippers.

Even more interesting is the Porte des Allemands, a bridge and gatehouse of a feudal castle belonging to the Order of the Teutonic Knights. Adjoining are remains of the castle itself; the gateway is really picturesque, flanked by the swift-flowing Seille.

I found the people very calm, in spite of the constant threat of war. The reason was always the same—the strength of the Maginot Line. It dominated all ideas. Thousands of labourers from the district had worked on its construction, and had spread the story of its massive power. Air raids might have to be endured, but, at least, the people of Metz were certain that their city would never again be captured by Germany. I was told that this idea had had a great effect on many people whose strict racial origin was indeterminate: the Maginot Line had decided them to become French.

I was in Metz again in April, 1940. Its atmosphere was unchanged: there was complete confidence. The proportion of German-reading news-seekers had suffered another vast decline. The men of Metz were playing their part solidly in the defence of France. Some of them may have had two ideas about Germany, but only one about Hitler.

One trifling experience near Metz still makes me shudder. I was lecturing on the subject of the Maginot Line to units of the British Army about to man its outposts, the idea being to give the troops a general account of the fortifications and their history. Metz was my headquarters: I lectured in huts and barracks, then was sent north-east, to the evacuated villages in the region of the Line.

One evening I arrived at one of these villages, to find an apologetic note from the commanding officer—his unit had suddenly been moved forward. Such incidents had to be foreseen, and I prepared to return to Metz. The British battalion had been replaced by a French; the French commander collared me—his men had just come out of the Maginot Line, and would be tickled to death to hear an Englishman's account of it. In a rash moment I agreed.

Three or four hundred French troops crowded in the local Salle des Fêtes. Now my French used to be good, but I have been lazy and neglected my vocabulary. The French sufficient for conversation is usefully inadequate for an impromptu lecture in a serious subject. Too late I realized my folly.

However, I managed: after talking to them for an hour, I patted myself on the back hard, and wound up.

Then I made another fatal slip. In my last sentence I referred to Mussolini: that was asking for trouble. Those Frenchmen rained questions on me for an hour and forty minutes. After that their hospitality was profound, and I never needed it more.

V

George plodded sedately to the south-east, over easy roads and through a pleasant countryside. Well ahead, the dark and lazy outlines of the Vosges promised sterner work. We halted at Morhange, where the French took a nasty knock in 1914. Completely under-estimating the German strength, they advanced to the attack in Lorraine, and at Morhange were flung back in complete confusion. These eastern provinces are places of death, the inevitable battle-ground in the long rivalry between Gaul and Teuton. There is scarcely a village over the widest area which does not bear some scar or memory of war.

The character of the country began to change: we were entering the foothills of the Vosges. Great forests bordered our path, sweeping majestically from the valleys over the crests of the long hills. Little lakes or over-grown ponds were freely scattered: some were undistinguished, others picturesque because of the beauty of their framing, the mixed green of meadow and woodland.

Even before Sarrebourg we had begun to climb: now we plunged boldly into the heart of the northern Vosges. There is an ancient cemetery at Lorquin, but the green forests were more inviting. About Abreschwiller the scene was really magnificent, great rocks lining the forest sides. For twenty miles we scarcely passed a human habitation as we followed the Red Saar; a meandering road, entirely enclosed in great forests, with the wooded hillsides sloping gently towards the dashing stream.

Then, through a clearing between the trees, I saw the Donon, highest peak of the northern Vosges. Of no great eminence (3,300 feet), it is imposing because it stands above its neighbours. The road began to twist and turn, gaining height. At last the Donon towered by my side: a well-marked path invited investigation.

"Can I leave my bicycle with you?" I asked of an aged forester.

"Of course. But why not take it with you?"

"Well, I can't ride a bicycle up a mountain!"

"No. But you can ride it down—the path is good enough."

The doctors had given me stern warnings about riding George uphill, but they had said nothing about riding him down. I began to push: sure enough, the surface of the path was reasonably smooth, though its gradients promised exciting moments in the descent. Nevertheless, George was a sensation when we reached the summit. It so happened that the last stretch was of moderate slope, so I got on and rode. The little group of hikers picnicking on the summit assumed that I had ridden all the way up, and gathered round in wonder.

There were girls in the party, and they shuddered as we stood before a great sacrificial stone. In the days when our Druids were gambolling about under mistletoe boughs, their confreres in Alsace were performing human sacrifices, slaughtering beautiful virgins for the delectation of the gods: a singularly inappropriate fate for beautiful virgins. On the Donon there is even a thing called a prehistoric temple, but to my inexperienced eyes it looked like a fake: some of its museum contents were genuine enough, for in ancient days the Donon was certainly a centre of religious mystery.

The company was good, the air fresh and keen after

the moist heat of the forest. I lay in the breeze: by my side was a French gym mistress who even on holiday was remarkably active: every few minutes she got up and turned half a dozen cartwheels: then returned to a denunciation of Hitler at the point where she had left off.

Someone started to sing: these young people were Alsatians, and they sang well—German fashion, seriously and methodically. I lay and listened in great content to the lovely folk-songs of Alsace. Then my gym mistress, lest I should be misled by the language of the songs, stood on the sacrificial stone and sang the Marseillaise—with such dramatic fervour that I would have followed her to war.

I had to make my excuses: George rattled down the steep path, taking complete command—I doubt if I could have stopped him. I remember a prolonged and only partially effective grip on the brakes: an occasional skid as we rounded an abrupt corner: one terrifying descent as we cleared the forest: then an easy coast down to Schirmeck.

I was in Alsace, but the people still spoke French. The watershed of the Vosges is not the lingual boundary, for in olden days French infiltrated through the valleys—freely in the south, more hardly in the north. Not until Lutzelhouse did I cross into German-speaking Alsace. Not that language offers a guide to a man's race, much less to his mind, as we shall see.

George was happy now: here was a perfect cycling road, its gentle slope following the course of a little stream. The little villages and towns were a delight, freely dotted with those ancient and picturesque houses in which Alsace is so rich.

After Molsheim the flat valley of the Rhine spread before us. Far ahead, a tapering spire beckoned us onwards: there was no need for urge. Metz is interesting, but Strasbourg is a good deal more.

VI

If Metz has turned towards the west, then it seemed that Strasbourg had turned towards the east. I made a mental note within an hour of entering the city that Strasbourg seemed to be much more German than it was ten years ago. Then I was always addressed in French first, now in German. An hour later I had corrected my first impression. Strasbourg had not become more German, but more Alsatian, which is a very different thing.

It is a very fascinating city. Some of the streets are modern and majestic, but I prefer those narrow winding ways which cluster about the cathedral, dotted here and there with glorious and ancient examples of Alsatian architecture. The cathedral itself is grand. Normally I am far more interested in people than stonework, but the tracery of Strasbourg always has a warm impression upon me, and its stained glass windows are as delightful to the mind as to the eye. The spire is a masterpiece, so delicately carved that at a distance it looks like a pillar of lace. And I am childish enough to appreciate the famous astronomical clock, which at the hours exhibits a series of puppet figures. Although immensely intrigued, I do not think that astronomical clocks ought to be sited in cathedrals. They are not conducive to holy atmosphere, for their best efforts savour of anti-climax. At noon great crowds gather round the clock at Strasbourg, for then the twelve apostles march out and make ovation to the figure of Christ. He raises His hand in blessing. So far as puppets can be dignified, this is dignified. But then a cock crows three times and flaps its wings. The religious significance is obvious, but in practice this is an effort calculated to cause the utmost amusement to a child of two years of age.

I have not a tidy mind, and hate to do my sightseeing methodically. I was wandering at random in and about the cathedral. For the third time I emerged to stare at the west façade, with its glory of statuary. My eyes were raised to the heights, and the magnificence of the scene compelled majestic thoughts.

Suddenly the atmosphere was rudely disturbed. A cacophony of noise descended about me, and I found myself surrounded by my seven priests who had filled my carriage on the outward journey. Forgotten were the glories of architecture in the joy of reunion. I must lunch with them—that was essential. They had to go to church. Would I care to come with them?

"But I am not a Catholic," I protested.

"That does not matter," they argued. "This particular church is for both Protestants and Catholics."

Out of curiosity I agreed. They led me to the church of St. Pierre-le-Vieux, which in the course of history has belonged to both creeds, and is now shared—a highly sensible arrangement.

Then I led the way to a famous house in the Place de Broglie. I confess that, despite my comparative sophistication, I can still thrill to the strains of the Marseillaise sung by a Frenchman who understands the meaning of its music, or by a crowd which comprehends its imperishable sentiments. Or by a band which does not waste effort in harmony, but emphasizes to the full its stirring tempo. We stood in the room where the Mayor of Strasbourg, Frederick Dietrich, entertained local people, and Rouget de L'Isle hesitantly confessed that he had written a revolutionary song. At first he was nervous: then the thrill of his music gripped him, and he electrified the company by its stirring strains. The next day all Strasbourg was singing his song: it spread rapidly. To-day there is some disappointment in Strasbourg. The marching song took its name from the men of Marseilles, who sang it to encourage them as they trudged the weary miles towards Paris. But it is claimed, with some reason, that it ought to be called the Strasbourgais.

Every Frenchman has hidden funds of emotion, even if he is a priest. My friends were paying their first visit to Strasbourg. For a while they were subdued, as is any man with a mind in the presence of history. Then their emotion surged forth. They grouped around the spot where Rouget de L'Isle stood, and burst into the strains of the Marseillaise. They did not sing well: two or three of them were hopelessly out of tune; nevertheless, the moment was inspiring, for the sentiments of the song were there.

It was their turn to undertake the duties of guide. They took me to see a body: I might have guessed that. If any Frenchman takes you sightseeing, he is almost certain to include a collection of skeletons in your itinerary. In the church of St. Thomas were several embalmed bodies which have been there for several hundred years and have kept remarkably well. More impressive was the tomb of Marshal Saxe. It is classed as theatrical, and as a tomb the criticism is reasonable enough. Nevertheless, it is a surprising piece of work. It shows the famous soldier descending a line of steps, at the foot of which is his coffin. France endeavours to detain him, while Hercules mourns the man who most resembles him on earth.

I was something of a sensation as I walked the streets of Strasbourg escorted by seven priests. They all wanted to talk to me at once—I could understand that after such a long journey together they were weary of each other's company. Sometimes their manners were out-weighed by enthusiasm, and one would push the other into the gutter to get a better place by my side. I was strongly tempted to stay with them, especially when

they promised to show me many more bodies and
skeletons; but I recalled my mission—that my real ride
had not begun, that this was just a physical preparation
for the hard work to come. So in the late afternoon
I made my farewell. I would do some riding in the
cool of the evening.

VII

In the exuberance of priestly company I had allowed
myself far too little time for the journey I contemplated.
Yet I halted at Obernai and again at Barr. Here were
many of the ancient picturesque houses for which Alsace
is so famous. There were dozens of others which were
equally picturesque but which were not so ancient, for
a tourist element has unfortunately touched part of Alsace
—Obernai especially—and not all the Alsatian architecture is genuine.

A heavy storm was gathering as I halted at Barr for
refreshment. It was a strange phenomenon, the clouds
driving from the west, the wind from the east. Before
me the first mountains of the Vosges, with their pine-
covered slopes towered almost abruptly. I was tempted
to spend the night in the valley, but there is a sensation
about heights which can never be resisted. I put it to
George, after the day's inactivity at Strasbourg. Indeed,
for him it had not been a happy day at all, for when
I produced him a portion of my clerical company insisted
on having a ride. Some were experts, some were not,
and one of them skidded violently, upsetting himself and
George, who does not like to be ridden by amateurs. I
may have imagined it, but when I picked him up outside
the café at Barr his front wheel was still itching for
the road.

We began to climb, a long winding road making its

way right round the other side of the mountain. Intermittent rain descended, and the wind, getting on top, beat down the clouds till they touched the head of the mountain. The time came when the gradient was so severe that I was constrained to dismount and push. By now great banks of cloud covered the sky, and brought with them an early dusk. It was almost dark as I reached the entrance to the convent of St. Odile.

Odelia was the daughter of a Duke of Alsace. I had seen the house where she was born at Obernai. She was born blind, but miraculously received sight at the moment of her baptism. In view of this miracle, she not unnaturally devoted herself to religious work when attaining years of discretion, and this convent was her principal foundation and her favourite residence. Certainly she knew how to choose a site, for her abbey is magnificently situated on one of the spurs of the easternmost mountains of the Vosges, visible from Germany itself on the other side of the Rhine and commanding a view of such magnificence that it has been deservedly frequented by tourists; or, in these dark days, by artillery observation officers.

The nuns made me welcome, for there is a great hostel for pilgrims attached to the abbey. There plainly, comfortably and cheaply I was lodged. As I stood at my little window the latent storm broke. The clouds were now as black as the night which was almost due, but they were suddenly riven by great streaks of lightning. The thunder rolled like a cannonade down the wooded valley. There is nothing more imposing and frightening than a thunderstorm among mountains.

The lightning punctured the clouds: they dropped suddenly to earth to clear the sky for the gentler stars and moon. I was attracted to a group of students from Strasbourg—attracted because after supper they had gathered together in a corner to sing some of the lovely folk-songs of Alsace. Then we wandered outside. Now

c

the night was marvellously clear.   On neighbouring spurs we could even distinguish the ruins of other abbeys or of the castles of the Robber Barons which once dominated this section of the Rhine valley.   Not far from the convent itself we found a section of the Mur Paien, a great historic fortification composed of huge blocks of unhewn stone, piled up to form a wall ten feet high.   In its day it would stop any enemy invader.   Even to-day it would call a halt to an advancing tank, which fears nothing so much as a stout blank wall.

Next morning I dropped down to Sélestat, one of my favourite Alsatian towns.   There is nothing spectacular about it, but its irregular streets, narrow and winding, have a delightful atmosphere of their own.   It has very few sights, as such—it scarcely compares with others of the Alsatian towns.   Yet I am not alone in my preference for Sélestat; the storks prefer it and its environs to any other corner of hospitable Alsace.   Always in the summer months you will see the storks, or hear them, their huge beaks clacking in the hours of dawn and dusk.   In the winter you will see their nests only; great bunches of twigs on a chimney pot.   It is supposed to be a sign of good fortune if the storks visit your house— not from the family point of view, but ordinary good luck.   You do your best to attract the storks to your house.   You hoist a cartwheel on your chimney, hoping that the stork will accept it as the foundation for his nest of twigs.   If he does so honour you, then you will willingly go without a fire under that chimney for the whole of the winter in the hope that he will come back again the following summer.   Usually he does.   There are peasants in Alsace who will tell you authenticated stories of whole generations of storks which have used the same nest summer after summer.

It was market day in Sélestat: the stalls were spread over half a dozen little squares and the streets between them. Some of them were parked on the steps of the churches, or in the gutters outside ancient houses with exterior staircases. The cattle market seemed to cover the greater part of the free space of the town. I wandered haphazard, joining this crowd and that, listening delightedly to the barker of a cheapjack's stall, always fascinating in any town. Eventually I sat down on a bench; the spirit was willing for unending mingling, but the soles of my feet demanded temporary repose.

I found myself sole auditor of a comedy. I had parked myself on the edge of the pig market. The farmer was there with a small pig—a very small pig. He was arguing with a gentleman who soon revealed himself as a local butcher. Normally I detest notes, but their conversation was so intriguing that I got out a piece of paper and took it down as near to verbatim as I could.

Farmer: Yes, M. Ladoux, I can thoroughly recommend this little pig. In fact, there is no need to tell you how good he is—you bought his brother only a year ago.

Butcher: His brother?

Farmer: Well, his half-brother.

Butcher: Half-brother is not the same as a brother, you know.

Farmer: No, but these two little pigs had the same mother, and the father of the second was the brother of the father of the first.

Butcher: H'm. Sounds too much like inbreeding to me.

Farmer: Inbreeding only affects the mind, not the body.

Butcher: I have to be so careful these days. My customers are very particular.

Farmer: But they will recall how tender was his brother!

Butcher: His half-brother! Now, had he been his full brother that would have been a different thing.

Farmer: But I insist, M. Ladoux, this little pig has a
    wonderful mother, a wonderful mother! Do you
    know she has had no less than twenty-six piglets in
    a single year.

Butcher: Ah, if you will excuse me saying so, M. Derocq,
    that seems to me like over-production. I am more
    concerned with quality than quantity. This sow of
    yours cannot possibly give the individual attention
    required by the growing pig to so large a family.

Farmer: On the contrary, this sow is a magnificent
    mother, and I can say with truth that this little
    piglet was the apple of her eye. Normally she is
    not gifted to favouritism, but this was certainly
    her favourite. In its earliest days she always saw
    that it had enough to drink. Later she restrained
    her own impatience at feeding time to point out
    the choicest bits of swill. Why, I have no doubt
    that her heart was broken this morning when I took
    it away from her. She will pine for it for months
    to come.

Butcher: Pine for it! Why, she will have had another
    thirteen by this time. It is a pity, M. Derocq, that
    there are no prizes for *nombreuses familles* among
    pigs.

Farmer (almost exhausted by the argument and rapidly
    changing its basis): I can tell you, too, M. Ladoux,
    that my own wife was particularly fond of this
    little pig and took especial care of it.

Butcher: Doubtless because it was ailing, M. Derocq!
    Anyway, it would be a great pity if you were to
    make a useless journey into Sélestat. Just to relieve
    you of the necessity of carrying this pig back all
    the way home, I am prepared to offer four hundred
    francs for it.

Farmer: Four hundred francs! My dear Ladoux, I have
    always been noted as a philanthropist, but this is

too much! I hope that I am not financially minded, but anything short of five hundred francs would be ridiculously like a gift.

Butcher: Four hundred francs, I said, M. Derocq. Or, perhaps to cover the expenses of the sale, we might say four hundred and ten francs.

Farmer: But, my dear M. Ladoux, four hundred and ten francs for a beautiful pig like this! Why, my wife had ideas far beyond five hundred francs: if I came back with less than five hundred francs—even so little as four hundred and ninety francs—I should never hear the last of it.

And so the argument went on. It must have lasted for thirty or forty minutes. There came the time when the prices offered and acceptable were only twenty francs apart. At this point I decided to do my good deed for the day. I got up and introduced myself. Any Englishman could depend upon a warm welcome in 1939. I admired the pig, which was certainly remarkably clean and had an intriguing tail. I felt him at the right place —I had been watching farmers and butchers doing this for half the morning. I hinted that in England I was a famous judge of pigs.

"Then you are the man we need," said the farmer.

"I agree," the butcher exclaimed. "We have been having an argument about the value of this pig. Now, what price would you put on the animal?"

I ran my fingers over its back again, twigged its ears and looked at its teeth. Then I considered solemnly— a hasty opinion would command but little respect.

"Personally, I should place four hundred and fifty francs as the value of this pig," I announced in solemn judgment. The butcher and the farmer looked at one another.

"Very well," they both said in a breath. Immediately

we adjourned to a neighbouring tavern for refreshment —which cost far more than the difference of twenty francs about which they had been haggling.

"There is one thing that astounds me," I said, when we were on convivial terms. "I can confess now that I heard your long conversation about this pig. Wouldn't it be much simpler to have a fixed price?"

"But if we had a fixed price, what would be the point in coming to market?" they demanded. And their query was unanswerable.

Near Sélestat is one of the prize comedies of Alsace. Commanding the Rhine valley, on an abrupt promontory of the Vosges, is the castle of Hoh-Koenigsbourg. In the days when Alsace was German, the castle was an abject ruin: nevertheless, the cost of its upkeep was considerable. Then a councillor of Sélestat had a brilliant idea: "We don't want the castle, and we don't like the Kaiser. I move, therefore, that we present the castle to the Kaiser." Naturally, this clever solution of the problem of the incubus was immediately adopted.

The Kaiser was so delighted at getting a present of anything from Alsace—normally he only got abuse—that he came down in person to take over the castle: and got a shock when he saw its condition. The council of Sélestat had to stand him a lunch, of course, and the Kaiser had to make a speech. To the horror of his secretaries, he refused to sit down when he had read his formal oration.

"I really am delighted at this magnificent present," he continued. "But I am sure you will agree that it is a great pity that such a fine old castle has been allowed to fall into such a sad state of ruin. This is what I propose to do: I shall gather the finest historic architects of Europe: they shall study the old plans and the old pictures. Stone by stone Hoh-Koenigsbourg shall be restored to its former glory. It will cost a lot of money, but no expense shall be spared: and the people of Sélestat shall pay the bill."

And they had to: people in Alsace couldn't argue with the Kaiser. While they were at it, however, they made a very good job of it. Hoh-Koenigsbourg to-day is a show place: they have made a folk museum of its spacious courtyard, re-erecting there ancient Alsatian houses and castles doomed to demolition by modern 'progress'.

VIII

Close by Sélestat is another fascinating corner of Alsace—the little town of Ribeauvillé, with the ruins of three castles on its wooded hill. In older days Ribeauvillé had a great and pleasing reputation, for its lord was the patron of the travelling minstrels of western Europe, and in his town they maintained the head-quarters of their guild. It is still there, the *pfifferhaus*, in the one long street which comprises the greater part of Ribeauvillé. On September 8th the minstrels would gather in Ribeauvillé for musical revelry and feasting, and the old customs are still faithfully preserved.

It must be ten years since I attended *pfifferdai* at Ribeauvillé, but I have not forgotten it. A long procession was the feature of the celebrations, the impersonators of the minstrels wearing the gorgeous costumes of older days. The procession was led by a bewhiskered lord of Ribeauvillé and his ladies, mounted on remarkably substantial horses. Drummers and fifers wore ancient uniforms: folk-dancers and singers made a leisurely but pleasing passage: the yodelling rivalled that of the Swiss valleys.

The modern representatives of the minstrel's art were not so attractive. Pride of place was given to a man who had come all the way from England to join in the festivities. He led the way carrying a portable hurdy-gurdy, which wheezed out an asthmatic version of 'A bicycle made for two'. The man was dirty, unshaven, and ragged: but he was English. Yet when I asked him *why* he had made the long journey from England, he was so evasive that the natural assumption was that he wanted to avoid the attentions of the police.

I rode over the gentle slopes of the foothills of the Vosges, between extensive vineyards, to Riquewihr. A generation ago this was the most charming village of Alsace, but the tourist agencies are doing their best to spoil it. There is a long street of ancient and picturesque Alsatian houses, only partially disfigured by souvenir shops and displays of picture postcards. I lingered long by a double gateway, and in the Rue des Juifs there is as striking a picture as France has to show.

There was interest on every hand. Many of the courtyards are unspoiled, gems of architecture beautified by the atmosphere of age. Here was an ancient wine press, less hygienic but more attractive than the new. Wine and tourists provide Riquewihr's income. It is a village of green men, for the vineyards have to be sprayed regularly with chemicals to exterminate pests, and the solution of copper salts is of a vivid shade of green. I do not know if the men of Riquewihr are extraordinarily clumsy, or only as clumsy as I am, but it seemed to me that they got as much green solution on their clothes as on their grapes.

The Rhine valley was attractive, with its succession of picturesque villages, their ancient timbered houses standing proudly against the dark background of the wooded Vosges. Yet this was poor preparation for the mountain passes of Savoy, so I turned west and plunged into the heart of the forest. The road ascended in sweeping curves towards the Col de Bonhomme: sometimes I descended to look backwards over the fine panorama of the Rhine valley to the Black Forest, sometimes just because the gradient was such that it was easier to push George than to ride him.

There are two little lakes just beyond the pass, situated strangely high. Lac Blanc is the more pleasant, Lac Noir the more inspiring. During the last war their banks witnessed stern scenes, for the French held one shore, the Germans the other. In their clear waters can still be seen the debris of war, grenades and shells, and rusting rifles.

I descended by forest paths to Fraize: much more exciting than the road, for there were occasional gates or stiles, and I was never quite certain whether I was going to be able to persuade George to stop. The scene was of great beauty: lovely pine forests lining the slopes of the green mountains: little streams leaping over obstructing rocks in graceful cascades.

Occasionally I would meet a woodman with his wooden shed, the *schlicht*. It glides easily over the thousand-year-old deposit of pine needles: too easily, so the woodman stretches himself in front, to use his spreadeagled feet as brakes. There must be a knack in it: when I tried, my feet did not act as brakes. On the contrary, in the first ten yards of my progress I knocked over the woodman and then collided with a tree. It was quite a painful apprenticeship, and I decided on the spot that the lumberjack's profession was not for me.

Fraize is a pleasant little town, but Gérardmer is a popular resort. For once popularity is justified, for it is grandly situated beside a pleasant lake, at the foot of one of the finest sectors of the Vosges. The adjacent valley is charming, and I forgave the sophistication of Gérardmer as I wandered about its lovely forest, freely scattered with streams and waterfalls, and with many a little lake nestling precariously high on the mountainside.

Now I was getting all the climbing I wanted. True, the passes were seldom much higher than three thousand feet, but I was doing an average of two a day. At the Col de la Schlucht I turned aside for a while to ride along the famous Route des Crêtes. The fighting line during the last war ran along the watershed of the Vosges. French military engineers built a remarkable road just below the crests, on the western side. One day I will ride right along this road, for it commands a continuous panorama of green mountains delightful to the eye.

There was a chalet on the Hohneck, I had heard, so I rode or pushed George—generally pushed—towards the summit. I found no crude mountain shelter, but a dignified guest-house in timber. Yet it was democratic, as all mountain hostels ought to be. I might engage a comfortable room with a bath: a floor above were private cubicles, plain but comfortable: higher still were communal dormitories, very inexpensive. I found there very good company, except that some of the performers on musical instruments were not so expert as they thought they were.

All about the crests were ample reminders of the last war: an occasional concrete pill-box, or a belt of rusty barbed wire. As I descended to the east, some of the villages were painfully new, monuments to the carnage of modern war. Kaysersberg happily escaped, for it has many ancient houses: in older days no war in Alsace was complete without a siege of Kaysersberg. The whole district reeks with war, for at Turckheim a great battle was fought and won by Turenne: next door is a scene of slaughter on a vaster scale, for at Les Trois-Épis, or La Linge, Frenchmen and Germans died by the thousand in 1915. Yet all about is as peaceful and as pleasant a countryside as nature ever fashioned.

I like Colmar: indeed, it must be classed high among

"Little Venice," Colmar

Storks in Alsace

RIBEAUVILLÉ AND THE THREE CASTLES

PFIFFERDAI, RIBEAUVILLÉ

the pleasant cities of Alsace. There is one quarter which is known as Little Venice: any scene with water in it is automatically dubbed Venice. Colmar's water quarter is nothing like Venice, but it is exceedingly picturesque. So are the ancient houses freely scattered about its streets, with their ancient timbers, colourful decoration, and grotesque statuary.

The main road to the south was straight and hot, so I wandered haphazard along country lanes. To the west the forest-clad mountains peered through the heat haze, assuming that strange blue tinge which is typical of the hills of Alsace. Despite the brilliant sun, the Vosges were strangely sombre: this is a quality of forests. In the far distance to the east I could see the parallel compensating range of the Black Forest.

I was thirsty: at a cross-roads was a group of three houses; one of them was bound to be a café. But it wasn't. This was a remarkable curiosity, the first time I had ever encountered such a phenomenon in France, so I halted to investigate. While I was talking to the lady of the centre house, my nostrils began to quiver. It was too hot to be hungry, I had thought, but the scent of Alsatian roast goose is irresistible. The lady noticed the twitching of my nasal muscles, and invited me into lunch. With the resources of its neighbours added, the centre house rapidly transformed itself into a café.

By this time I was inside French-speaking Alsace. The French language has passed over the mountains with difficulty, but easily permeates through the Belfort Gap, between the Juras and the Vosges. If Strasbourg is largely German, Mulhouse is overwhelmingly French —it was significant that throughout the last war the Germans ruled this district as hostile territory. From the aspect of the picturesque, Mulhouse cannot compare with the northern cities of Alsace, but economically it

is more important than most; there are manufactures of
hardware and cotton goods.

Yet there is one feature of ancient Mulhouse which is
really intriguing. Outside the gaily decorated Town
Hall hangs the Pierre des Bavards, a gossip's stone,
shaped like a head. In older and more direct days, people
convicted of slander or backbiting gossip were made
to perambulate the town on market day, with the stone
hanging round their necks. It might be worth while
renewing the method in an attempt to suppress the flood
of rumours which are so unsettling to minds already
strained by the tension of war.

Another feature of Mulhouse is more modern but just
as practical: the town was the centre of an early
experiment in housing—a French experiment, by the
way, though the Germans frequently claim its credit.
Pleasant residential suburbs were built: workmen paid
rent for their pleasant houses—which became their own
after a fixed period of years. The communal bakeries
and workhouses have served as models for more modern
schemes.

IX

The heat of the Rhine valley became oppressive: it
was almost painful to touch George's iron frame. We
turned to the mountains again, halting at Thann, a very
pleasant little town at the foot of the wooded valleys.
During the last war it was of some importance: in the
early days the French invaded southern Alsace; and,
though they were soon driven back, they held a corner
of the province for the whole of the war: Thann served
as the capital of the occupied territory.

We climbed up a rough mountain road: the slopes
edged abruptly from the green valley. Soon familiar

scars disfigured the scene, for this was a place of renown.
It will be recalled that the Vosges front was classed
as a 'quiet sector' during the World War: it was generally
held by reserve or recuperating divisions. But one
place was mentioned continuously in the war com-
muniqués: we remembered it because of its unwieldy
name—the Hartmannsweilerkopf. It changed hands a
dozen times during the war, and the reason for the
struggle is immediately clear once the summit of the
mountain is reached, for it commands an enormous
stretch of the Rhine valley.

Wisely, the French have left the battlefield as it was,
a maze of tangled barbed wire, battered trenches, and
broken concrete: sheltering beneath the eastern spurs
are the German rest billets, some of them dug into the
mountainside. On the crest are striking war memorials
of the regiments who fought over the scarred summit of
the Hartmannsweilerkopf.

Some idiot told me that I could get George across
country to the Ballon de Guebwiller, the highest mountain
of the Vosges. He was right eventually, but it was
mighty hard work: frequently I had to push, and often
to carry. I pointed out to George that, admirable
companion as he was, he was scarcely built for mountain
climbing. He retorted that I was deliberately climbing
mountains for practice: why did I not keep to roads,
which would be sensible? Presumably I did not intend
to push him up an Alp?

The mountains of the Vosges are generally called
ballons. The word has nothing to do with balloons,
but is a corruption of *bois long*—long wood. Even to-day
the Vosges are well wooded; once they were entirely
forest-covered. Now the actual summits are generally
bald, rounded knolls of grass: there is very little conventional mountain scenery on the Alpine pattern—no
imposing peaks or gaunt stone cliffs. The Vosges are

green mountains: in the south there is scarcely a sign
of rock. The rounded summits tend to give an
appearance of more modest height than bald figures
can prove.

I hugged roads religiously as I worked my way to
the south. It was hard toil, for my path rose and fell
continually as I plodded through the very heart of
the Vosges. The scene was grand, the toil eased by the
shade of the trees and the fresh mountain breeze. For
miles the only sounds disturbing the silence would be
the song of birds or the sharp echoing of the woodman's
axe. Shepherds lounged on the high pastures, carving
industriously at wooden figures while the sheep nibbled
contentedly at the sweet mountain grass. So pleasant
a pastoral scene I had never encountered. Yet here
men fought and died by the thousand.

The Ballon d'Alsace is the baldest of all the
mountains of the Vosges: its forests are scantier, its
pastures wider, than those of its fellows. Its summit
is the least imposing, a grassy plateau, yet it commands a
view which was worth the hard work involved in gaining
it. To the east were the mountains of the Black Forest,
dark and sombre: to the north the Vosges, with that
strange bluish tinge in their haze: to the south, faintly
discernible in the far distance, the monster peaks of the
Alps.

It was a grand descent to Belfort: I had scarcely
to turn a pedal. The history of Belfort is romantic
and stirring, but it is a very dull town. It has stood a
dozen sieges, including one which lasted throughout
the war of 1870–1. The giant lion, carved out of the
rock face of the citadel cliff, is symbolical of the place,
which commanded the famous 'gap' through which
invaders sought to pass. Yet, though I can usually
thrill to history, I confess that I have always been bored
by Belfort.

Though not nearly so important in a military sense, Montbéleard, ten miles south, is much more impressive. Here is a huge citadel of solid strength, including a castle and schools within its walls, perched high on a sudden eminence dominating the town and the adjacent valley. Otherwise the town is not especially interesting—except that by virtue of an ancient German feudal descent it is Protestant in character instead of Catholic.

I was looking round the memorials, a feature of every French town. One at least was unusual: it was erected to the memory of a Corporal Peugert. I confess that I had never heard of him, but the memorial was justified: he was the first Frenchman to die in battle in 1914.

From Montbéleard I followed the valley of the Doubs. The afternoon's ride had been disappointing scenically, but here was the promise of things to come. I passed an imposing cliff formation on the right bank: now the valley began to narrow, forest-covered hills approaching to the water's edge.

I halted for the night at L'Isle sur Doubs. Even its iron-working factory was romantic in the soft evening light, and the air of the valley was gracious. Nor was conversation lacking. An Italian commercial traveller was staying the night at the hotel, and he was unwise enough to embark on a eulogy of Mussolini. His host was restrainedly polite—at first: but even hospitality cannot be expected to accept indirect insult without protest. Soon the Italian was surrounded by a circle of locals, all of whom were better debaters than he was. He was quite glad to go to bed early.

It was a lovely ride the following morning. There was a white mist rising from the river in the hour after dawn, enhancing the charm of the quiet scene. Sometimes the valley was wide and pastoral: sometimes it closed in, with great white rocks forcing their way through the continuous greenery.

After Baume-les-Dames the scene was even more picturesque. The Ladies of Baume were noble ladies who founded a convent there nearly 1,400 years ago: they chose their site well. The river twists and turns continuously, avoiding the fatal clash with the protruding hills. Sometimes the road leaves the river bank and rises over the intervening hills, commanding a picture akin to the dales of Derbyshire.

We were attracted by a board which called our attention to a grotto. The cave itself was of no special interest, for it housed no dragon and its guardian had no imagination. It showed us, however, that there was a ridable towpath by the riverside. This was more friendly, more intimate, than the main road. There was a warm, moist breeze along the valley, and the sight of the river was cooling.

Yet the path rapidly deteriorated: evidently the section by the grotto had been well made merely to entice unwary travellers along it. George negotiated its eccentricities with difficulty: once I skidded violently, and was only saved from sudden immersion because my belt caught on the stub of a giant thistle. It was good of the thistle to save me a wetting, but painful.

An old man sat fishing: at least, a rod lay by his side, but I suspect that he was asleep as I approached. The path was now impossible: I asked him if there was a path by which I could regain the main road.

"But why?" he asked. "It is more pleasant by the river."

"Yes," I agreed. "But soon I shall have no tyres left."

"Ah, but the path gets better in another three hundred metres!"

And he was right, to a yard!

The valley widened, less spectacular: the more frequent villages were plain but substantial, yet the gaps between were still gloriously green. I continued along the tow-path, till I had another skid—an unusual accident. I saw a snake leisurely crawling across the path, and naturally made a spurt to ride him down. At the moment of impact, however, he suddenly turned length-ways, and George's front wheel went the length of his back. I might have recovered balance, but my eyes were fixed on the snake, which looked at me with a sardonic smile as I wobbled and fell: rather like the expression on the face of a cat sitting just out of range of a barking dog on a chain.

X

Besançon was magnificent: it is gloriously situated in a great amphitheatre of wooded mountains, commanded by an imposing citadel. The foothills of the Jura Mountains may not be spectacular, but they are exceedingly pleasant, and approach to the easy outskirts of the city.

Its buildings are not so impressive as its long history would presume. There are some scanty Roman remains, and one of the dullest cathedrals in France. An outlying tower, however, has an astronomical clock which makes that of Strasbourg a mere toy. It shows the eclipses over thousands of years, the time in various parts of the world and an encyclopædic volume of other informa-tion useful to those who might need it. One hand only moves once every four hundred years!

When I think back on Besançon, there are surprisingly few outstanding features impressed in my mind. Yet my recollections are of the most pleasant: the charm of Besançon is its magnificent situation and the quiet atmosphere which only old age can impress upon a pleasant city. Of all its historic buildings the one which intrigued me most was the house where Victor Hugo

D

was born.   If Besançon had done no more for humanity than to produce Victor Hugo, all her long labours would have been well justified.

George looked ahead in anxious apprehension as we turned to the south-west.   The Vosges had been deceptive because of their forest-clad slopes: they looked like hills, but turned out to be mountains.   The Juras looked quite a different proposition: the map indicated that we faced a spot of real climbing.

The road mounted gently, then it followed the course of a lovely river valley, flanked by white limestone cliffs crowned with trees.   Sometimes it narrowed to a picturesque gorge: scenically the sequel was disappointing, for the road crossed an open pastoral tableland, green and pleasant, but not panoramic.

We halted for the night at Pontarlier.   I thought it undistinguished, but there were many visitors.   In the winter it is much frequented, for the smooth slopes of the Juras offer admirable ski-ing grounds.

I had put in a fairly full day.   The morning ride had been easy, and Besançon pleasant, but the long continuous climb to Pontarlier was fatiguing.   My idea of an evening's entertainment was to sit at a café and maybe strike up an interesting conversation.   Instead, I met Alphonse.

"What?   You leave Pontarlier to-morrow morning? Ah, then you have no time to lose.   Come, finish your drink quickly, and let us set off."

"But I was going to have another drink after this," I said weakly.

"Later, later!   Now, I must plan this out——"

I resigned myself to my fate.   I was hopelessly in the toils of an organizer.   I could almost see his grey matter working.

"Now, we have no more than two hours of daylight left.   We must hurry."

"I don't feel like hurrying."

"We must. Otherwise my plan will not be completed. Here is a walking-stick—you will need it. Now, I will explains things to you as we go. You can make notes if you like—there is no copyright in my remarks. Now, this is a tributary of the river Doubs."

"But I saw the Doubs at Besançon."

"Yes. This is the same river."

"But at Besançon the Doubs was flowing from east to west: this flows west to east. There must be a big splash when they meet."

"The Doubs forms an enormous loop as it passes among the mountains. It flows in all directions."

"It is a lovely river."

"For my part, I prefer a river which knows its own mind. The Doubs has no plan—it just wanders on. Now we are climbing."

"I had suspected that!" I commented, for we were toiling up a steep and rough track. "Where are we going?"

"I shall show you. In my mind I have organized a rapid tour. We have so little time that it means very hard work."

I groaned. I dislike hard work at all times.

"Now, this was once the Fort de Joux."

"I see. It has had a bit of a bashing."

"It has interesting associations. Napoleon came here. There was a battle here in 1871."

"My dear Alphonse, I know I am weak at dates, but I do know that Napoleon wasn't alive in 1871."

"Who said he was, idiot? This was another battle, in the Franco-German war. Napoleon did not fight here."

"Ah, then the place has real distinction!"

"Mirabeau was imprisoned here—the younger, not the older."

"I didn't know that there were two of them!"

"I perceive that your studies of French history are incomplete. I will plan you out a course of reading. There was another interesting prisoner here—Toussaint L'Ouverture."

"What, the negro patriot from St. Dominique?"

"I always knew the English were strange! You did not know that there were two Mirabeaux, yet you know of Toussaint L'Ouverture!"

This casual incident somewhat rattled Alphonse. Like all organizers, he had assumed that I was completely dumb. He hurried me to points of vantage, but the fire had gone from his non-copyright remarks. As we neared the hotel he recovered his spirits.

"I have a little time in the morning," he explained. "I can just rush you round one or two places. My plan is this: we will set off at six——"

But my own plan was better: to set off at five—with George, not Alphonse. I do not appreciate organization.

I turned back to look over the pleasant lowlands left behind. Even this peaceful scene was scarred by the suggestion of war, for I noted forts perched precariously on the crests. Nor could I class them as unnecessary; the drums of war were beating in Germany, and a swoop through Switzerland was not merely possible but probable. This extension of the Maginot Line might be the first to see service.

Actually it was the last—attacked from the rear by German storm troops breaking through the French armies of the north. Who could have prophesied the tragedies of June, 1940? Not even Hitler himself.

XI

There has never been a frontier province in Europe which has not been the scene of continuous strife. Alsace and Lorraine, by virtue of their border position between Gaul and Teuton, have not escaped that unhappy lot.

For several centuries Frenchmen and Germans have disputed about their natural frontier, the French claiming the Rhine, the Germans insisting that the watershed of the Vosges mountains was the natural boundary. Both arguments are fundamentally insecure, for there is no such thing as a natural boundary.

When, three thousand years ago, the human swarm spread from the east, the settling tribes did not halt on the right bank of the Rhine, but passed over to the green meadows on the further bank. No river was ever intended by nature to form a barrier between races; rather it is a kind of artery around which a racial body can form itself. Thus a considerable portion of the people of Alsace are of the same racial origin as the Germans on the right bank of the river. (The question of Lorraine is quite different. In any case, only about one-fifth of Lorraine was involved in the transfer of 1871.) In older days, however, the race of a people meant very little, since they were at the disposal of a feudal overlord. In later years the mind rather than blood has been the decisive factor.

Nor is language a true guide. About two-thirds of the people of Alsace and a much smaller proportion of the people of eastern Lorraine speak a German dialect as their first language. According to Hitler, this is an adequate reason why they should find themselves under German rule. But it is no argument that a country has a right to claim territory inhabited by people who speak its language. If so, Switzerland would immediately disappear from the map, divided between France, Germany and Italy. Germany might even claim Holland and part of Belgium; Spain and Portugal between them would claim the greater part of South America: and, of course, Britain would naturally claim the United States. Or, maybe, since U.S.A. is now so predominant numerically, the claim might be the other way round. A common language is no evidence of common ancestry: there are hundreds of cases in history of forced changes of language.

Yet if a boundary of the spirit could have been formed, then the frontiers of 1869 and 1919 would have been found approximately correct. Cultural development has advanced more during the last two centuries than during the previous ten. For the greater part of its formative years Alsace was under French rule and influence, and to-day its spirit is largely French. It is impossible to mistake it, even when its outward form is German. Throughout modern history Alsace has been among the leading homes of progressive thought. It was far more significant that it was in a house in Strasbourg that Rouget de L'Isle first sang that song of liberty, the Marseillaise—that fact is far more significant than the other, that the people who lived in that house spoke German as their first language.

After centuries of rule by local princes Alsace became French in 1697, and remained French until forcibly seized by Germany in 1871. The natural reaction of the Alsatian was one of resistance, a violent protest against forcible seizure, being handed over from one country to another like a flock of sheep. Naturally, this vigorous resistance could not be maintained, and after twenty years of struggle the local patriots scrapped the idea of reunion with France and substituted instead the vision of an antonomous state within the German Empire. It

would have paid the Germans to have given heed to this
demand; instead, they treated Alsace as conquered
territory, and complicated the position by planting three
hundred thousand German immigrants in the province.
Nevertheless, spasmodic German attempts at assimilation
in Alsace-Lorraine met with some success, but it is significant that when the Germans crossed the Rhine in 1914,
they were warned that they were entering hostile territory
and must conduct themselves accordingly.   Hundreds of
Alsatians and Lorrainers were imprisoned for the duration
of the war as suspects, and thousands were exiled to
safer parts of Germany.

The restoration of Alsace-Lorraine to France was
hailed by the world as elementary justice—a reverse of
the doctrine of might over right.   It is worth while
noting that the German complaint ran that Germany
surrendered on the basis of President Wilson's Fourteen
Points, which subsequently were not implemented.   Yet
the restoration of Alsace-Lorraine was one of the
points.

It had been interesting to note the progress of opinion
in France.   Immediately after 1871 there was continuous
talk of revenge; gradually this died, as it was bound to
do, and if your acquaintance with France before 1914
was superficial, you might be pardoned if you thought
that revenge was a forgotten policy.   True, the Statue
of Strasbourg in the Place de la Concorde was veiled,
but there was no more talk of marching to the liberation
of the lost provinces.   It is not true that Alsace-Lorraine
formed one of the causes of the world war: it is true
that the problem was likely to keep the war going once
it had started.   Once France was at war, the recovery
of Alsace-Lorraine became a major war objective.

But deep in the heart of every Frenchman the old idea
always prevailed.   It was not merely a question of
sentimental aspirations, but of injured pride.   It seems

that it is impossible to inflict a major humiliation on a great power without inviting revenge. There was a time when Britain withdrew from the Sudan—but it was quite certain that we would return. In 1896 the Italians were defeated by the Abyssinians at Adowa. Revenge was only postponed. In 1871 the Germans humiliated the French: the tables were turned with a vengeance in 1919. From that date the Germans in their turn have never ceased to writhe under the humiliation of Versailles, and the present war is the direct result.

What of the people of Alsace-Lorraine themselves? The Germans claimed that a plebiscite should have been held—though this was not even hinted at in the Fourteen Points. No plebiscite had been held in 1871. For my own part, I am inclined to wish that a popular vote had been taken. For if the German settlers had been excluded —and this would have been no more than just, since they had but recently been planted by the Germans—I am convinced that the plebiscite would have shown an overwhelming majority in favour of France. I was one of the men who marched beside the French soldiers into the recovered provinces in the last days of 1918, and I shall not easily forget the rapturous welcome given to the incoming French troops.

The German settlers were given the opportunity of returning to their own country. Some exercised this option, but others remained, and they have provided a serious problem with the passage of years. From the first moment of reunion difficulties were encountered. Currency was in a state of chaos; the value of the German mark in Alsace-Lorraine dropped almost to zero, and financial ruin threatened. The French Government tackled the problem with great courage and generosity: it shouldered the burden of the depreciated marks. The legal chaos was straightened out—for the provinces, of course, were still under German law. The best of France's administrators were seconded to the needs of the provinces. Germanic ideas were treated with remarkable tolerance: energetic action was taken to heal the war scars, and the Alsatian villages were among the first to be rebuilt.

The religious difficulty was more fundamental. The Alsatian is a fervent Catholic, and in Alsace the hold of the Church was strong, and atheist France was suspect. The French attitude was conciliatory if not entirely logical—the Church in Alsace still retained its old powers. In spite of this, the clergy of Alsace were generally to be found in the opposition camp—until the rise of Hitler persuaded them that there was a more dangerous enemy just over the Rhine.

There were two forms to the opposition movement: one party, small but dangerous, demanded return to Germany. This party was comprised largely of the descendants of the planted German settlers. The other was far more important, an antonomous movement, favouring self-government for Alsace within the French Empire.

At first it made little headway, for the French administration was so tolerant that it detached many of those who had merely been suspicious. Complete freedom in religion and education began to have beneficial results. The autonomous movement in its turn took several forms—and received a bitter blow when it was revealed that one important wing was backed by German money. The rise of Hitler provided the hardest blow of all. Public opinion in Alsace has always tended to the Left, and there is a very strong Socialist element. Dreams of independence were rudely dispelled when it was realized that separation from France meant inevitably incorporation in Nazi Germany.

Since that time the autonomous movement has been

more accommodating in its relations with France, but its extremist section has taken a definitely separatist tendency. Even before the rise of Hitler, there were men who were working furiously for the return of Alsace to Germany—some of them were tried and imprisoned for sedition in 1928; the evidence revealed German complicity. After Hitler's rise to power, local Germans of Alsace were freely used as agents of propaganda and as spies, and in the early days of the present war more than one of the leaders of the separatist movement were caught in acts of open treachery and were shot.

Visiting Alsace immediately before and during the present war, I found the feeling overwhelmingly in favour of France—apart, of course, from the descendants of the German immigrants. It was necessary to evacuate the population of the towns and villages from the battle zone, a belt of territory adjoining the German frontier. I talked with many of their people, and found that they had a very clear appreciation of the course of affairs. They were filled with deep resentment for Hitler, and an equally deep appreciation of the solicitude of the French Government for their welfare. Many of them were quartered in central France, living in the homes of local people, for the first time in contact with folks of real French stock. I do not know whether this contact has been sufficiently prolonged to secure the widespread results which it promised.

To-day German troops are again in occupation of the historic frontier province, and the swastika flies from the cathedral tower of Strasbourg. French street names have been removed: French newspapers forced out of circulation. The German settlers of Alsace have been given their lead, and the antonomist factions are being wooed. The idea is obviously that Alsace-Lorraine shall 'demand' incorporation with Germany. Such a demand will doubtless be made: it may even appear to be 'unanimous'; but it will be a lie. Do the dictators think us fools, that we cannot see through their fakes?

Maybe the final *dénouement* will not be made until the war is over. The German peace terms have not been formulated, but if Hitler wins—or even draws— it is no less than certain that he will demand Alsace-Lorraine. This would be double tragedy: it would make a further war almost inevitable, to heal once again the broken pride of France. It would be a bitter blow to hundreds of thousands of Alsatians and Lorrainers, whose spirit is the very essence of democracy. Their own outlook is exceedingly clear: if you will study the ancient and picturesque houses so freely encountered in Alsatian towns and villages, you will find in them traces of the architecture of eastern France and western Germany. That is the Alsatian idea—that their province is not there to separate France from Germany, but to join these two rival states.

Where there is progress of the spirit there is a disgust with war. The Alsatians have a double reason for apprehension, because of their position as a frontier province and because of their high progressive level, more desperately devastated by war than a primitive state.

It is always worth while looking at war memorials. As you wander about these villages of France, you will notice the village memorial—the statue of the *poilu* with the inevitable inscription: 'To the sons of —— who died for France in the World War.' In Alsace the inscription is different. It has to be different: picture the situation in 1914; the young men were of course serving as conscripts in the German army, but thousands of them slipped over the frontier to fight for France. It was difficult enough, as some of my readers know to their cost, for an English mother to sit at home while her sons were at the war: imagine the

anguish of an Alsatian mother whose sons were fighting
on opposite sides! More than once I have sat in an
Alsatian village and have traced cases where Alsatian
brother faced brother on the same part of the front.
It may easily have happened that brother killed brother.

So the inscription on the Alsatian war memorials
cannot read: 'To the sons of —— who died for France
in the World War.' Instead it runs: 'To the children
of ——, *victims of the World War.*' The difference in
phrasing is striking. Then follows not one list of names,
but three: those who died fighting with the Germans,
those who died fighting with the French; and the third—
most pathetic of all—a list of Alsatian men, women and
children who were killed when the tide of war surged
over their village.

CHAPTER TWO

SWISS INTERLUDE

I

SWITZERLAND is very like the picture postcards: I cannot decide whether I thought of this first, or if somebody else said it earlier.

It is the neatest and tidiest country of Europe. Even its mountains are under proper restraints. It is admirably planned and organized—which is probably why I like Switzerland rather less than so pleasant a country really deserves. I have never succeeded in finding any spot from which it is impossible to see an hotel: if there are two houses, one is an hotel, the other a chalet to let.

I have managed to lose myself in every country of Europe except Switzerland, where there are so many signposts to the square mile that the feat is impossible. Even the footpaths are branded so that the veriest nitwit could not stray. Appreciating the low intelligence of the average human being, a benevolent Swiss council even halts the wayfarer at the best points of view, and tells him what to look at.

Even if you are deliberately perverse, it is difficult to wander from the paths, which are bounded by a fence and a precipice. The freedom of the Pyrenees is sadly lacking: there you can walk for a hundred miles without touching private property. Although the Swiss mountains are far higher, they seem tame: like animals in a zoo, there to be looked at.

Everything is commercialized, yet in no country is

commerce so frank, pleasant and sincere.   You get value
for money, and service from people who really know
what service means.   They charge you for it, but give
full measure.   The only ramp I ever met in Switzerland
concerned nationality, when a man calmly informed me
that a charge was eight francs if I were English, eleven
francs if I were American.   I asked for an amended
quotation as I was a Hottentot, but was unable to
make him understand.

I have been back to Switzerland several times.   Its
scenery is probably the finest in Europe, yet I know
a dozen other countries I would rather visit.   Its people
are friendly and admirable, yet I feel more at home
with Balkan gypsies.   There is a clash of temperament
and atmosphere between Switzerland and me: I am out
of place in this orderly land.   The fault is mine, not
Switzerland's.

One small feature may explain the foreign atmosphere
of Switzerland.   As I wandered its lovely valleys, there
seemed to be something missing.   At last it dawned in
upon me—there were no war memorials.

II

We had made a narrow escape from Alphonse, who
had descended unexpectedly early with a new plan.   I
abandoned breakfast and escaped through another door.

The rise was gentle, and George rode easily through
the glorious cool of the morning.   We admired the gorge
of La Cluse, and glanced upward at the forts topping
the rocky cliffs.   They were ancient, as forts go, but
looked substantial enough.   A breakfast at Jougne, and
the frontier was at hand.

I always judge the civilization of a country by the
ease or otherwise with which a bicycle can cross its

frontiers. In some parts of Europe this appalling process takes several hours: in Switzerland about thirty seconds. The frontier guards looked at George, admiring his gears: "Though you won't need them for the next hour," one of them said.

He was right. A glorious coast down a rapid but easily negotiated descent. Many a time I have been bitterly disappointed: after toiling up to a mountain pass, I have eagerly mounted George, looking forward to an exhilarating joy-ride downhill. Instead, my hands have ached with fierce gripping of brakes, and my hair has mounted to the perpendicular as we rounded acute corners at appalling angles.

The Juras are not majestic, but they are always green and pleasant: except when the sun hid behind clouds, when the scene assumed a strangely sombre aspect. The Swiss villages appeared more substantial than the French: maybe because they had not had to expend so large a proportion of their incomes and energies on war.

Yet even peaceful Switzerland could not escape the scourge of Hitler's coming. With the menace plainly realized, the Swiss built forts along their German frontier. Hitler protested that this was unneutral, so Switzerland built a few forts on the French frontier too. I laughed aloud as I passed them by, beautifully camouflaged in shades of green: for the business end faced Germany, not France!

The road wandered up hill and down dale, but George was happy. The hills were pups after the passes we had already tackled. Maybe I was now getting my first wind, for the continuous ascents had ceased to distress me. My route was rather formal. The terrace of the donjon at Orbe was very Swiss, precise and ordered. Yet the difference in the cost of living was marked. At Besançon the previous day I had lunched very satisfactorily on the equivalent of one and sixpence. At Ouchy for a similar meal I paid four shillings. Why? Experts murmur to me about the gold standard, but a cow and a potato are still a cow and a potato even if they cross a frontier.

Lausanne was very much of a tourist resort, admirably organized. I liked best the older quarters of the town, perched high on the hillside. From a dozen points in Lausanne there is a magnificent view—amply indicated by signposts. The eastern end of the lake of Geneva is magnificent, enclosed by high and picturesque mountains: the protruding castle of Chillon is one of the most famous picture postcard views in the world. The Geneva end of the lake is insignificant.

I do not pretend that I enjoyed my ride to the west. The road was too popular: I was submerged in a procession of cars and buses: rather like the Great West Road on a Sunday afternoon. Instead of the free mountain air of the morning, I now breathed exhaust.

From time to time signposts indicated views of Mont Blanc, but the lion was sulking in his den of clouds. Mountains usually are when I want to look at them. I had been to see Mt. Blanc previously, but had never succeeded. Once the summit was actually visible, I believe, but the hall porter omitted to call me.

III

I halted at Nyon. Here Mr. Eden discovered the only way to talk to the dictators: it is a pity that the lesson was not heeded. During the Spanish Civil War, submarines were sinking neutral shipping in the Mediterranean. Everybody knew that the submarines were Italian, but Mussolini's envoy naturally denied it.

"Very well," said Mr. Eden, in effect; "nobody owns

these submarines. Therefore they are pirates. So we sink them on sight."

And orders were promptly despatched to the British and French navies accordingly—and the sinkings ceased in a night. It is galling to think that we knew the only way of arguing with egoists, but did not subsequently employ it.

I waited for Mt. Blanc to emerge from the clouds: I knew I was looking in the right direction, for the sign-posts told me so. I began to suspect that the picture postcards were faked, the summit of Mt. Blanc being painted in afterwards. But an old man assured me that there *was* a view of the mountain over the lake. Probably he had seen it when a very small boy.

"What did you do about the language?" people often ask when I return from a journey. The question does not arise in Switzerland, where children are taught English from menu cards in their cradles. Nyon bristled with advertisements for afternoon tea. (There was even one appalling 'Ye Olde Englishe Tea Room'.) Yet the amazing thing is that ladies tell me that none of these foreigners can make tea. I don't understand that. There is no high mystery about making tea—I can do it myself. True, I have to be told each time how many spoonfuls to put in, and how many for the pot, but in the end I usually get tea, even if the strength is experimental. Wherein, then, lies the difficulty?

Geneva has always been famed as a centre of intellectual culture, but it is a rather dull place. Officers of the League of Nations complained to me that it was difficult to entice really important ministers to headquarters. I suggested that the remedy lay, not in the nature of the business, but in the lack of attractions in the city itself. There is a famous view of Mt. Blanc, but foreign secre-taries don't want to stare at a mountain for ever: be-sides, the mountain isn't often to be seen. There is a

E

cathedral, a museum, and some statues—none of them
exactly appealing to the *joie de vivre* of Cabinet Ministers.
There is an illuminated fountain reminiscent of Wembley,
and a boating and bathing station at the meaner end of
the lake.   If they would make me publicity manager of
Geneva for a couple of years I would undertake that
Prime Ministers would fall over themselves to head
deputations thither: if my advertisements mentioned
museums and monuments, it would be at the bottom,
in very small type.

I can, however, give one very high mark to Geneva:
its method of collecting household refuse is the most
hygienic I ever saw.   Each house has a large metal
container with an automatic lid: this fits into a kind of
funnel in the collecting lorry, and the refuse is forced
out by suction.   Not a speck of dust escapes into the
road.

The palace of the League of Nations is a grandiose
affair, but its atmosphere was lifeless; the gloom of
tragedy overhung it.   Yet it was not the League that
failed, but the Nations.   Many of its members never
pretended to believe in it: others did—and they were its
worst enemies.   Yet when this present war is over, and
the hurly-burly of its aftermath subsided, we have either
to recreate the League or make something very like it.

In the immediate post-war years, the Swiss were rather
proud of the fact that one of their cities had been chosen
as the headquarters of the new League.   In 1939 I found
them wishing heartily that it would remove itself somewhere else.   Hitler had condemned the League, and
Switzerland was nervous about Hitler.   Only in Geneva
itself was there even moderate enthusiasm, for the League
has considerably increased the tourist traffic of the town.

CHAPTER THREE

SAVOY

I

GENEVA is only just inside Switzerland. Perhaps that is why the Germans were so suspicious of it as a League headquarters.

Three miles after leaving Geneva I was back in France. There were big mountains ahead, and half a dozen times I wrongly identified Mt. Blanc: what I thought was the summit turned out to be white clouds instead of snow.

It was market day at Bonneville, a little town enclosed in vine-clad hills. I wish I could take down French in shorthand: I would love a verbatim version of the patter of the barkers and cheapjacks, who can be even more fluent in French than in English. The salesmen at the stalls are excessively persuasive; once I betrayed my interest so keenly that I apparently became the purchaser of a pair of lace curtains. The lady kindly took them back: I was quite confident that she would soon sell them again. She was so persuasive that I believe she would have sold a Bible to Hitler.

The road followed the Avre valley. At first it was very pleasant; after Cluses it was magnificent—a tremendous gorge, often a mile wide, between enormous cliffs of grey granite. There were occasional cascades, many high on the mountainside, with lace-like effects of spray in their long drops. Occasionally a break in the cliff face would reveal a cloudy vista of great mountains to the east.

Cluses is a famous watch-making town. I was taken into one factory; because I am completely unmechanical, I was fascinated. It was a good thing that the proprietor was not so fluent as the market woman of Bonneville, or I might have found myself the purchaser of half a gross of wrist watches.

I halted for lunch by the roadside, a few miles short of Sallanches. I munched my fodder in great content, for the scene was inspiring. Though the distant giants were still enveloped in cloud, the near prospect was grand.

I sat for a while, thinking. I don't believe I dozed, but when I think I am often oblivious to my surroundings. Suddenly I realized that an old man sat opposite, on a heap of stones on the other side of the road. He, too, was munching: finished, he sat on to admire the scenery. I called across a greeting.

"This is a grand spot," I added.

"Aye," he agreed. "Nearly forty years I have worked along this road, but I never cease to marvel at the glory about it. Did you ever see anything so majestic as Mont Blanc?"

"I'll tell you that when I've seen it!"

"What do you mean, when you've seen it?"

"Well, whenever I look, it isn't there."

"What on earth are you talking about?" he cried. "Turn around!"

I turned around: then gasped. The clouds had blown away. Mont Blanc was suddenly revealed in all its inspiring glory. I took back all I had ever said about conventional scenes.

The old man was astonished at the warmth of my handshake as I made to move on. So often we turn our back on things of beauty. Now the mountain was continuously in view, with a different aspect at every turn of the road. The nearer I approached, the more inspiring towered its majesty, snow-covered at the peaks, its grey slopes slashed by great glaciers.

The road began to climb seriously, flanking the lower slopes of the massif. Instinct drove me upwards to Chamonix. The place is no more than a maze of hotels and shops, but there remain one or two signs that it was once a Savoy village. The fountain in the main street is grandly unsophisticated: just behind is a wooden trough, in use until recently replaced.

Why do the shops at holiday resorts stock such expensive merchandise? I put the poser to a shopkeeper of Chamonix. He explained that people on holiday are in a mood ripe for spending. A man will cheerfully pay ten guineas for a cuckoo clock when at home he would begrudge ten shillings for an alarm. Tourists are particularly susceptible. They like to cluster their homes with things they 'picked up' abroad—it gives them the cachet of travellers with their friends. Some of the things they 'pick up' are substantial, including wooden bears weighing a couple of hundredweights.

"And what about carriage and customs dues?" I asked.

"We prefer not to discuss such mundane affairs until the sale is concluded," he chuckled.

All the business is done at night, he explained. The streets are deserted from 7 to 9 p.m. while everybody feeds. Then the shops open again. They know no eight-hour day: they *must* open at night, for during the day everybody is out of town on excursions. Why not close during the daytime? I demanded.

Eventually I made a hurried departure. The constant threat of war had seriously reduced the trade of Chamonix. The proprietor began to turn the conversation into dangerous channels: I detected a certain look in his eye. I am a tender-hearted man, easy to move. Had I not escaped I might have become the owner of a carved wooden bear weighing about two hundredweights.

II

When I got down the following morning, the hall porter was tapping the barometer.

"It's going up," he announced.

He was an optimist: the barometer might be going up, but the rain was coming down.

"What does one do at Chamonix on a rainy morning?" I demanded.

He murmured something about drinking coffee until the rain stopped.

"I am not here for an orgy of coffee-drinking," I protested. "Find me something to do, or I mount my bicycle and coast down to the valley below, where I may possibly find respite from this remarkably cold brand of rain you favour here."

Without great conviction, he suggested that I should take the mountain railway to the Mer de Glace—it might carry me above the rain-producing clouds. His argument appeared to me sensible, and he gravely presented me with a pair of cotton socks to pull over my shoes.

In the train was a party of Belgian visitors, a dozen or more, mostly girls. We chattered hopefully as the train mounted through the clouds. Yet a second layer must have floated above, for the rain was firmer and colder than ever. We sheltered miserably for ten minutes, but I am not good at waiting.

"Well, you will please yourselves," I said, "but for my part I have come to see the Mer de Glace, and I intend to see the Mer de Glace."

There were murmurs of appreciation from the feminine section of the audience at my intrepidity, and they streamed after me into the rain. It was not a very successful expedition, for visibility was limited to a hundred yards: however, it was exciting, for the rain made the ice more slippery than normal, and our cotton socks seemed strangely ineffective. I picked up two or three girls, until I decided that they were falling down merely for the pleasure of being picked up by the intrepid Englishman.

I do not like girls who are absurdly shy, but I confess to being startled when one of the Belgians suddenly said: "I love you!"—in no intimate whisper, but a hearty exclamation. It appeared, however, that she was merely airing her English, which consisted of one or two phrases picked up from the talkies. When it was explained to her what her phrase meant, she was only mildly concerned: she was glad that it was no worse, she said.

I dumped them at their hotel, promising to drop in for dinner, and strode off, by this time so wet that a few additional gallons mattered little. I lost my direction completely: first I followed a mountain stream, halting only at a camping ground. Here was an amazing assortment, from luxury caravans to Boy Scout tents, in every glaring colour. The camping habit is one of England's gifts to open-air life: other people invented it, but we made it fashionable.

Yet camping in Alpine rain is not the most exhilarating fashion of passing a holiday. I saw a batch of newcomers to the site, and pitied them. Like nearly all hikers, they carried far too much on their backs, and were dog-tired: and now they had to pitch their tent while the rain added to their misery.

I struck across the valley. Here was a hamlet of substantial farmhouses, with exterior timber staircases. The atmosphere was so unsophisticated that I boldly knocked at the door of the first house, and was welcomed inside.

"Are you a tourist?" they asked.

SWITZERLAND

GENEVA

CHAMONIX &
Mt BLANC

SAVOY

St JEAN DE
MAURIENNE

ITALY

COL DE
GALIBIER

COL DU LAUTERET

BRIANCON

GUILLESTRE

BARCELONETTE

ENTREVAUX

MENTON
NICE   MONTE CARLO

MARSEILLES

MEDITERRANEAN   SEA

"In a way, yes. At least, I am on tour."

"That is strange; tourists never come here. It is on the wrong side of the valley. The view isn't so good from here."

"I'd rather talk to people than look at views," I said. "You are Savoyards?"

"Yes."

"You know that Mussolini wants you, of course?"

"Yes—but we don't want him, do we, Benito?" demanded the lady of the house.

"Benito!" I echoed.

"Yes. Oh, there is a lot of Italian blood in Savoy. At least, Lombard blood—that isn't the same thing. But Mussolini, and Fascists, and castor oil—bah!" She spat vigorously and accurately into the fire.

I looked at her in interest. She might have passed as an Italian 'type' with her dark skin, black hair, and fine features. Yet her French was flowing, and I found that she knew no Italian at all—only family names preserved ancient connections.

"Most of the people here are of mixed ancestry," said Benito. "You expect it in a frontier district. But what is blood? If it is everything, then there is no Switzerland. Things of the spirit count more than those of the body. We are French. Let Mussolini come for us if he wants us—we shall know how to put the monkey back on the organ."

"You know, if we wanted to buy Mussolini off, we needn't give him Savoy," said another man. "We've only to move the frontier a few yards. All he really wants is Mont Blanc. All these Fascists are after is records. They are jealous because the peak of Europe's highest mountain is in France——"

"Incidentally, it isn't Europe's highest mountain," I put in. "There's a peak in the Caucasus——"

"Never heard of it, and I don't believe it," he went

on. "Anyway, give him Mont Blanc to boast about, and he'd be happy."

"For five minutes!" said Benito. "Give him nothing —not a sausage. If you do, he'll want a saveloy."

The conversation degenerated into a discussion of records. I explained that I sought none myself—that I had no ambition to be the first man to ride a bicycle up Mont Blanc. They appeared to regard a ride to Tunis as an equally imposing feat.

III

After dinner, rain still descending, my Belgians decided to go to the pictures. There were two picture houses, one normally patronized by the visitors, the other by the inhabitants. We chose the second, and it was worth it.

Not that the pictures were good. They were Hollywood productions 'dubbed' in French. As the Frenchman never says one word where two will do, the conversation was one long gabble, and the lip movements didn't fit. There was one grand moment when the villain continued to talk for a few seconds after he was dead!

But two incidents made up for the indifferent programme. There was a newsreel, and Mussolini appeared in it. The Savoy form of disapproval is neither restrained nor polite.

The second comedy was non-political. Savoyards are fond of their dogs, and often take them to church: also to the cinema. There had already been an incident, when a terrier had nipped the leg of a sheepdog. I explained to the Belgian girls that it was part of a long-standing canine argument as to the respective merits of Greta Garbo and Marlene Dietrich. Dogs are intelligent, and have their preferences like other fans.

I approve heartily of friendship with dogs, but the cinema-going habit ought to be discouraged, I think. The last film was a 'Western', with vigorous action scenes on horseback, and much shooting between cowboys and Indians. Even boys join in such scenes vociferously: how could dogs expect to be restrained? They had already barked at the M.G.M. lion: now the cinema became a free and easy. Dogs hurriedly sorted themselves out into cowboys and Indians, and fought a noisy battle under the seats. My Belgian girls stood on the chairs, as if mice were underfoot; and my reputation for intrepidity mounted rapidly as I surveyed the howling scene with unrestrained amusement. After five minutes chaos some sort of order was restored.

Then the operator, with kindly intent, ran the film backwards to the point where the pandemonium started, so that the audience should not miss anything. It was weird to see dead Indians getting up and then being shot, while fallen cowboys recovered their horses in a fashion which would have amazed a mere circus rider. The dogs, however, accepted the second showing as an encore, and the subsequent fight was as vociferous as the first. Although one of my Belgian girls was bitten in the leg, I haven't laughed so much for a long time.

IV

The rain had degenerated into a drizzle next morning, and not all the optimistic blandishments of the hall porter could detain me longer. If Mont Blanc wouldn't play, I would show my independence.

In some mysterious way the news penetrated to the neighbouring hotel—probably the Belgian girl who confessed that she loved me had bribed the hall porter. I had a grand send-off from a bevy of ladies in an artistic assortment of pyjamas.

It was a good drop to Le Fayet: I was so occupied in navigating George that I did not notice where the change occurred, but down in the valley the drizzle was replaced by bright sunshine. This was good, for I was now at the beginning of my Alpine journey. For many days I was to follow the Route des Grandes Alpes.

I found that out at an early stage, for the road mounted rapidly to St. Gervais. Nevertheless, the scene was exhilarating: the near mountains were modest enough, but the lateral valleys revealed intriguing glimpses of snow-capped peaks. There followed a glorious ride through the Gorges d'Arby, where grey stone cliffs burst through the steep bank of dark trees.

At Albertville I thought to halt: I had covered no more than forty miles, but half of them had been spent climbing up mountainsides. However, Albertville seemed to hold no special attraction, and the map promised an easy ride along the valley of the Arc. George and I are very good at following rivers, even against the stream.

The latter part of the day was the best, as in the soft light of evening we approached St. Jean-de-Maurienne. The scene was really picturesque, and the situation of the little town rivalled that of Besançon—at the confluence of five lovely valleys, enclosed by green mountains shot with grey stone: in the background a prospect of snow-capped heights.

Here was a pleasant town of old Savoy. About the main street were narrow alleys: many of the houses had an outside staircase; others had no front entrance at all— a dark tunnel led to the back of the house. Some of the courtyards were really picturesque, their picture value enhanced by the inevitable French untidiness and refusal to part with anything which might conceivably be used again.

The little cathedral had a tiny bell tower which was almost a joke, but its woodwork and cloisters were very fine. I sat on a stone shelf and was cool: a priest looked at me curiously.

"Yes, it is seldom that we have visitors in the evening," he said, when we got into conversation. "In the middle of the day, yes, for the autocars halt here to give their passengers lunch."

I led the talk round to political subjects. He was not so forceful in his language as the farmers of Chamonix, but his opinions were identical. I spent the evening wandering from café to café, eventually being invited into homes. I had scarcely need to talk. Mention of Mussolini's name was quite sufficient to provoke the liveliest scene. I wish he could have been there!

v

The morning's ride began well, for the road to St. Michel-de-Maurienne was easy in its gradients. Then a real climb began: the road ascended in great serpentines. I halted periodically to admire the grandiose view. The higher I mounted, the more frequently and the longer I halted—naturally, for the view was finer, I persuaded myself: the fact that I was tiring may have had something to do with it.

I had topped five thousand feet when the road suddenly began to descend. This was the false pass, an inevitable and deceiving feature of a mountain road. A short descent to Valloire, and the climb began again: first gradual, then really steep. I reached the point when George refused to go any further, and where I had not the heart to urge him on. So I got off and pushed.

Here was a military camp, tents pitched on a flat shelf on the mountainside. There is always refreshment in a military camp, so I halted. It was necessary, too, for hours of solid travail awaited me. The road was rough and narrow. Every few hundred yards was a temporary widening, labelled 'Garage', where a car could halt so that another might pass.

The keen mountain air was a tonic, and the preparation of the last weeks now justified itself. This was the first serious climb of the journey; soon I would be approaching nine thousand feet. It is no despicable feat to get a bicycle up to nine thousand feet, even if you have to push it for the latter part of the journey. I had plenty of energy left as I pulled out the map to look at the last stages of the climb. In my pocket was a loose piece of paper: the instructions the doctor had given me—and the first order read that on no account was I to walk uphill! Probably he had intended to add that the first ten thousand feet didn't count.

Just ahead were two other bicycles parked by the roadside. The sight spurred George to action, and we rode deliberately up the slope. Two girls sat by their machines: one looked hard in front of her, the other was visibly distressed.

"Anything wrong?" I asked.

"Yes," said the hard staring one. "She's all out—I told her so!"

"I shall be all right in a minute!" the other protested weakly.

"You won't! We've been here an hour already. Do you know if there is a bus? No traffic has passed us at all."

"I don't know. There's a chalet on the pass, I believe."

"She'll never get to the pass. I knew she wouldn't—I told her so."

I dumped George. The girl was evidently in a bad way: her heart was pumping furiously. I don't understand mountain illnesses, but obviously the sooner she received attention the better. It would take me at least an hour to get to the pass and bring help, and it was impracticable to depend upon passing traffic—there might be no more for the rest of the day.

"Can you push two bicycles?" I asked of the hardy one. Her name, it had transpired, was Emma: it would be.

"Yes."

"Right. Then I'll push Marie Therese."

Fortunately Marie Therese was no heavyweight, so I was able to hoist her into George's saddle. She clung about my neck, half fainting. Behind us strode Emma, pushing two bicycles with ridiculous ease: she was tough, that girl.

For myself, I confess that I soon began to tire. I had covered no great number of miles, but a climb of eight thousand feet can be exhausting. And now to push a girl up to the climax of the pass! We halted frequently.

"She ought never to have tried it—I told her so," Emma declared, at each halt. The fact that she was right made her comment the more irritating.

The road disappeared into a tunnel—here was the pass of Galibier: at its exit was a chalet. The people there seemed to understand: somebody carried in Marie Therese and gave her something to drink. Emma refused all refreshment: to accept would be a sign of weakness.

They put Marie Therese to bed, but to my surprise she descended to dinner two hours later.

"Surely you ought to have stayed in bed!" I suggested.

"I told her so!" said Emma.

"I wanted to see you," whispered Marie Therese. She looked at me adoringly, and I got very nervous. This was an unusual journey: first a Belgian girl confessed that she loved me after five minutes' acquaintance, and now Marie Therese, who didn't say anything in words, but talked with her eyes.

Verbally she was not a good conversationalist: she resembled an animated doll. Her pet method consisted of a look of wonder prefacing a remark like "Did you really?" or "Oh, dear!" But at any rate her unsimulated interest was more attractive than Emma's contributions to the conversation, which consisted almost exclusively of "I told you so."

While there was still some light, we strolled gently to the old pass, a few hundred feet above the tunnel. Marie Therese clung tightly to my arm. The view was marvellous. To the east was a grand group of wild mountains. The deep valleys were already plunged into sombre shadow, but the setting sun still picked out the grey peaks, flecked with snow. This was Alpine scenery at its grandest. I wanted to sit down and think, but a man must be alone for serious thinking. He cannot do it sitting between two girls, one of whom echoed "Did you really?' and the other "I told you so."

Marie Therese's recovery was remarkable: maybe it was the tonic they gave her to drink at the chalet. She professed a great solicitude for me: insisted on going into my cubicle to make certain that the bed was aired. Emma looked on disdainfully: her philosophy was above such femininities.

I felt somewhat responsible, so promised to see them down to Briançon if they would promise to climb no more passes after that. The day's journey promised to be easy. First a descent in great serpentines to the Col du Lauteret: it was a grand coast, but needed careful negotiation. What should have been a pleasure became a nightmare, for Marie Therese revealed herself as a veritable amateur of a cyclist. I marvelled that she did not break her neck. Nor was Emma's monotonous comment encouraging. I would not care to write a topographical description of the scene about. I have a hazy recollection of continuous mountain magnificence,

PALACE OF THE LEAGUE OF NATIONS, GENEVA

BESANÇON

ON THE COL DU LAURERET

"I SAT DOWN TO THINK"

but a far more vivid mental picture of Marie Therese and her wobbling wheels precariously rounding a hairpin bend.

The Col du Lauteret is much lower than the Galibier—a mere six thousand nine hundred and sixteen feet. Nevertheless, it is a very attractive place; utterly desolate in every direction, with a fresh vista of great mountains at every point of the compass. Alpine flowers relieved the immediate scene: near the chalet is an Alpine garden, which saves visitors the trouble of wandering about to find their own flowers. Nearby was a cairn of stones: to my surprise I found that it was erected to the memory of a famous Englishman, Captain Scott. This was the district where he experimented with the motor sledges which were to prove failures on his Antarctic journeys.

I am not good at describing Alpine scenery: nor is it necessary to waste valuable paper, for a picture is often more satisfying and informative. Yet neither the photograph nor the written description can compensate for the real thing, with all its vigorous majesty.

There is something unruly about mountains which has a sure appeal to me. There is nothing regular in the craggy heights, each striving to out-top his neighbour. Only at a distance do they sometimes present a calm and solemn appearance: at close quarters they reveal their savage menace. The mood of the mountain is treacherous: a day begun in quiet sunshine may terminate in tempest.

Briançon was a welcome contrast with the stern majesty of the mountains: a pleasant and aged city, perched on a hillside. Vauban's walls still surround the old quarters, enclosing streets so narrow and steep that wheeled traffic is impossible. Main drainage is elementary, even by Balkan standards. Down the middle of each sloping street is a runnel of rushing water, locally called a *gargouille*, calculated to carry away any

F

unwanted garbage. It cannot always carry off the odour, however.

The Grande Gargouille, the main street, enclosed a gulley through which water rushed at a good thirty miles an hour. Water gushed from fountains: little streets adjoining had Clovelly-like flights of steps, twisting at picturesque corners. In the soft light of the evening, I was scarcely surprised when Marie Therese waxed exceedingly sentimental: I was saved by the protective presence of Emma, who didn't worry Marie Therese, but did me.

"Well, to-morrow our partnership ends," I announced, as we walked back to the hotel.

"What, are you going?" pouted Marie Therese.

"I told you so," said Emma.

"You must carry on with your tour. I have worked out a route for you which avoids the high passes. To-morrow you can set off for Guillestre."

"And you?"

"I stay here for a day or so. I have met an old acquaintance here, a French officer. He has invited me to stay with his regiment in the mountains."

"What? Among all those rough soldiers?" demanded Marie Therese, wide-eyed.

"I was once a rough soldier myself."

I made my adieux that night, forbidding Marie Therese to get up in the morning to see me off. Nevertheless, I was scarcely surprised to see her in the hall when I descended.

VI

The next few days were vastly interesting. Briançon is an important military centre, only ten miles from the Italian frontier. The town is surrounded by a ring of forts, perched high on the mountain cliffs. They were first designed by Vauban, but have been modernized, and ought to be capable of resisting any artillery the Italians would ever drag over the Alps.

Most impressive were the French mountain tanks, specially designed for climbing. It was strange to see these vehicles manœuvring easily at seven thousand and eight thousand feet, moving up steep slopes without apparent effort.

The frontier between France and Italy is not difficult to defend. Apart from the coastal road, there are but four roads crossing the Alpine barrier. While small patrols could penetrate by unmarked paths among the high mountains, a modern army must cling closely to roads. The French defences were impressive: forts hewn out of the living rock, well armoured, equipped, and stoutly manned. Even in winter the forts had been kept garrisoned, supplies being carried up by ski.

The French army, in these summer days of 1939, was already on a war footing: I noticed that officers and N.C.O.s wore abbreviated *galons* on their arms, so that snipers should not pick them out at a distance. There were considerable parks of artillery, much of it mechanized—and the tractors, like the tanks, were amazing climbers.

The French forces were always cosmopolitan. Here were Moroccans apparently quite happy in the new environment of an Alpine valley. Here, incorporated in a French regiment, were Italians, haters of Mussolini. Never have I heard such venom as they talked of him. They were mostly Lombards—the practical north never quite appreciated the glories of Fascism like the easily-moved south. They declared that the manufacturing north-western corner of Italy was overwhelmingly Franco-phile in sympathy: they were the cousins of the Savoyards of France.

Yet my most interesting hours were spent with a battalion of Spaniards, enlisted by the French from the Spanish Government soldiers who sought refuge in France. Now the attitude of the French troops was admirable: they did not seek war, but were prepared if it came. These Spaniards, mostly Catalans, were thirsting for blood. When I remonstrated gently, their answer was forceful.

"It's all very well for you, but you don't understand. For two years we have been fighting the Italians, literally with bare fists. Now we have rifles and machine-guns, and we can show them exactly what we can do. And we *will* show them. I don't envy any wops who find themselves up against us."

Neither did I.

As a final novelty, my friend led me to the shoulder of a mountain: the frontier was less than a mile away. Through the glasses we watched: there, on the eastern mountain slopes, was Mussolini's army on summer manœuvres.

VII

The whole scene was so interesting that I stayed days longer than I had anticipated. But when I returned to Briançon to recover George, Marie Therese was waiting for me. Unhappily, Emma had lost patience and gone. I couldn't stand the sight of her, and her refrain was irritating, but at least she spelled safety.

"I thought you would need looking after, when you came back from those soldiers," said Marie Therese. It was a very warm afternoon.

Nevertheless, next morning I was early astir. The road to Guillestre was easy, ascending only to avoid a deep rocky gorge. I halted for breakfast by a lake of extraordinary greenness.

Guillestre was a picturesque and ancient town; a feature of the church were the laughing lions at the foot of the pillar: they are weathering rapidly, and in another hundred years their features will have faded. But their backs are as firm as ever.

Immediately I faced a big climb. The rough road swept upwards in great loops, and commanded a wonderful view over the valley long before the pass was reached. A group of roadmenders gave me an excuse to halt, and I joined them in an early lunch. Their repairs, I remarked, were somewhat spasmodic.

"What would you?" they demanded. "It takes all summer to repair the damage of the previous winter, and then the next winter comes!"

I agreed that it was rather disheartening.

I was intrigued when I heard them refer to the local residents as Mexicans. It appears that this district is much favoured by returned emigrants from Mexico, who have made their fortune and returned to France. I had remarked in one village, Queyras, that it acknowledged the philanthropy of the Arnaud Brothers, who were not musical clowns, but successful merchants who had returned as benefactors to their native village.

I was lucky at Barcelonnette, which is normally an undistinguished town, with roads patterned regularly about its one straight main street. The town was *en fête*, the annual saint's day. The good people took their pleasures simply but enthusiastically. An army band was playing: the French army is democratic, and no one grumbled when the children mingled intimately with the musicians.

The children's races were amusing, as they always are. Down the streets they raced in sacks: standing in rows they sought to prove the power of their lungs by bursting balloons in one terrific gust of breath. The adult sports were more serious. George had already attracted the

attention of the cycling fraternity: now I was formally
invited to enter for the great event of the day—eighty
times round the town, they explained, a mere hundred
kilometres. And this after I had toiled wearily over a
mountain pass. I have every confidence in my own
abilities, but know my limitations. I am no racer at
the best of times, and was now in no condition for a test
of endurance except of lounging in a deck chair.

The side streets were given up to a great *Concours de
boules*. All over the town were grave-faced men carrying
two steel balls in leather straps or mats. Most of the
balls were patterned, some with expensive mosaics.
Bowls are a passion in France, though the game differs
vastly from ours. No smooth grass rink is needed: the
by-lanes were divided into rinks by logs of wood about
thirty yards apart, and any irregularities of the ground
only added to the skill of the game. I never knew that
it was possible to get so excited over a game of bowls.
Drake would have enjoyed himself at Barcelonnette. And
he would have appreciated the spirit of the local men
when, as usual, I introduced the subject of Mussolini's
aspirations into the conversation.

And when I returned to my hotel, very late, I found
a telegram from Marie Therese, hoping that I had had
a pleasant journey, was not too tired, and was taking
care of myself. I wondered how she knew which hotel
I had chosen: I discovered that she had sent her telegram
to half a dozen of them to make sure! That girl almost
deserved to succeed.

VIII

George admitted quite frankly that he was becoming
somewhat satiated with mountain scenery; there comes
a time when one mountain looks very like another, and

at a much earlier stage pushing up one mountain strongly resembled pushing up the last. Fortunately I was able to assure George, after studying the map, that only one more serious climb faced us before we reached the sea.

I do not know if the fête at Barcelonnette had sapped my energy, but I found the climb more exhausting than the others, although the pass was not nearly so high—a comparatively small matter of seven thousand three hundred and eighty-two feet. (It is understood that I do not guarantee the accuracy of these figures. I did not measure the mountains myself, but made a note of their altitude from the inscriptions on the spot. These, however, were in metres, and I am maybe a foot or two out in my mathematical calculations.)

The road was very narrow and in places remarkably rough. In its early stages, too, it was populated, not by vehicles but by interesting people. It would have been criminal to pass them by, although technically speaking I was now out of Savoy. I was crossing a sort of no-man's-land between Savoy and Nice, both coveted by Mussolini. It could scarcely be expected that such a nut would escape the crackers.

Most amusing of my morning's acquaintances was a postman. If I were not hurrying, he was positively somnolent. Indeed, as I passed him by he was fast asleep by the roadside, but he must have dozed lightly, for the swish of George's wheels woke him up. He eyed us in great disappointment.

"I thought you were a car," he said.

I hastened to query his remark. Surely we did not look a bit like a car.

"No, but it was the sound of your wheels. I have to deliver letters to one or two houses up the mountain. It is a long way to walk."

"It is more than that," I agreed. "It is uphill. Do I pass the houses? Can I deliver the letters for you?"

"No, you don't exactly pass them," he explained eagerly, "but one of them is only about an hour's walk from the road. Now if——"

But I cut him short gently, explaining that I could not possibly leave George unattended by the roadside for a couple of hours.

"I am very unlucky these days," he said, bitterly. "As often as not there is no traffic comes along the road, and I have to walk: the trouble is that I wait so long that it is always late before I get started. Even when I do get a lift, something happens to it; either it has a puncture or the engine won't face the hills, or something like that. Why, do you know, once last winter, just before the snow closed up the path I got a lift on a lorry and it ran right over the cliff."

"Indeed! Were you hurt?"

"Oh, no, I jumped clear: the driver was killed, of course, but I was all right. However, I got into a lot of trouble because my bag of mail was beside the driver, and some blood got on the letters."

"I can imagine that that would be very disconcerting to the recipients."

"Yes, some people make a fuss about nothing," he agreed bitterly. "There were one or two parcels in the sack, too. One of them contained a clock: the owner grumbled like a madman. How on earth could he expect a clock to fall over a precipice and not to break, that's what I should like to know."

He rambled on, telling the woes of rural postmen in mountain districts. At last I had to cut him short, and left him there waiting for a lift which might never come; for I have at least learned one lesson in my wanderings, that in mountain country you must break the back of your journey by midday or you will never arrive at your destination, if you have one.

The road followed the course of a mountain stream far

below us. When I got really going, I had to admit that fatiguing though the climb was, it could not compare with those of the previous day. Nevertheless, in spite of the moderate altitude of the pass, I found myself above the snowline, for there was a considerable snow field near the shelter hut. The air was keen and fine, and the view about was magnificent in every direction. As I lounged, in great content, a lorry came toiling up the path: beside the driver sat my friend the postman, grinning amiably.

"So you didn't drive this lorry over the cliff?" I asked.

"No," he smiled broadly.

"Here, what's this?" cried the driver suspiciously.

"Nothing, my friend," I assured him. "It is only that our friend the postman is a lover of excitement and prefers abrupt descents to winding paths."

"That's wrong," said the postman. "I always take the winding path—it was the other man who chose the abrupt descent. Anyway, it's a winding path for you, all right," he continued.

"Why"? I asked.

"Well, you go downhill all the way to the sea from here."

"What!" I cried, and opened the map to the breeze. He was right. I chuckled to George as we studied the situation. According to the map—of course the map might be wrong; I have frequently found them optimistic —a stream rose just below the pass. All we had to do was to follow this river Var to Nice.

IX

But George refused to be exhilarated. He had often been comforted by the idea of riding beside a river, only to find that there was no room for a road alongside the stream and he had to ascend high on the mountainside, to rejoin the stream farther down. Nevertheless, the postman was right. We swept down the mountainside in great serpentines. Then the descent was more gradual. Since we had only six or seven thousand feet to drop, it was obvious that we could not coast all the way, for the sea was eighty miles to the south. Nevertheless, we never went out of top gear for the whole of that eighty miles.

The scene changed at every turn of the road. At first the valley path was wild and green; but then it narrowed to a wild and savage gorge, with red rocks rearing themselves precipitously from the banks of the rushing stream. It was a majestic scene and, though the pleasure of the easy ride was tempting, I descended frequently along its course to admire its splendid savagery.

A charabanc halted, and thirty-two tourists descended. Cameras clicked merrily: one or two of them may have achieved results by some fluke, but the scene was beyond the range of the average amateur apparatus. The guide gathered his little flock around him: they looked at me curiously, doubtless by this time I was dirty, for the road was dusty. The tourists were English, and two of the young men were making witty remarks about my appearance to the girls by their side. I took no offence: I am fond of a good laugh myself, and if I gave them amusement, at least I could count it my good deed for the day.

It appeared that by accident I had chosen one of the stock viewpoints. Probably I ought to have recognized it, for on examination it was liberally strewn with discarded cartons which had once held photographic films.

"You see that rock over there, ladies and gentlemen?" the guide proclaimed, pointing. "No, not that one; the red one on the other side; well, that was a scene of a great tragedy. A honeymoon couple came along here——"

The two fellows and their girls giggled. Evidently their sense of humour was not very original.

"A honeymoon couple came along here," the guide continued; "the husband climbed on to a promontory and the wife stood on that rock to take his photograph. She slipped and fell to her death in the valley below."

Thirty-two necks craned forward to look at the fatal spot.

"She had only been married two days," said the guide; and, being French, there was real pathos in his voice, despite the fact that he must have repeated the story a thousand times.

Thirty-two necks craned forward even more eagerly. I had no doubt that at least thirty-two postcards would leave for England that evening.

The two young men attempted some facetious remark, but they had completely misjudged their moment. I looked at the two girls—one of them was staring wide-eyed across the valley, the other unashamedly weeping. I forgave their earlier titters, and was thankful that Marie Therese was not with me. I could well imagine the effect of such a tragic story on that sentimental soul.

I was now in the province which is known as the Low Alps; it was true that, immediately after the gorge had terminated as suddenly as it began, the mountains began to behave themselves as befitting the approach to the Riviera. Only once more did they rebel against respectability. We passed one other short gorge, a last burst of wildness; then we were in the Maritime Alps, highly sophisticated after centuries of wild freedom.

After days in which the interest had been almost exclusively scenic, it was a pleasure to chance upon a little town, of which I confess I had never heard, but which I found exceedingly charming. This was Entrevaux. Its situation is remarkable, on the slope of a mountain overlooking the Var valley. The town itself is completely enclosed within strong walls, its narrow streets and ancient houses mingling about a solid stone church. Dominating the town is a colossal fort high on the rocks above. During the last war it was used for the internment of German officers, an old man informed me.

"I suppose it is unnecessary to say that Vauban built the fort," I suggested.

"More than that," he replied. "Vauban lived here."

Immediately I decided to stay the night. Since my journey was a superficial study of the defences of France, where Vauban stayed was good enough for me.

I sat by the moat with its ancient drawbridge. Here was a quiet scene of peace. Only when I glanced upwards to the citadel could I think of war; the atmosphere was softer than I had known for many days, for a gentle breeze was straying up the valley. The vegetation had already changed: the hardy pines of the mountains had been displaced by the gentler olives. There were even suggestions of that semi-tropical vegetation which is one of the delights of the Riviera. At the appropriate hour my host came to tell me that dinner was ready. The company at the table was charming, but I was glad that I was not fastidious in food. In spite of all their skill in cookery, no race can murder mutton like the French.

We were in Nice by breakfast next morning: the map said we had covered forty miles, but I would never have believed it.

X

I don't wonder that Mussolini would like Nice. It isn't merely pleasant, but beautiful as well; and it has one advantage over many a hundred other resorts in the beauty of its hinterland. There are, of course, sophisticated pleasures by the dozen, but if only as a centre for those who like organized excursions, Nice and its Riviera neighbours must be classed among the *élite*.

To me the most attractive part of Nice is not the fashionable Promenade des Anglais, but the old town, with its narrow streets of tall houses. The visitor to Nice wants to trap the sun, the resident tries to keep it out. There are few really ancient buildings: the charm is one of atmosphere, simplicity as a neighbour to sophistication. The cathedral is very undistinguished. Three hundred years ago the dome suddenly collapsed: among the many people killed was the bishop. I noticed an occasional worshipper glancing upwards in some apprehension: even a priest gave an anxious peep.

I dumped my pack and rode light-heartedly along the coast towards Italy, for if Mussolini takes Nice he must necessarily take Monte Carlo and Mentone as well. It is a glorious ride, skirting the picturesque coves which make the coast so memorable. After the continuous green and grey of the mountains it was comforting to gaze on the blue of the Mediterranean, a shade which people consider quite impossible when they see it on the coloured picture postcards.

I do not pretend that Monte Carlo is one of my favourite resorts. To me the Casino is one of the most pathetic places in the world, a gigantic monument to human frailty or folly. I completely miss the thrills of the society novel as I gaze around the tables at the soured faces of the habitués; and I can only look with sorrow on the casual visitors who throw away a pound or two just to be able to say to their friends that they have gambled at Monte Carlo. To me the magnificent aquarium is far more interesting than the Casino; the faces of the fishes seem to be more intelligent than those of the gamblers, and there is a definite resemblance between the octopuses and the croupiers.

An American, a crude but accurate psychologist, proclaimed that a mug was born every minute. Quite a number of them eventually come to Monte Carlo. The number of 'infallible' systems for breaking the bank is legion. For a shilling you can have full details of a scheme which will make you a millionaire in a couple of hours. The author of the booklet, you must assume, is a philanthropist, since he prefers to hand over the information to you rather than to keep it greedily to himself. The truth is that he is far more likely to get rich on your shillings than on the profits of his 'system'.

Other players invent their own. You see them slavishly making notes of all the numbers which turn up. I never saw such unhappy faces as those of the professional gamblers.

Yet Monaco could be a pleasant place. Indeed, to the natives—who do *not* gamble—it is. Nor do all the visitors flock to the Casino. In its day the Society of Sea Baths, as the Casino owners euphemistically disguise themselves, have made huge profits. Their day is nearly over: they have catered for a clientele which will soon be extinct.

I chanced upon acquaintances at Monte Carlo and promised to return for the evening. First I pressed on to Mentone, the first French town over the Italian frontier, and my favourite among the resorts of the Riviera. Here I swam deliciously; the pull-back of the waves gives one an uneasy feeling, but the bathing is exhilarating.

Although I had promised George that he had come to
the end of his climbing, I persuaded him to mount to
the Grand Corniche, and he had to agree that it was
worth it. Sophisticated the road may be; it had far too
much high speed traffic to be comfortable, but it is one
of the finest roads in the world. So grand, indeed, that
I continued to the end and had to ride back to Monte
Carlo again.

I had to chuckle as I passed through Villefranche.
After his return from Munich, the municipality was so
grateful for what appeared to be peace that it named
a street after Mr. Neville Chamberlain. It does not do
to take these compliments in France too seriously; it is
quite probable that the name of the street will be changed
again in a few years' time. If ever Mr. Chamberlain did
something which France didn't like, it would certainly
be changed immediately.

Now the reader will have gathered that I am not
particular about clothes. My sole repertoire on these
rides consists of shorts and shirt, with a pullover and an
old pair of flannel trousers for cool evenings. When my
friend proposed an evening visit to the Casino, therefore,
I demurred. I had no objection to visiting the Casino
again, but I knew very well that I would not be admitted: the hall porter of the hotel was called in to
conference, and after making a grave examination of that
portion of my wardrobe which I was actually wearing,
agreed that there might be a little difficulty.

"This is a special night, too," he added. "I am afraid
evening dress is essential for the Great Room." However, the hall porter was a man of resource, as all good
hall porters should be. He summoned the head waiter,
who confessed that hidden away in a trunk was an old
dress suit which he had not worn for many years. It
would doubtless be rather shabby, but if the regulations
merely said evening dress, then not even at the Casino

could they halt a man merely because his clothes were out of fashion. I am not in the least particular about such things: my own evening dress, worn sparingly, has sufficed for my needs for many years, and will, I hope, continue to give me gallant service for years to come.

I admit that the head waiter's suit was slightly old-fashioned. He was about my size, but either had put on weight since it was made or else they used to cut the trousers somewhat more tightly than is the present fashion. However, as he said, it was a dress suit. Trouble arose when I tried to don one of his shirts, to find that my neck was several sizes larger than his. By this time he and the hall porter had entered into the spirit of the thing: the hall porter produced a colossal collar —he was an enormous man who would have gladdened the heart of a Guards recruiting sergeant. It certainly gave me plenty of neck room, but I preferred it infinitely to a tight squeeze, for the evening was warm. Unfortunately, he had no dress shirt; here, however, the head waiter announced triumphantly that he had a paper shirt; at least, he added, it was not exactly a shirt, but a front. These things, he explained, are much used by waiters inasmuch as they save excessive laundry bills. I could wear my own shirt and the paper front at the same time.

And cuffs, too? Alas, he had no cuffs, but ingeniously suggested that I should roll up the sleeves of my own shirt and go without any cuffs at all. I was still wearing a dress suit, he pointed out. I allowed them to wreak their will on me. As I emerged, I could not claim that I looked like a tailor's dummy—unless I were posing for a model of the Edwardian era. The experienced and sophisticated commissionaires of the Casino wilted visibly as I approached, but I took advantage of their discomfiture to march boldly through.

It was not a successful evening so far as I was concerned. I have already said that I do not enjoy the sight of other people throwing money away, if only because they find no pleasure in the process themselves. I was even more troubled about my suit—or, rather, the head waiter's suit. I strongly suspected that in its long incarceration in his trunk it had rotted—both the cloth and the stitches. After long respite from tails I forgot to flick them gracefully from under me as I sat down—and, when I rose abruptly, one of the tails remained on the chair.

I am not to be perturbed by small details like that, however. I rolled up the piece of cloth and put it in my pocket for, obviously, if I could not return the suit in one piece, I must at least return the pieces. A few minutes later, however, I discovered a greater tragedy in its elementary stages. The seam of the seat of the trousers was coming apart.

There are limits to my courage. I would walk about the Casino at Monte Carlo minus one tail, but not with my shirt hanging out of my trousers. I sat down abruptly and remained in a sitting posture for the rest of the evening. Then, when my friends were satiated, one of them kindly went back to the hotel to bring a coat for me, so that I might escape without dishonour.

My friends found the incident extraordinarily amusing, but I have confessed that I am fond of people with a well-developed sense of humour. I had an unexpected revenge the following morning. As we sat in the pleasant garden the workmen came round with hoses, pails and brushes, washing down all seats and pavements. One of my friends, a lady, commented that this was an excellent idea which she would like to see adopted in England. She got so interested in her theme that she sat down on one of the wet seats. When she rose she was visibly disconcerted, bearing all the traces of an accident.

G

XI

But it was time for me to hurry back to Nice, for the boat for Corsica was timed to leave. A couple of hours later I could have kicked myself hard. The boat was already full, and no further tickets could be issued. I ought to have remembered that the Corsican boats are always overcrowded. I remonstrated with an official of the Fraissinet Line.

"Well, you can't make places on the boat," he replied.

"No, but you could put on more boats," I suggested.

It has surprised me on many occasions: the steamship company concerned spends quite a lot of money in advertising—and it has something to shout about, as I hope to show, for Corsica is one of the most beautiful islands in the world. Yet, having attracted its visitors, it is unable to carry them over!

I booked a place on the boat for the following day, and prepared for a sojourn in Nice. My last visit had been paid during the season—that magic space of weeks in which the prices of everything in Nice are multiplied three or four times—or more. Why it should be essential to go to Nice during a set period and a crime to be seen there at any other time is one of those things which I do not understand. In summer Nice is certainly very cheap. Nevertheless, there was something wrong with its atmosphere. It was never planned for tourists, but for careless aristocrats of a type which is rapidly passing away. There was a strangely unreal atmosphere about Nice as crowds of ordinary homely people sought recreation there—rather like a man in evening dress and opera hat sitting on a workman's bus. There is no reason on earth why he shouldn't do, but he doesn't fit.

In the evening, Nice offered ample entertainment at

ridiculously cheap prices. At one of the Casinos was
staged a competition for amateur performers, of the type
which is so popular in France, and England too. In
France, however, the audience is more downright, and
the management with wise foresight had exhibited large
notices imploring the audience not to guy the performers.
In spite of that, one or two of the amateurs had a fairly
rough passage. I confess they asked for it. There was
one girl who sang—at least she opened her mouth and
noises emerged. Another man gave imitations, but made
the mistake of telling us what the imitations were after
he had made them instead of before. The prize of the
evening went to a cheeky little girl of eight or nine, a
born coquette who would give somebody a good deal of
trouble when she was ten years older.

And in view of the political situation, it was interesting
to note that the biggest reception went to a spectacular
patriotic scene in which the centre of the stage was
occupied by a *poilu* wearing the old tricolour uniform of
France.

XII

The original county of Savoy was entirely on the French
side of the Alpine watershed, and was part of the Bur-
gundian kingdom. Later its counts acquired the neighbouring territory of Piedmont, and their interests tended
to stray to the other side of the Alps. The people of
Savoy proper were of mixed stock, French predominating.
In the interminable series of wars and treaties of the
seventeenth and eighteenth centuries, leading to the dis-
memberment of Burgundy, the French frontiers were
gradually extended at the expense of Savoy. But the
eastern part of the county did not become French until
1860.

It was the result of a deal, and the man who gave the province away was Cavour. At that time Italy was disintegrated, struggling for liberty against Austrian oppression. In return for French help, Cavour promised Savoy and Nice. The French help was small, but the Italians won their war of liberation and handed over the payment without protest—indeed, without demand.

An arrangement of this kind might be considered immoral to-day, except by Hitler and Mussolini, but it was common enough then. And it was made between realists who knew perfectly well what they were doing. To-day there is no question about the character of the two countries; they house many thousands of people of Italian stock, but they are overwhelmingly French. In culture this is especially noticeable. Indeed, it could reasonably be claimed that, even on the other side of the Alps, the people of Piedmont have been more affected by French culture than by Italian. And to this day the general sentiment of the north-west corner of Italy is very Francophile.

Nice, like most Mediterranean cities, had a more varied history. Its first recorded conquest is by Greece—the same sea rovers who temporarily overcame Corsica. They rapidly conquered the primitive native Ligurians, and established the settlement of Nike. In course of time Nike degenerated into the softer Nice.

The Greek colony flourished until the coming of the Romans; then it began to decline. When it lost the protection of the Roman legions, it was harassed by barbarians and destroyed in the sixth century. Local nobles gradually took control, but the city and its environs were too small to enjoy independence. It was taken and retaken again and again by the princes of Savoy and the kings of France.

Mussolini's historians make great play of the fact that on Napoleon's overthrow in 1814, Nice threw itself into the arms of the new kingdom of Sardinia. The historians failed to note the cause of this event—that the Nicois are a people of peace, and did not enjoy conscription into Napoleon's army. What Mussolini does not mention is that as a result of the bargain with France for assistance in the wars of liberation in 1860, another plebiscite was held. Over twenty-six thousand people voted for return to France and only a hundred and fifty-nine votes were recorded against. Since that time the story of Nice has been one of expanding prosperity. And not even an Italian apologist could doubt the sympathies of the people to-day.

CHAPTER FOUR

CORSICA

I

THE arrival of the boat is the event of the day at Calvi, and the entire population turns out to supervise its parking. On the boat I had made the acquaintance of two Belgian cyclists, two English youths and three Scottish girls making their first daring venture abroad. As I had visited Corsica before, I was naturally regarded as an authority. My dignified descent from the steamer at the head of my troupe was unfortunately spoiled by a ship's rope concealed in the maze of human legs, over which I tripped ignominiously, George falling heavily on top of me.

After a series of scrums we got clear of the crowd and began to look for an hotel. I had anticipated trouble, for Corsica is as inadequately supplied as Marseilles. For myself accommodation did not matter very much; it was a warm evening. The two Belgians and the English youths had surely once been Boy Scouts, but in my innocence I assumed that the girls must have suitable accommodation. We did not find it, tramping wearily from hotel to hotel only to find the whole lot full. Later, when the crowds had returned from the quay, it might be possible to get lodgings at cottages. In the meantime, however, I determined to take action on the principle of the thing.

I halted for a moment to put on my trousers in order to assume a more dignified appearance, and marched boldly to the Mairie. The Mayor was at home and received my complaint. Corsica expended considerable sums on propaganda persuading people to visit the island. Such propaganda I was prepared to back, but what was the use of persuading people to come if there was no accommodation for them?

The Mayor lifted his hands in hopeless dismay. "The trouble is that everybody comes at once," he declared.

"Even in Corsica people must be aware of human habits," I countered. "Anyway, the question is, where is my party to spend the night?"

Again he lifted his hands in silent eloquence.

"Tell me," I continued. "What is the fine for assaulting a gendarme in the execution of his duty?"

"Why do you ask?" he demanded.

"If I hit a policeman you're bound to bung me in prison, and presumably the rest of my gang as accomplices."

Perceiving my determination, the Mayor donned his jacket and led our trek.

"There may be room at the Casino," he murmured.

"The Casino?" I echoed primly. "I have young girls in my party, Mr. Mayor!"

But he led us up the steep cobbled streets into the old town of Calvi, enclosed within the citadel walls. We followed him through a maze of narrow streets, till he halted before a tall building of dignified aspect. This, he announced, was the Casino.

"But it was the Bishop's Palace last time I was here!" I complained.

"Yes: it has changed hands."

It was now tenanted by a volatile Russian, apparently one of those amazing exiles who pop up at most unexpected places. He took pity on our plight and allotted us rooms. Mine was once the bishop's study: my bed was a couch, and in place of wallpaper I had thousands of ancient volumes in four languages: a place of great dignity and peace.

There is a feeling of comfort which comes to the wanderer when he has found a habitation.

We sauntered through the picturesque streets of old Calvi, stumbling along the cobbled stairways within the citadel, looking for a street whose name I had forgotten. By persistent enquiry I found it, and concentrated my party, guide-fashion, before a ruined cottage of history: for, here in Corsican Calvi, Columbus was born. I know that you will have read in your history books that his natal place was Genoa, but any Corsican will soon prove to you that this is a delusion. There is, of course, the circumstantial evidence that Corsica was owned by Genoa at the time. Nevertheless, for so remarkable a survival the house is in a pitiable state of repair. Although adorned by a suitable commemorative tablet, only a few portions of the walls of the ground floor remain, and these looked as if they might collapse at any moment.

I complained to a local worthy. "What a terrible condition you have allowed Columbus's house to fall into—you ought to be proud of it."

"That's just the trouble," he replied. "We are still discussing among ourselves whether the discovery of America is something to be proud of or not!"

We ranged ourselves on the opposite side of the street, like the true tourists we were, determined to get our own snap of Columbus's home. About us was a maze of rubbish, decayed offal—and worse. I had years before discovered that in Corsica sanitation meant emptying everything out of an upper window. Even as I photographed Columbus's house, precariously poised on a disused spring mattress, the lady next door emptied a pail of slops over me. She apologized, it is true, which was very nice of her, since it is an unwritten law in Corsica

COLUMBUS' BIRTHPLACE, CALVI

THE GULF OF PORTO

THE HARBOUR, AJACCIO

PORTO VECCHIO

that you should not stand under the eaves of a house except on your own responsibility.

There were squeals in the street as we took refreshment at a café. A wild boar was charging down the main street of Calvi: true, it was only a little one. The behaviour of the lady visitors was rather amusing—they stood on chairs, screaming, and lifted their skirts, as if the boar were a mouse! My Scottish girls stared at them in disdain. "What a fuss over a pig!" they said. The Belgians regarded their intrepidity in open-mouthed admiration: one of them was well-read, and agreed that girls who were accustomed to such fearsome creatures as the pibroch and the haggis would naturally scorn a mere boar.

We climbed to the top of the promontory and surveyed the lovely scene. The west coast of Corsica is the finest stretch of coastal scenery in Europe, and now at sunset it was at its loveliest. The rich blue of the calm sea reflected the incredible crimson of the setting sun.

"You would say a river of blood, across the sea," whispered one of the Scottish girls.

"No, one cannot think of blood in a peaceful place like this," said another. "I cannot imagine crime at Calvi."

"Yet Calvi has been the scene of battle a hundred times in its history," I pointed out. "Why, here one of the outstanding incidents of British history occurred, for it was at Calvi that Nelson lost his eye."

There was an immediate movement down towards the quay to photograph the spot where this happened—at least, I presumed this was the intention, for naturally it was far too late to look for the eye. One of the Belgians restored the party to sanity, however; as we were scrambling to our feet he asked mildly: "And who was Nelson?"

II

The two Belgians asked if they might ride with me on the morrow. One was strong and active, the other was not. They confessed, however, that they were looking forward with some little trepidation to their ride, which would be the first they had ever made in mountain country—their native Belgium being largely flat. It would be very comforting if they could spend their first day with an expert.

Naturally I could not resist such a compliment, and soon after dawn next morning we were on the road. It was a grand ride through completely deserted country: here was the real Corsica, the land of the *maquis*—a great expanse of flowering shrubbery covering hundreds of square miles. In the spring the *maquis* is at its best, a blaze of colour with sweet scents which are carried by the breeze far out to sea. Now most of the flowers had withered and died, yet the green leaves, already beginning to turn to brown—for autumn comes early to Corsica—against a background of deep red cliffs, made a scene which is unique in Europe.

I assured my friends that they would have ample practice at mountain riding. Corsica is as hilly as Belgium is flat: more so, indeed. Football is not a favourite game on the island, for it is almost impossible to find flat spaces big enough for the game. The mountains in the west rise abruptly from the sea, and soon reach respectable heights—seven to nine thousand feet. Only along the east coast is there a narrow flat strip of land: the rest of Corsica is entirely mountainous. A consecutive mile of level road is a real novelty.

For the first ten miles my Belgian friends were content: the road was a bit rough, but had a surface of tar. After

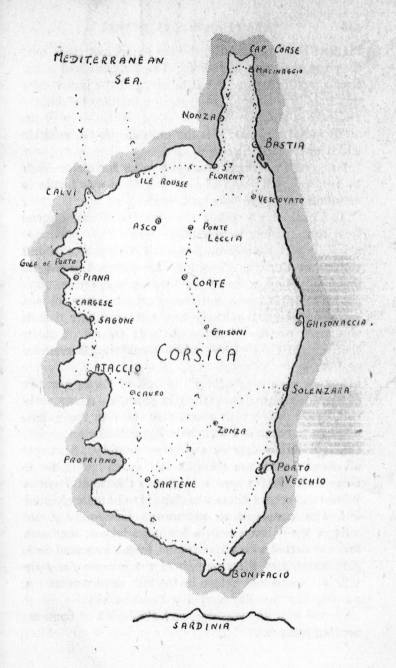

MEDITERRANEAN
SEA.

CAP CORSE

MACINAGGIO

NONZA

BASTIA

ST FLORENT

ILE ROUSSE

VESCOVATO

CALVI

ASCO

PONTE LECCIA

GULF OF PORTO

PIANA

CORTE

CARGESE

SAGONE

GHISONI

GHISONACCIA.

CORSICA

AJACCIO

CAURO

SOLENZARA

ZONZA

PROPRIANO

SARTÈNE

PORTO VECCHIO

BONIFACIO

SARDINIA

the first hour, apparently, the tar barrel had given out; then the road was appalling. The Belgians had never struck anything quite like it before, and the junior rider was frankly concerned, as every few minutes he skidded violently in a rut.

"It is not the ruts: it is the precipice by the roadside which scares me," he confessed.

I agreed that there was some cause for alarm: only by performing a series of acrobatic feats was I able to maintain my equilibrium on George.

The road struck across the great headland, dipping from time to time to greet the glorious bays which are a feature of the north-western coast, one of the wildest corners of Corsica. Save for an isolated *bergerie*, we scarcely passed a house in the morning's ride. The younger Belgian was entranced at the glory of the scene, and even the husky one had to admit that it was much prettier than the coast at Ostend. I knew that a sight awaited him which would shake even his reserve.

For we were approaching the Gulf of Porto, grandest of Corsica's bays, unequalled in Europe. A steep red cliff, freely flaked with green, falls sheer to the water's edge: in the cove is a little beach guarded by an ancient Genoese watch-tower on a tiny promontory. Scattered all about Corsica are these ancient watch-towers, for in older days Corsica was subject to raids from Barbary pirates and other visitors who claimed to be more civilized, but who were just as predatory. Consequently, the villages were always built a few miles inland; the coast-line was dotted with watch-towers, from which men could give warning of the approach of the invaders, and the villagers could take refuge in the hills until trouble had passed. To this day very few Corsican villages are to be found near the seashore, and almost all of these are modern creations.

The two Belgians succumbed completely to Porto,
as I knew they would. We lunched on the beach, after
vain endeavours to swim. At Calvi the sea had been
calm, but in this bay great waves charged against the
smooth layer of hot white sand. It was impossible to
swim, but very easy to get wet.

As we climbed the winding road on the south side of
the bay I prepared them for another of the sights of
Corsica. The Calanches of Piana are so remarkable that
I could forgive the tourist agencies for building an hotel
in their vicinity. An enormous pile of red rocks falls
almost sheer from three thousand feet to the blue sea.
The vagaries of wind and weather have worn the rocks
into the strangest of shapes—mitred bishops, gargoyles,
Turkish warriors, birds, dogs and a whole medley of
devils and angels. In the moments of the hours of
sunrise and sunset, the shadows make the weirdest
patterns of light and shade in blends of colours which
almost shatter the complacency of the eyes' appreciation.
On every hand is an eerie picture compounded of the
Peter Pan drawings of Arthur Rackham and the grotesque
caricatures of Cruikshank. Weird animals lurk in unexpected corners, while leering devils peer from overhead. The variety in gargoyles is incredible. I do not
wonder that Dante got his inspiration for his *Inferno*
from this scene. It can be one of the most remarkable
in the world: of course, it can also be very little out
of the ordinary; it all depends upon your outlook.

III

The junior Belgian by this time was showing some
signs of strain, and I tried to persuade him to spend
the night at Piana. For my own part, I proposed to

push on to Cargese, which is far more interesting. He insisted on continuing: his husky friend was in excellent condition. Fortunately we were not pressed for time, and in the cool of the evening made our ascent of the last hill before the last drop to Cargese. We had halted for tea at Piana, and made a sumptuous meal off bread from the village oven. Each village of Corsica has its stone ovens: some of these belong to single families, others are communal and are used in turn. The oven is just a chamber built of rough stones; the interior is filled with *maquis* which burns fiercely, emitting great heat; the fire is kept up continually for an hour or so, until the stones of the oven floor are tremendously warm. The fire is then damped and lumps of dough inserted, and soon the most appetizing odour assails the nostrils of a passer-by. Hospitality is profound, and an instinctive sniff means that you are presented with a generous lump of bread. It is remarkably filling, and has a slightly bitter taste. Practically no wheat is grown in Corsica—there is not enough earth on this rocky island—and chestnut flour is mingled with imported supplies. The taste is not unpleasant when you get used to it.

Cargese is a village of Greek ancestry and tradition. It was founded some centuries ago in an attempt to establish a substantial Greek colony in Corsica. To this day Grecian traits are observable in the features of the people, and the older men and women still speak a Greek dialect. There is a Greek church which is more prosperous and better attended than its Catholic neighbour. It houses some pictures, curiously painted on wood, which were brought over by the first Greek settlers: some of them, it is claimed, date from the eleventh century, others even earlier. They did not look it, but it may be true. If further proof of the Greek origin of the village is needed, the local war memorial supplies it, for the names are a curious mixture of French, Italian and Greek.

"Alas, the hotel is full!" said the landlady of the only inn in Cargese.

"I expected that," I replied. "It was full the last time I came. But you found me a place to sleep in the village."

"Now I remember you!" she exclaimed. "You are the Englishman who met the bandit Caviglioli!"

"Quite right," I agreed. "So now, of course, you will find us accommodation."

"Naturally."

She fed us well, and found us beds in peasant cottages in the village: but after dinner, when I tried to talk about the Corsican bandits, conversation immediately flagged. Corsica is very anxious to forget the last unhappy episode in the history of the vendetta: I shall discuss it later.

The Belgians were not yet acclimatized, but I insisted that we push on in the morning. Mountains are not conquered by looking at them. First came a spin along a magnificent *corniche*, flanked by red cliffs. A bathe and breakfast at Sagone freshened us for a stiff climb up a wooded mountain: a grand scene. Sagone itself is one of the pathetic places which has seen better days. Indeed, at one time it was the seat of a bishopric, but you would never guess that now.

An old man sat in silent contemplation by the road-side: we joined him. For a while we were content to look at the glory about us: then we began to talk.

One point of our conversation struck me forcibly. The old man claimed that Corsicans were men of their own countryside, who never travelled.

"But," I protested, "I have met Corsicans in France, Morocco——"

"Yes," he agreed. "But they only travelled because

they had to. Look at me: my war service took me to
Turkey, Greece, Bulgaria, Syria and Algeria. You
would call me a travelled man? Yes, but I have
never even been to Corte, thirty miles away: not
even to Calvi. Only once have I been to Ajaccio, and
that was to catch the boat for France when I was
called up for military service. No, I am quite content
to stay here."

"It is hard work, getting a living?" I suggested.

"Not for me. I have a small pension, and can live
very cheaply. I have a garden: it is growing. It will
not grow any faster if I work all day in it."

In spite of his contemplative and unenquiring mind,
his knowledge of the country was profound. He led us
into the forest to meet an acquaintance of his, a hunts-
man. His booty for the day was interesting—two falcons
and one eagle. These birds are a menace to the peasant
properties of Corsica. They will swoop like dive bombers
on a chicken roost; rabbits and even hares are not safe
from their deadly clutch.

There is a particular glory in a scene which is a combination of mountain and forest. No land in Europe can
compare with Corsica for wild beauty. There is nothing
tame and sophisticated, once the few beaten tracks are
deserted. My Belgian friends, who had never known
anything wilder than the Ardennes, were visibly startled
when a family of wild boar scurried across our path, only
a few hundred yards ahead. I was more concerned when,
turning an abrupt corner, I found myself facing a wild
cat, who made no secret of his hostile intentions. Trees
were at their grandest, and in their generous shade we
lazed away the heated afternoon hours.

Nevertheless, it was a great mistake to drop down to
Ajaccio late in the evening. In the countryside you can
curl yourself into a ditch and sleep without interruption,
except possibly from field mice and rabbits; but in a town

if you attempt to sleep on a bench the police are morbidly inquisitive.

We wandered hopelessly round Ajaccio seeking accommodation, passed on from one hotel to another. By this time the junior Belgian was visibly distressed. He was slight, pale and good-looking, so at the sixth hotel I insisted that he should go forward and demand accommodation; the other two of us were too hardy in appearance to command pity. The stratagem worked. The proprietress of the hotel, though claiming that every room was full, agreed to offer us a shake-down in the laundry. I do not pretend that this was perfect accommodation: even when not actually in use, a laundry has a steamy atmosphere which is somewhat unpleasant.

When more pleasant days return, Corsica will really have to look seriously into this question of accommodation. Its hotel service is hopelessly inadequate, and the boats are a joke—not one-tenth of the people who wish to bring their cars over to Corsica ever succeed in doing so. There is no sense in spending good money attracting visitors to the island and then turning them away.

IV

Ajaccio is a pleasant town, but it is not Corsica. Imagine a small section of the Riviera dumped down on the Corsican coast, and you have an excellent impression of the island's capital. From the health point of view, its claims are even more extravagant than those of Nice or Cannes: its mean temperature is two degrees higher. Certainly in winter it is an amazing place. By the sea you can lounge comfortably in a deck chair, while by travelling ten miles inland you can enjoy winter sports under ideal conditions.

The centre of Ajaccio is the Place de Diamant, covered

H

with a dusty gravel and exposed to the full force of the sun during the heat of the day. Fortunately for non-energetic persons, three sides of the square are shaded by four rows of sycamore and mimosa trees, plentifully interspersed with stone seats, which form an admirable gossip centre for the inhabitants. The fourth side of the square faces the sea over a submerged casino. Close by is a statue of Napoleon, contemptuously called "The Inkstand". Napoleon is represented on horseback, surrounded by his four king brothers on foot in Roman costume; and Napoleon's horse is unfortunate. Why have sculptors never solved the mystery of equine statuary? Whenever they design a horse there is a row about it. This particular horse has no shoes. We were told that the sculptor was so mortified when this was pointed out to him that he committed suicide. I don't know if the story was true: I have heard similar ones, including the suicide of the man who carved the Duke of Wellington on a horse with no stirrups. If faults of this kind are to determine the fate of artists, the mortality among sculptors of horses must have been appallingly high.

Naturally there are plenty of other statues of Napoleon about Ajaccio. Indeed, whenever I chanced across a street which had no statue of Napoleon I took a photograph of it as a curiosity, and considered writing a letter of complaint to the local town council. It is, of course, natural that the good people of Ajaccio should be very proud of their fellow countryman. After all, Napoleon must be ranked among the greatest figures of world history. I was somewhat surprised when I found his birthplace (when I say I found it, I take no credit for any detective work; it has never been lost). It was not a pretentious-looking place, just a plain stone building in a narrow street; yet the interior was surprising. Rooms are large and spacious—might even be classed as salons or small halls; their dignity and the quality of the furniture dispel some illusions. I had always looked upon Napoleon as a man of the people—had pictured him as a comparatively poor boy who had through his own force and ability made his way in the world. Yet on viewing his home, I was not surprised to learn that his father was a prominent lawyer in Ajaccio, and one of the leading notables of the island. He was, indeed, Paoli's right-hand man in his struggles for freedom, and there was certainly no question of poverty in the family.

As we wandered about the narrow streets of the old town, we got the curious impression that we were receiving an official welcome. It appeared that the inhabitants were decorating the streets for our benefit, hanging out bunting on poles from window to window. Closer inspection, however, dispelled this pleasant idea. In old Corsica the streets were narrow and houses small. The idea was a double one, to crowd as many houses as possible within the shelter of the town walls, and by the height of the houses in the narrow streets to gain precious shade. The houses are devoid of backyards, so that when the housewife has finished her washing she hangs out a pole across the street, supported at the other end by arrangement with the lady opposite.

We saw the procedure actually in operation. It seemed to be a popular event, though it happened hundreds of times in a day. The children, in particular, would gather in the street below and proceed to identify each garment, however intimate, as it was hung on the pole.

"Look! There's Jean's shirt! And his pants—they need darning. There's Louise's vest—and her pink petticoat—and her green knick——"

I led my friends away: the junior Belgian was too young.

The harbour of Ajaccio was very attractive. It is claimed that Nelson rated it as better than that of Malta—

though I had an uneasy suspicion that I had heard something similar at Calvi. Evidently Nelson went about giving testimonials to all the Corsican harbours. But the beauty of the bay needs no Nelson to commend it. The ordinary human eye will do very well.

Fishermen were mending their nets along the whole length of the quay. Cork is produced in large quantities in Corsica, and there were large piles standing on the quay waiting for shipment. This makes the repair of nets a simple matter, for when you find that some of your floats have disappeared you have only to go to the nearest pile and borrow a chunk of cork.

Yet the most pleasant part of Ajaccio is the road to the west, towards the Iles Sanguinaires. First it passes the town's cemetery, a remarkable place, where every family of any importance has its own sepulchre. Then the road skirts the sea, with a background of green hills, and innumerable bathing beaches.

The junior Belgian was unfortunate. We had swum out to some rocks and he was fifty yards away from us. We heard him shouting in dismay and noticed that he was gazing anxiously into a nearby pool of water. I was not surprised when we reached his side, for there was an octopus. There are many of these in Corsican waters. They are not big enough to be dangerous, but are exceedingly loathsome: the toad of marine life.

v

George and I parted company with the Belgians at Ajaccio. They were in a hurry, and must plan their tour of Corsica carefully to include the greatest number of show-places within their limited span of days. We preferred our own haphazard method, and headed to the south.

Genoa to negotiate. Sampiero was able to intercept her on her mission of peace: then followed the crime which is the blot on his escutcheon. To Sampiero country was more sacred than love; and, tortured by the thought that the wife he worshipped had willed to surrender to Genoa, he killed her—strangling her with her own garter, according to popular legend.

His remorse fanned his desperate mood. Once more he landed in Corsica, sinking his ship behind him in the Gulf of Valinco. This time he had no army, but a number of guerrilla bands formed at his call. The mountainous country favoured their exploits: the Genoese power almost disappeared in a series of lightning raids and remorseless annihilations. The bravest mercenaries of Europe, led by its most famous generals, failed to subdue the unflinching spirit of the desperate bands.

Treachery succeeded where force had failed. Lured to the little valley of Eccica by false news of a rising, Sampiero found himself surrounded by overwhelming forces—led by three brothers of his dead wife, who had vowed vengeance on him, and had joined the Genoese in order to execute it. He fought to the last, but his own armourer had been bribed, and had misloaded his pistol: the miserable man completed his treachery by shooting his master in the back. Thus died Sampiero, on the 17th January, 1567, at the age of sixty-nine.

This is the bare story of an island patriot; the priest, a Corsican, made it live. Later I saw the statue of Sampiero at Vasteica: his impetuous figure is rushing to the battle, and his hard eyes glare across the valleys to the mountains beyond, calling his countrymen to arms against tyranny.

Yet the tangible result of my pilgrimage was rather disappointing, as my clerical friend was bound to admit. In fact, he declared that he would bring it at once to the notice of one of the Corsican patriotic societies. It was a monument we had come to see, purporting to commemorate the actual scene of death of Sampiero. Actually, with some considerable difficulty and only with the help of one of the oldest inhabitants, we found a small stone tablet a hundred yards or so beyond the village, almost overgrown with bracken and other specimens of the encroaching *maquis*. Certainly, though Corsica may honour her heroes in her heart, she is not demonstrative. Sampiero did more for Corsica than ever Napoleon did, and he has statues by the dozen!

VI

George and I continued to climb. The country through which we passed was pleasant enough—a miniature Corsica, indeed, with hills replacing the more violent mountains of the north. On every hand spread the *maquis* in endless profusion, its summer hues a delight to the eye, even if the scent of its flowers had long been sapped by the fierce heat. As we reached the pass, we looked back over a grand prospect of the bay of Ajaccio. Yet while we wondered at its beauty, we were also amazed when we calculated how long it had taken to cover so little a distance—as flies the proverbial crow.

I never knew a day in Corsica without its incident. Near the Col de San Giorgio, we caught up one of the small and extremely uncomfortable motor buses which ply about rural Corsica. Evidently something was amiss, for the passengers had gathered in the road, forming a rough circle about the conductor and another man, who were arguing violently. The adverb is really too mild for Corsican arguments: imagine people of mixed Italian and French descent, who have only recently abandoned the vendetta as an instrument of personal policy, and it becomes obvious that quiet discussion is seldom encountered. After a brief interval as observer, and remarking the disquiet of elderly ladies who wanted to get on to market with their eggs and butter, I offered my services as arbitrator.

The case appeared simple enough. A Corsican farmer had boarded the bus at the foot of the pass; he was on his way to a day's shooting among the mountains, and carried his gun with him. As is common, he parked it between his knees, the barrel pointing upwards. Unfortunately, the lady sitting next to him was excessively stout, so that her lap was unable to support the parcel she carried. As it slid off her knees, it touched the trigger and the farmer's gun went off. Luckily for him he was leaning back talking to a man in the seat behind, or his face might have gone off with it. As it was, a shower of pellets penetrated the thin roof and came to rest in a bag of mail up above.

The conductor thus had a double claim—for damage to his roof, and for the trouble he would encounter when the postmaster-general of Corsica found pellet holes through a couple of hundred letters. I agreed at once that he had legitimate grievances, but the allocation of responsibility was far more difficult. As the bus driver pointed out vehemently, the farmer had no right to bring a loaded gun on to a public bus; the farmer in turn insisted that fat women who could not hold parcels had no right to travel on buses at all.

The conductor—he was also the driver—refused to move a yard until the question was settled. I am afraid the old lady influenced my decision, which was not strictly legal, for she announced that it was no good saying anything to her because she hadn't got any money anyway. Thereupon I suggested that the farmer should pay a moderate sum. Under impatient persuasion from the rest of the passengers, he agreed. Yet

I am of the opinion that I moved on too quickly, for as I mounted George I heard the argument begun afresh with even fiercer intensity—they were now discussing the amount of reparations the conductor was entitled to claim.

The road was disgustingly haphazard, and did not know its mind for ten consecutive miles. I can understand a road which climbs steadily to a pass and then descends just as properly on the other side, but this switch-backed continually, so that the exhilaration of each coast was soon damped by the necessity of a further climb. The sun was rising rapidly, and as the mean height was no more than two or three thousand the day promised to be very warm.

According to the map we had covered no more than eighty kilometres by the time we arrived at Propriano: nevertheless, the continuous climbing was so exhausting in the afternoon heat that when I found myself on a sandy beach, my natural instinct was for a prolonged dip in the warm sea. Then, finding a shady olive tree, I lay down to think and promptly went to sleep. I accepted the incident as an omen, and stayed at Propriano for the night.

Propriano is not outstandingly attractive. Its harbour is important, serving a considerable area of southern Corsica and carrying on a large trade in timber, leather, wine and charcoal. It was the time of the wine harvest, and there were scenes of activity on the green slopes of the neighbouring hills.

Not that the wine harvest is picturesque in these days. There was no music, no bare feet dancing on the grapes in the great presses. I have never fancied Italian wine since I once witnessed such a festival in an Italian vineyard, for the local feet were not scrupulously clean. In Corsica in these practical days a mechanical press is favoured. Towards it lumbered the long, narrow, two-wheeled cart, specially fashioned for the transport of the grapes, lined with a tarpaulin sheet; the cart can penetrate into the heart of the vineyard itself, halting at the ends of the rows of trees, and the grapes are carried to it in baskets on the heads of the workers. At the pressing places I saw them unloading the grapes on to a tarpaulin square actually in the road; then they were fed by hand into the machine, a portable affair not unlike a chaff cutter with rollers instead of knives. Two men took turns at turning the handle: the grapes were flung into a narrow metal funnel, and passed between two iron rollers. The wine streamed into a vat below, while the empty skins fell on a kind of chute and were gathered into sacks.

VII

The evening was as hot as the day, and I sat in the sea for an hour at a stretch, dipping my head under the water every few minutes to keep cool. At dawn in the morning I was on the road. The map suggested another violent journey, but I was determined to break the back of it before the sun found its strength.

By the roadside were two isolated menhirs. According to legend—which flourishes as freely in Corsica as any southern country—a monk and a nun in Sartène fell in love with each other. Forgetting their vows, they eloped: yet when they fled down the mountainside, they turned for a last look at the monastery and convent they had left behind. Perhaps at that moment, too, they remembered their broken vows, for as they stood silent in awe they were turned into pillars of stone. I do not guarantee the accuracy of the legend, but the pillars of stone are definitely there.

Sartène is a good specimen of the Corsican hill town.

Its situation is magnificent: rising on a series of terraces high above a great valley stretching away towards the sea; it claims to be the most Corsican town except Corte. As is usual, there are now two towns in Sartène, an old and a new. Some of the new streets are almost imposing, for the houses are large and substantial. The older part is the more interesting. In older days Sartène was noted for the quickness of its tempers—and this was indeed a distinction in Corsica, where men argued with swords, or, later, bullets. There were two quarters of Sartène which used to live in deadly enmity. Not content with continuous fighting through the centuries against Genoese, Romans, Greeks, Barbarians, French, Spanish and the other successive invaders of Corsica, and not content with the individual vendetta which periodically decimated the population, the inhabitants of the Borgo quarter had a permanent blood feud with that of Ste Anna. It is significant of the violence of Corsican history to recall that formal peace was only made between these two districts less than a hundred years ago.

It was a grand ride as the road bored its way between the mountains to the north. Though there were occasional descents, we were making height every hour. From time to time we passed a hill village, gloriously situated in a forest clearing on the side of the mountain. Some of them were isolated until a generation ago, for the road is comparatively modern; until recently it was no more than a mule track. If you are searching for Corsican types you will find them among the older men of this district: the austere costume is still worn, the tight trousers, the black jackets, the broad-brimmed black hat which has almost a Mexican touch about it.

Zonza in these days is classed as a resort, for there is an hotel there, and an hotel of western European standard is something of a rarity on Corsica. I had thought to stay there, but it looked too big and cosmopolitan. Of

course, there were inns in the village, but hours of daylight remained and the pass of Bavella was no more
than ten kilometres ahead. I decided to press on.

Unfortunately at this stage the road, which had
hitherto been good, relapsed into an appalling state of
disrepair. Not merely stones but miniature rocks lay
about freely, and progress was slow and laborious. All
estimates of time were soon falsified as I toiled towards
the pass, for even on the moderate gradient it was
almost impossible to ride. The rocks reflected the heat
of the sun, making it formidable even in its declining
hours.

But the Col de Bavella was worth any effort. It is
one of the grandest scenes in Corsica. Happily, the forest
breaks within a few hundred yards of the pass, revealing
to the eye such a panorama as only a poet who is also
an artist could possibly describe. A great group of
mountains, grey-tinted with red, dominates the scene.
Like a great jaw of upturned teeth the mountains surge
across the skyline; intervening lie broken valleys, fissures
of rock peeping through the shallow earth on every hand.
Here and there are stretches of *maquis*, still holding to
some of the tints of the earlier months. Even more
attractive are the isolated trees which scatter the landscape, weather-beaten, sloping and top-heavy from the
continuous pressure of a wind always blowing from
the sea.

I looked back along the road which I had traversed;
the view was not so magnificent as the nearer scene, but
its panorama was grandiose. In the evening the distant
mountains which I had crossed looked strangely dark
and sombre, yet it was possible to count six ranges of
mountains between Bavella and the sea.

Over the pass I found a strange village—not without
pleasure, for refreshment was welcome. Every house
was no more than a shack of timber or corrugated iron,

a temporary summer home for a family which, in the
winter, inhabited the unhealthy coastal plain.   In the
summer, when the snows have gone from the mountains,
there is work to be done, quarrying, lumbering, charcoal-
burning and the like.   The Corsican has the herding
instinct: he does not care for isolated cottages: even in
the mountains he prefers to live in a village, though it
may mean a walk of many miles to his daily labour.
The word 'walk' applies only to the poorest classes;
generally only the donkeys and the women walk; the
men ride.

The road descended steeply: its surface continued to
be appalling, and I got more thrills than I needed as
George negotiated hairpin bends round angles of a
hundred and seventy degrees; yet the scene was so
magnificent that I halted continuously.   After the village
on the pass I met no living soul for hours.   The road
wound down the mountainside, passing through a lovely
pine forest: this was a place of peace, undisturbed even
by the note of a bird.   In the twilight hours the jagged
mountains of Bavella were a grand picture; no Dolomite
ever blushed more prettily than these rocky monsters,
catching the last rays of the dying sun.

But even as I stood in open-eyed wonderment, darkness
fell suddenly; for I was on the eastern side of the pass
and had dropped far down its steep slope.   Probably
there would be light on the western side for an hour to
come, but in the forest the road now loomed as a dim
ribbon, its irregular stones indistinguishable from the
rock which bordered the roadside; and when I switched
on my lamp I could scarcely pretend surprise when I
found that the continuous shaking had shattered its
delicate bulb.

The descent was a nightmare journey, along a pre-
cipitous road through forest and gorge.   The gradients
were appalling—for one stretch twelve per cent—and the

road indescribable. My hands showed great weals as I gripped George's brakes. And, in spite of all caution, half a dozen times we struck a rock and fell abruptly. To this day I give credit to George that his stout wheels did not buckle. Twice as I picked myself up I recoiled when I realized that I had fallen off on the wrong side, and that less than a foot separated me from some chasm of unknown depth, singularly uninviting in the dark.

By this time the blackness of a southern night had descended—this was no question of the sunset shade on the eastern side of a mountain. It was about five hours later than I had anticipated when I rode into Solenzara, but when I saw its feeble lights ahead of me I broke instinctively into the Hallelujah Chorus.

Nor, apparently, was I alone in regarding the descent as a nervous ordeal.

"You have come from Bonifacio?" asked the welcoming host.

"No."

"From Bastia, perhaps?"

"No, I have come from Propriano."

"What! To-day?"

"Yes."

"But which way?"

"Over the Bavella pass."

"You have crossed the Bavella path in the darkness?" he cried incredulously.

"Yes. At least it wasn't dark when I got on the pass, but it was soon afterwards—too soon."

The landlord retreated to the public bar. Within a few minutes I was surrounded by his local cronies, who wished to share their hospitality with the man who had ridden a bicycle over the Bavella by night.

VIII

In contrast there was nothing spectacular about the ride the following day. For miles I rode easily along the narrow coastal plain, only rising gently as it swayed inland over a headland towards Porto Vecchio. I had been warned not to linger on this plain, which is the only unhealthy portion of Corsica. Mosquitoes breed in the shallow lagoons, and malaria is rife. All the local inhabitants who can, retire to the hills for the summer—either to work among the mountain forests, or else to sleep in some hillside cottage, descending by donkey to their business by day.

The bay of Porto Vecchio is exceedingly beautiful, though in grandeur it cannot compare with the gulfs of the west. It is surrounded by low-lying cliffs, broken by great boulders at their feet. Near the little harbour were signs of activity; fishermen at work, a cork factory with great piles of rough bark ready for export, piles of charcoal. Riding at anchor in the harbour were two or three beautiful little sailing vessels. The trade of Porto Vecchio is not sophisticated; in the manner of its carriage it differs little from the fashion of a hundred years ago.

The road from Porto Vecchio to Bonifacio is unlike practically every other road in Corsica. It might have been planned by Napoleon himself, for it is plotted in a dead straight line for all practical purposes, contrasting weirdly with the continuous zigzag of the mountain routes. The neighbouring hills were of the homely kind, and of no great height. To the left at intervals the sight of the sea struck along a lowland valley. A stiff breeze was blowing: I noticed that the gardens and vineyards were protected by high stone or reed walls, but all the

trees bore inevitable marks of continuous conflict with
the unruly elements. They had had the worst of it;
the seaward side was devoid of branches and leaves,
and it was almost eerie to see groves of pines and
olives leaning away from the sea in almost regimental
precision.

The first vista of Bonifacio was amazing: it is one
of the quaintest towns in Europe; the houses enclosed
by the citadel walls perch precariously on the very edge
of the cliff: the chalky rock has been continually worn
away by the weathering of centuries. Whole streets
actually overhang the sea and it seems that at any
moment they will topple into the water below. The
chalk strata were a fascinating geological study, and
there was an eerie sensation at the foot of the cliff with
a mass of rock and a dozen houses protruding above
my head.

Bonifacio is almost entirely enclosed within the walls
of the citadel—there is a little new town outside down
by the harbour. Before I had been in the town for an
hour I began to understand why the cliffs had crumbled.
There is always a wind in Bonifacio, for it stands on the
southernmost point of Corsica, and the wind makes for
the gap between the island and Sardinia. Had an English
policeman seen me staggering about the streets of
Bonifacio, he would certainly have arrested me. As I
lunched, doors were rattling, curtains touching the ceiling,
and the hanging lamp looping the loop. Yet when I
mentioned something about the wind to the innkeeper
he said: "What wind?" and went outside to see if he
could find it. But by our standards it blows a gale at
Bonifacio from Monday to Saturday. On Sunday they
have a tempest.

(When I got back to England and was telling a dear
old lady about Corsica I mentioned how in Bonifacio
I was very troubled with the wind.

I

"You should have taken a little oil of peppermint, you know," said the dear old lady.)

The streets of Bonifacio are narrow; so narrow, in fact, that when I halted to do up my shoe-lace the entire traffic of the street was necessarily held up behind me. A recalcitrant donkey will arrest the traffic stream more surely than a policeman's arm in Piccadilly. To make matters worse, some of the doors open outwards, and that means that if anyone carelessly leaves a door open a traffic block again is the inevitable result.

I wandered into a church, where it was alleged was housed a piece of the true Cross. I would never like to disturb people's faith, but in my travels I have seen enough pieces of the true Cross to make a good-sized fence. I have heard it alleged that their multiplication was miraculous. As I stepped outside a Curé accosted me.

"You are a stranger to Bonifacio!" he declared.

I agreed, congratulating him on his rapid and accurate discernment.

"What have you been doing in the church?"

"I went in to see the piece of the true Cross."

"Ah, then come along with me; come to my church: I can show you better things than that. I can show you Bonifacio as well; I have been here for thirty years."

I looked at him in some pity; to be relegated to Bonifacio for thirty years was surely the punishment for some fearful crime or indiscretion; but he led me proudly to his church, to display images mounted on platforms, which are carried shoulder-high in religious processions. He admitted that there was some difficulty in navigating the corners of the narrow streets, of course. He even admitted that more than once one of his effigies had been blown from its stand by a gust of wind.

He was a cheery old soul, and one of the few Corsicans who were prepared to recall the old days of banditry

He told me that twenty-five years ago bandits were particularly prevalent in the region. Nor were all of them the *bandits d'honneur*—the men who fled to the *maquis* to escape the consequences of the vendetta. Once he told me he had been stopped along the Sartène road by an armed robber who had demanded his purse.

"Did you give it to him?" I asked.

"Give it to him?" he cried. "Why, I would have given him the whole church if he had asked for it!"

He also told me how the Bishop of Ajaccio had fallen in love with his little church.

"You are a lucky man, M. le Curé," said the bishop. "You are a lucky man to have a church like this."

"Very well," replied the Curé. "I will not be selfish: give me your cathedral, and you shall have my church."

The Curé took me round to show me the staircase of the King of Aragon. When Bonifacio was being besieged by the King of Aragon in 1420, he found it impossible to make a landing owing to the great height of the cliffs; he therefore ordered his engineers to land a small party of men under cover of night on one of the rocks at the foot of the cliff, and to construct a staircase whereby the troops could ascend. This staircase, comprising a hundred and forty-five steps, was actually completed in one night, according to the story; personally I do not believe it. In any case it was quite useless, for the king ought to have known that a few men could hold it against an army. As it happened, the engineers were spied just as they were about to complete the staircase—a woman, of course, happened to be looking—and the whole scheme collapsed.

This siege of Bonifacio must have been remarkable. The King of Aragon resorted to methods prohibited by the current Hague Conventions: he used poison gas, burning sulphur near the breaches in the wall; the city replied with mediæval *flammenwerfer*, consisting of burning pitch and lime flung into the faces of the enemy.

All this time Bonifacio awaited relief from Genoa; the horrors of famine became fiercer daily, till at last an arrangement was necessary. If the Genoese fleet did not arrive within forty days, said the Bonifacians, they would surrender their city.

"It was the women who saved Bonifacio," said the Curé. "They had fought throughout the siege; they perfected the stratagem when the forty days and forty nights were expired.

"'Surrender the city!'" cried the Aragonese.

"'But, no!' said the besieged. 'We have received Genoese help during the night—look!' And, true enough, troops of soldiers were parading the rampart— the women of Bonifacio dressed up for the occasion. The King of Aragon made one last desperate onslaught, but the women fought beside their men. Four days later the Genoese arrived, and the King of Aragon had to retire."

The Curé produced a book written by a local historian describing the horrors of the siege. The straits of the famine were really terrible.

"The people in turn ate rats and dogs," quoted the Curé. "When these were exhausted, the married women —the historian writes—gave freely the milk of their breasts to their friends and relations."

This story seemed to me to be hardly drawing-room, and I hinted as much, but he blamed the local historian. He agreed that it was a most unsatisfactory commissariat method, liable to lead to many complications.

The Curé had a service to prepare, so I wandered down to the new town bordering the harbour—if anything, the new town is dirtier than the old. On the roofs of houses, on the balconies and even on the pavements, wooden trays of grapes and figs were lying about drying in the sun.

Around each tray clustered an army of flies, the dusty wind depositing sand by the ton and microbes by the million. The little dogs found in the trays a convenient lavatory. I have completely lost my appetite for raisins and dried figs since I left Bonifacio.

I wanted to visit the sea caves for which the town is famous. The boatman demurred; he said it was too rough. Apparently the caves can only be visited in calm weather. Eventually I persuaded him to try, promising to pay for the excursion, even if we did not actually get inside the caves.

The craft was on old tub to which some sort of out-board motor had been fixed, and after a few false starts we went rushing the length of the harbour at a good four knots. My skipper must have been a grandson of Long John Silver, but uglier and minus the parrot and with an arm missing instead of a leg, though the length of his moustache almost compensated for it. The crew con-sisted of a boy of about eighty-seven or eighty-eight years of age; his luxuriant whiskers grew at right angles to his face, only the tip of his nose and two little eyes showing from the mass which engulfed them. To get food into his mouth must have been a complicated task; the difficulty was, in fact, proved by the particles of dinner still adhering to the southern hemisphere of his whiskers. He steered the boat as seriously as if he were piloting a warship up the Dardanelles—and, when we reached the mouth of the harbour, I began to appreciate his caution, for immediately we were buffeted by about a dozen different currents. The waves were running high, driven by the forceful wind. We lost speed; indeed sometimes it seemed that we went backwards: while the boy steered, Mr. Silver kept the engine together with the aid of pieces of string. Waves broke over the boat; we were wet through.

Turning the headland, however, we came into sheltered

water, and almost before I knew it the first of the caves was displayed to my view.

It was disappointing—nothing but a hole in the rock, with a few very ordinary stalactites hanging down; nearby, however, was a bigger and better cave. Mr. Silver and the boy announced it unanimously as 'the Bath of Venus'. It was certainly beautiful enough for the purpose, although Venus herself was missing. There were many dainty stalactites descending in fairy columns, weathered gracefully by the continued inrush of eddying winds. All sorts of shapes had been carved by nature at the sides of the cave; below was a great pool of beautiful green sea, so clear that the minutest object in its depths could be easily discerned.

Yet even this was not the show-place. Mr. Silver and the boy held an anxious consultation. Was the sea so high that it was impossible to force the entrance to the Sdragonato? I joined in, urging them to make a dash for it—promised that I would not hold them responsible if they drowned me. Apparently they were not worrying over that: it was the question of damage to their boat which concerned them.

Eventually we made it. Skilfully taking advantage of a trough in the waves and shouting to me to lie down, they steered the boat beneath a low arch in the cliff. At first the cave seemed ordinary enough; but then "Look down!" commanded Mr. Silver. I looked down.

Never have I seen anything so beautiful as the floor of this Grotto of Sdragonato; a kaleidoscopic mosaic of colour—rose, purple, crimson, mauve, sky-blue, peacock-blue—a gorgeous medley of every hue of the spectrum. All the shades were of incredible brilliance: you have seen those ornaments which are alleged to be made from butterflies' wings; imagine them as the sea floor in a romantic cave, seen through ten feet of clear green water and comprising a hundred square yards of butterfly wings of every hue, in a tesselated pattern, gloriously blended. That is the Sdragonato.

I do not know how it is done: I do not think that anybody has ever satisfactorily explained it. Some say it is a queer lighting effect, for there is a hole in the roof of the cave—strangely enough, of almost the exact shape of Corsica, complete even with the Cap Corse peninsula. Others say that is the natural colour of the little pieces of rock down below. Another theory is that the rock is overgrown with lichen of varying hue. You can believe which you wish—the essential fact remains that it is a picture of exceeding beauty.

In the cool of the evening I walked out towards the lighthouse of Cape Pertusato. A rough road ran parallel with the cliff, and the view was continuously magnificent. To the south, only seven or eight miles away, was Sardinia, its low hills approaching to the sea edge. The view was so clear that I could even see the smoke of the charcoal-burners' fires on the other side.

I have seen sunsets in mountain valleys and eastern plains, but none so impressive as that sun which died over the Straits of Bonifacio. The blue waters gleamed with the reddish glow during the short twilight; almost within a few moments, so it seemed, it was dark. The dimmed gleams of the charcoal-burners' fires on the Sardinian side were now romantic. The lighthouse itself added to the piquancy of the scene as it began to cast its white shaft across the narrow straits, so dangerous to mariners, the scene of so many wrecks. As I sat there I thought of my namesake, the Cardinal, who was inspired by this romantic spot to write his famous hymn "Lead Kindly Light".

IX

The morning mist lingered as we sped away from
Bonifacio towards Sartène. It was still hanging as our
road swung finally to the north and plunged into the hills.
We had halted to see the famous lion of Roccapina. It
was almost hazy in the half light of dawn—a rocky
mass rising almost directly from the sea, surmounted
by a great stone lion which might almost have been
transferred from Trafalgar Square, so perfect were its
proportions.

At Sartène we crossed a previous route and, after
crossing a wide valley, began a serious climb. The mountains of southern Corsica are not so tall as those of the
north, but the passes are just as laborious. They differ
from those of Savoy, however, in that the approach is
generally lengthy—it is not a question of a sudden climb
by abrupt serpentines.

The Col de Vaccia, like every other pass in Corsica,
commanded so lovely a view that we were constrained to
halt. So long that charcoal-burners accepted us as part
of the scenery, and approached for conversation. They
were sleeping by the pyres, they said; it was a fine night,
and there seemed to be no reason why I should not join
them.

Sometimes I have wondered if I would like to be a
charcoal-burner: while providing an active life, it affords
ample opportunity for contemplation. It is a great pity
that the rewards are so meagre.

I saw my friends at work on several stages of the
fascinating process of taking smoke out of wood. Some
were laying the foundation of pyramids—a thick layer of
twigs and small branches. With two holes left near the
ground to admit the air, and an open space in the middle

to serve as a flue, the pyramids were built in sheltered
spots so that the wood would not smoulder too freely.
Gradually the pyramid was built up, high and conical.
Then it must be turfed at once, lest rain should come.
The pile of twigs, branches and billets of timber stacked
in three vertical layers, was encased in turf; a narrow
spade ripped up strips of turf from the ground; the
charcoal-burners plastered them round the sides of the
timber pile till the entire pyramid was enclosed. It is
heavy work—about four tons of timber have to be burned
to gain one ton of charcoal; it is skilled work, too, for any
miscalculation may ruin the whole pile. The demand at
the moment was large, I was told. Charcoal is needed
for the canisters of gas-masks!

One of the pyramids had just been turfed, and my
friends worked hard mixing water with earth to form mud,
daubing the cracks of the turf. Then buckets of water
were flung on the turves, for they must not burn—they
must contain the fire, and keep air from the timber so
that it would char without burning.

Other pyramids were smoking, and the charcoal-burners
watched the colour of the smoke carefully. Its colour
betrays the condition of the interior as a man's tongue
will reveal secrets of his digestion. The smoke must be
thick and white: if it is blue, then the wood is burning too
quickly and the combustion must be checked by closing
the ventilation holes at the bottom. It is because the
winds of central Corsica are variable that it is necessary
for the charcoal-burner to stay by his fire by night as well
as by day, regulating its combustion as carefully as a
stoker regulates his furnace. It is essential that the
pyramid shall burn slowly and regularly: the combustion
proceeds gradually from the top to the bottom and from
the centre to the outside. As the central portions burn
away, fresh wood is thrown in the hole at the top. Then,
after four days' combustion, the pile must be covered

again with turf or ashes and left to cool for two or three days. After this it can be opened, water or sand being thrown on any portion still hot.

I passed an interesting evening but a restless night. There were fifteen or twenty charcoal pryes within easy reach, in different stages of combustion. Thus, while it was fascinating to inspect the process in all its stages, my companions had no continuous rest. I never saw such easy sleepers; it seemed that they were able to set a clock inside their brain which woke them after an hour's repose; then they would work solidly for a while, flinging water on the outer turves or regulating the draught, so that the interior was no more than a slow smoulder.

I regretted that I had not their gift: I can go to sleep at any time, but cannot guarantee continuous and accurate wakening. For the latter part of the night, therefore, I made no pretence, but kept awake and joined any of the charcoal-burners who found a job to do. Their conversational range was somewhat limited—charcoal-burning is a poorly paid occupation, and some of the least intelligent of Corsica's peasants are to be found among its ranks; many of them, indeed, are Italians.

The beauty of the scene next morning soon made me forget the restless night. I was still surrounded by forests and mountains, but for a long stretch the scene was more delicate in its beauty—no wild magnificence but a more intimate charm. The very infrequent villages were generally perched on the mountainside. The houses were of solid stone construction, substantial and gloomy. Animals wander freely about the ground floor. Pigs are everywhere in a Corsican village, especially at nightfall, when they come trooping home from the forests.

The Corsican pig is no adipose and repulsive specimen, but an agile creature whose back legs are longer than his front, and who can cover the ground at a remarkable

CORTE

BONIFACIO

"The Lizards Liked My Whistling"

The Tavignano Valley

pace. There is a strain of wild boar in him: indeed, natural inter-breeding is common enough even to-day.

Throughout the day I made but slow timing, for frequent halts were compelled by the magnificence of the scene which greeted my eyes on every hand. The Col de Verde is one of the finest viewpoints of all, with grand views over the fading *maquis* and distant prospects of the wilder mountains to the north.

Then the descent was rapid. I was passing through country which played a great part in the history of Corsica in the older bandit days. I had already passed one village which had staged for me a pretty comedy ten years earlier. I had heard that it was at Palneca that the famous or infamous bandit Bartoli lived. Anxious to meet a real bandit, I had made for the village. Yet when I got there I was nonplussed: how did one begin a search for a bandit?

The woman in the village shop came to my rescue. It is always a good plan to patronize a village shop. As I lingered, making the purchase of a packet of biscuits a lengthy operation, a man came into the shop: he wore rough breeches, a black jacket and a broad-brimmed black hat. His features were very Italian, and his black moustache was stiff.

"Good morning, M. Bartoli," said the lady of the shop.

I went outside the shop quickly and began to think. Suppose I challenged him—would he think that I was a policeman and shoot me as such? Yet a risk must be taken.

"Excuse me, this is M. Bartoli, is it not?" I said when he emerged.

"Yes, monsieur," he replied, raising his hat courteously.

I almost dried up for a moment, but as a measure of precaution I offered my hand and we shook hands in Corsican fashion.

"I hope you will not consider it impertinent," I continued, "but would you mind telling me: are you *the* M. Bartoli?"

He stared at me for a moment as if he did not understand—in fact, he said so.

"I don't quite comprehend," he said. "My name is Bartoli—it is a common name in this village—but if you mean am I the head of my family, then I am not. There is my father walking down to the wood-mill. I suppose one would call him *the* M. Bartoli. On the other hand, of the hundred men in the village I should think quite fifty of them are named Bartoli. Ours is a large family. The other fifty are called Santoni: they are also a large family. And most of them are cousins of ours."

That killed my first attempt to run to earth a Corsican bandit. I had not the nerve to ask fifty men in turn if they were *the* M. Bartoli I sought. Later I was to meet him under very different conditions.

I descended upon Ghisoni—quite literally, for the gradient was steep—and found it a larger village of a more affluent type. Alongside the ancient houses constructed of the native rock were others far more modern, made of symmetrical pattern with cement. What was more, there was electric light throughout the village, of sufficiently strong voltage to make it possible to read by the light of a lamp if you held the newspaper within two or three feet of it. This is more of a feat than it sounds, for I refer, of course, to French newspapers.

Certainly the dinner at the inn was unusual. The soup was conventional enough—the hostess did not even bother to give it a name. It was just soup, and good, even if it had no fancy title. Next followed the wing of a bird served on a piece of toast: the bird tasted something like soap, but on enquiry I found that it was blackbird. This is considered a great delicacy in Corsica. The birds are shot wholesale, and are usually made into some sort of potted meat. Next followed lobsters, which are a course of every Corsican dinner, and are very good eating. There was no butcher's meat available in the village, but the hostess served a plump partridge which was really good. And the local cheese made from goat's milk puts gorgonzola in the amateur class.

x

The sun had relapsed behind the western mountains and the short twilight was nearly over. Across the valley towered the two great rocks Kyrie and Christe Eleison. I could have sworn earlier in the day that they were grey, but as they now caught the last rays of the dying sun it seemed that they were a medley of crimson. From the forest on every hand peered little patches of light crowned by pillars of ascending smoke, the fires of the charcoal-burners. In flashes greater flares lit the sky, where stretches of *maquis* blazed carelessly or purposefully: the last of the goats and sheep were straggling along the roads to their homes; the donkeys, their day's work over, sprawled lazily about the streets: a scene of rural beauty and great content.

Another rise and fall the following morning, and I turned aside to Vizzavone, the loveliest forest in the whole of Corsica, nestling about the lower slopes of Monte d'Oro—the 'mountain of gold'. It is the most sophisticated of Corsica's beauty spots, but all its hotels and marked paths cannot spoil the magnificent medley of mountain and forest. So vast is the expanse of wild land that it is easily possible to lose the visitors frequenting the hotels, for most of them are conservative in their habits. I left George and plunged haphazard into the forest. The invitation to the heights was irresistible.

The glory of the scene encouraged a cheerful spirit, but

a couple of hours later I chanced across an Englishman in the depths of melancholy. He sat by a little stream, half-heartedly handling a fishing rod: I could quite understand his despair, for to me fishing is a dreary occupation.

"I presume you have had no success," I said, as I surveyed the scene. Maybe I was a little unkind.

"It isn't that," he replied. "I suppose the fishing's all right, but it's the way they do it."

"I haven't got you."

"Well, I only arrived here yesterday. They told me I would get good fishing here, and they were right: I had a fine morning's sport; the trout here are fine little fellows, and I got eight or nine. But then a man came up to me. I couldn't understand him; he spoke in some foreign language."

"Probably Corsican," I said.

"Yes, maybe. Anyway, it was foreign. It was not English, I am prepared to swear to that."

"I can believe you," I assured him. "He was probably a native."

"No, do not say a native," he shuddered, "that word is too good: say an aborigine. When he saw my catch, he took me by the arm and led me away. I thought that he was going to show me a better place to fish; instead he led me to a spot where the stream formed a pool—and there was a net across it. Imagine—a trout stream and they were netting the fish! I think I shall go back to England; this place is not civilized."

I tried to argue with him. What was sport to him was food to the inhabitants. Opinions about such matters are largely conventional, and every people is at least entitled to do as it likes. For example, I pointed out, at one of the *bergeries* they had told me how they were troubled by foxes, which did a lot of damage to the goat kids.

At the word foxes he brightened up considerably. "Is there any chance of hunting?" he cried.

"Well, not unless you hunt foxes on donkeys," I said, surveying the broken mountain country.

"No, that wouldn't be hunting!"

"Anyway," I pointed out, "it isn't necessary, because the shepherds dispose of the foxes in their own way. They shoot them if they get a chance, and poison them if they can't."

My friend recoiled. "Shoot foxes! Poison foxes! No, this is too much! Netting trout was bad enough, but this—I shall go back to England!"

XI

The country about Venaco has been compared with the Highlands of Scotland, and its semi-barren upheavels of rock and moor may bear some slight resemblance. To me the most interesting thing in the village was an *arca*. Corsica does not have cemeteries as we know them: generally there is not enough depth of soil to dig graves. Each family has a little chapel or vault on the edge of its village for the reception of its dead—the collection of chapels is generally well outside the village, for Corsicans are a superstitious people, and for all their valour are nervous of ghosts. In previous centuries a communal tomb was provided for those who could not afford their own: this was an *arca*. There remains one at Venaco which was in use within living memory. It is but a small building, with two square holes in its flat roof; through these holes the bodies were pushed, and I saw on the floor a pile of human bones and skulls.

Further south I had heard a grim story of another *arca*; no legend, but a tale from life. There was a Corsican youth who suspected that his girl was not so faithful as she ought to have been—she had allowed her eyes to glance at another man. Such indignity was an offence against Corsican pride, and deserved a stern reproof. As they made their moonlight walk, the youth fell upon the girl and bundled her through the roof into the *arca*. In the morning, armed with a rope, he went to rescue her, grimly musing that by this time she would have learned her lesson. He was right. From a pile of skulls and bones he drew not the buxom lass of the previous night, but a haggard, white-haired madwoman.

The Corsicans work their women hard, in the stern fashion of the south. I sat on a wall at Venaco, talking to a local farmer. As we chatted, his wife, sister and daughter worked hard, carrying on their heads heavy baskets of grapes from a cart to the press. But they were *his* grapes, he pointed out. To emphasize his ownership, he presented me with a large bunch—and a nice mess they made when they squashed in my haversack.

A man walked by us, carrying two large wire cages filled with rats; there must have been twelve or fifteen of them. I do not pretend to like rats, and I looked at them in some loathing. He announced cheerfully that he proposed to put an end to them: I agreed—that is the proper fate for rats. Nevertheless, I was not quite prepared for the method of execution. In the middle of the main street, and surrounded by what appeared to be the entire population of the village, the two cages and their contents were soaked in petrol, and a lighted match applied. I got on to George and rode hard into the country to get clean again. For a long time the squeals of the tortured rats pursued me.

XII

Corte is the most Corsican town in Corsica, ensconced on a hill, with the roof of one house almost touching the foundations of the next. This was the town of Paoli, the Corsican patriot, who very nearly made his island an English protectorate. His house is perched high on a great green rock inside the walls of the citadel. It is plain and substantial, but it means a lot to Corsica.

There is no privacy in the ancient parts of Corte; the houses date back hundreds of years, perched precariously on the mountainside. They mount one above the other: from the kitchen window of one you gaze at a few yards' range full into the bedroom of another. They are crowded and jumbled: the streets are but narrow and winding alleys, picturesque crumbling corners on every hand. One block of tenement buildings, 'the House of the Three Hundred Proprietors', has an amazing drainage system, all the pipes being built outside the walls, in a surprising pattern of sanitation. From the summit of the rock I gazed about in sheer delight. This is one of my favourite viewpoints of Europe, the heart of the Corsican Highlands.

Corte teems with history. I wandered around the house of Paoli: it is called a palace, but is really a cottage. His bedroom and study are still kept as show-places, though the old part of the building is used as a school. Austere rooms they are, reflecting the stern spirit of the man who very nearly won freedom for Corsica. The schoolmaster talked as he sensed my mood.

"He is Corsica's greatest son. Napoleon? No, Napoleon was great to France and to the world, but not to Corsica. Paoli is our Washington, our Cromwell, our

K

Garibaldi.   You know him well, do you not?   He was no
stranger to England.   Ah, but for a slight turn of fortune's
wheel, Corsica might have been English now, just as
Malta is.

"Paoli was a young man in exile at Naples when his
country called him.   For centuries Corsica had lain under
the yoke of Genoa and its burden was heavy.   Then
Paoli came: the whole island rallied to him.   This was in
1765.   Within two years he had driven the Genoese from
Corsica except for a few coastal fortresses like Calvi and
Bonifacio.   Then for eleven years he was the ruler of
Corsica: he made Corte his capital.   Here he founded
its university; he completely transformed the administration and the law.   He struck at its weakest point—the
vendetta.   How could Corsica fight her enemies when
Corsicans were fighting one another?   Without hesita-
tion he condemned to death men who were found guilty
of vendetta killings.   This had never been done before,
and has seldom been done since.   He even executed one
of his own family for that crime—an example which the
lowliest could understand.

"By 1768 the Genoese had despaired of Corsica, and
like a pack of cowards they sold it to France as if its
people were but a plantation of slaves.   What could
little Corsica do against the might of France?   The battle
of Ponte Nuovo was our Sedan.   Corsica was conquered
and Paoli sought refuge in England.

"He was welcomed there: he became the friend of your
Dr. Johnson, a great man—you know that Boswell stayed
here in Corte?

"Paoli was in exile for many years until the revolution
came to France.   Then he returned home, appalled at the
state of the island.   Alas, once again the Corsicans were
divided between themselves.   There were two sides, the
Paolists supported by the English and Republicans supported by the French.   Paoli won—your Nelson was a

great man, and Corsica honoured him.   The French fled
or surrendered.

"The English actually took possession of Corsica.   Ah,
if they had but made Paoli its governor it would have been
English to-day!   But they sent out another commander,
General Elliott.   He did not understand Paoli; he took
a dislike to him from the beginning.   Paoli retired to
England in despair.   Had your governor but known it,
with him went English power in Corsica.

"At least he was honoured in England.   The King
gave him a pension.   There is a tablet to his memory in
Westminster Abbey: you have seen it, of course?"

"Not yet, but I will."

The schoolmaster walked down the steep slope with
me.   Here was yet another reminder of Corsica's vivid
history, the house of General Gaffori.   Yet it was Gaffori's
wife who brought it honour.   Gaffori was away at the
war, fighting the Genoese among the Corsican mountains.
In his absence they besieged Corte and seized a portion of
the lower town.   Their armies were encamped about
Gaffori's house, defended by a troop of soldiers—commanded by Gaffori's wife.   There were men among the
soldiers who weakened when they saw that the forces
about them were overwhelming; but Corsican women, as
we saw at Bonifacio, are of the fibre of their men. Madame
Gaffori stood, a lighted torch in her hand, over a barrel of
gunpowder.   Were there one word of surrender, she
threatened, then the torch would descend into the barrel
and the whole house and its garrison would ascend to the
heavens.   Such argument could not be resisted.   The
soldiers turned to face the Genoese forces and held the
attackers at bay until Gaffori, hastily summoned by a
courier, rushed to Corte and drove the Genoese headlong
from its valleys.

XIII

Half a dozen valleys meet at Corte, and two of them are the loveliest in Corsica. I like best the Tavignano, a wild valley; on either hand the rocky sides of the mountain descend, meeting in an acute angle in the gorge below. The mule path is hard and flinty, unkind to the feet, but the scene is magnificent in its light and shade. This is the wild Corsica of the story books, unchanged and unspoiled.

Parallel with it is a valley of gentler charm, that of the Restonica. Its waters amble casually over great boulders in their course. There is a local legend that the waters of the Restonica have peculiar bleaching properties. In sterner days Corsican warriors used to bring their swords and leave them in the stream for cleansing. Presumably the magic properties have now departed, for I put a couple of dirty shirts in the stream with disappointing results.

I never tired of wandering about the valleys around Corte. Goats stared at me in undisguised curiosity: shackled donkeys, their fore and hind legs tied together that they might not stray, hopped awkwardly towards me, with anticipatory glances at my pack. Innumerable lizards sped across the path.

The lizards of Corsica are friendly creatures. They scurry about the roads and paths, almost unconcerned at the coming of a stranger. Their colouring is a pleasing medley of shades, greens, blues and browns, with delicate markings.

As I sat by the side of the stream I was so filled with the joy of life that I began to whistle. I do not pretend that my whistle is musical, but it is at least substantial. Soon I found that the lizards were coming to hear my recital. One of them clambered on to the rock within a couple of feet of my mouth so as to get a front seat. After two minutes it seemed that I was about to attract the largest house of lizards ever congregated in Corsica.

It was explained to me later that lizards will always turn out to hear a good whistle. Their natural ally is the grasshopper, who makes a whistling noise in peculiar fashion, it is alleged, by rubbing his back legs together. At any rate the lizard knows that when the grasshopper —who has sharp eyes—is whistling, then no enemy birds are about. Consequently he can come out.

It was a good thing that the hour was early, otherwise one of my lizard visitors might have made me sign the pledge. My gaze developed into a stare, for I could have sworn that he had two tails. As a matter of fact, he had. If you try to grab a lizard by his tail, it comes off in your hand, while the lizard scurries away. He is not concerned: from the soft place where his tail has been, he will soon grow another one. I was told that the two-tailed lizard is not an uncommon phenomenon. It might be that your grab of the tail was not firm enough, and you only pulled it half out. Nevertheless, once even a portion of soft tissue is exposed, the lizard proceeds to grow a second tail.

It must be a bit of a nuisance sometimes: nevertheless, many a lizard owes his life to his tail. When the birds are swooping upon him, and he cannot get away in time, he just shakes off his tail and escapes with the essential part of his body, while the birds gobble up the succulent tail. The whole process is most ingenious, for the muscles continue in action even after the tail is separated, making it swing about violently. The bird is attracted by this flurry, and in the excitement the lizard gets away unnoticed. It is a kind of reversed camouflage, like a dummy pill-box to attract enemy fire.

XIV

As I plodded northwards from Corte I discovered that one of my shoes needed the essential stitch to save the necessary nine.   At the next village I halted and made for the cobbler's shop.   It was locked and empty, and I had to do a little detective work to trace its owner.   Alas, he had just been arrested as drunk and disorderly by the local gendarme!   I prepared to carry on, but the local people would not hear of it.   A woman ran for the gendarme and explained the position.   He examined my shoe with the eye of an expert, agreed that a stitch was necessary, yet he doubted if his prisoner were in a fit state to apply it.   However, it was worth trying.   He brought back the cobbler from the local lock-up to the shop, gave him a cup of coffee, so strong that it poured like syrup, douched him freely in cold water and told him to get on with the job.   The sobering effect of this administration was remarkable, and a few minutes later my shoe was repaired.   I am glad to say that I was able to persuade the gendarme to drop his charge, pointing out perfectly truly that the cobbler was now quite sober, otherwise he could not have made as neat a job as he did.

Ponte Leccia is an insignificant village, but the Clapham Junction of Corsica.   Here the narrow gauge railways from Bastia and Calvi meet to forge through the mountains towards Ajaccio.   Not that the station is particularly busy—about three trains a day in each direction. The Corsican railway is almost a joke, except to the Corsicans.   It was a present to the island from France, and cost a huge sum of money, so difficult were the mountains for engineering work.   To the Corsican the arrival of the infrequent trains is a social event, and everybody in the vicinity stops work to stroll down to see if any friends should happen to be on the train. Visitors are not quite so pleased with the railway, for the trains have a habit of being inordinately late. I remember years earlier running to catch a train, which to my amazement was about to puff out some minutes before the scheduled time. Not until I was ensconced in a carriage did I discover that I had really caught the previous train, some four hours late!

Away to the west is one of the most Corsican villages in the island, Asco. Only within the last few years has Asco been connected with civilization by a road—when last I visited it, nothing but a mule track led to its glorious site on the slope of Monte Cinto, the highest mountain in Corsica. The village is primitive. It has no street, but only a series of narrow rough alleys. The people are almost a tribe apart. Until a hundred years ago, in fact, they formed a little republic of their own, semi-independent under the guardianship of one of their own people, who was called the *Savio*—the Saint. He was paid a salary for acting as president of the little republic, and according to legend when he died his funeral ceremony was a thing of wonder. The republic of Asco, indeed, provides a most interesting study, for it was founded in Roman days and retained the Roman code of law long after the rest of Corsica had been subjected to foreign invasion. Asco escaped because of its inaccessibility.

A little group of men gathered about George. Bicycles are by no means unknown in Corsica, but rarely encountered in the mountain villages.

"It is hard work on a thing like this," one old man hazarded.

"It can be," I hedged.

"You ought to sell it and buy a donkey," he urged. "With the money you got for the bicycle, you could buy a very good donkey; they are not expensive; you can get

a good one for seven hundred francs, or a donkey of the Cross for eight hundred francs."

"A donkey of the cross?"

"Yes, that is one, the grey donkey there. Do you not see that he has a black line right down the middle of his back, and another black line at right angles across his shoulders. He is a donkey of the Cross; he is descended, so they say, from the donkey that carried Christ into Jerusalem, so he is worth a hundred francs more than the ordinary brown donkey."

I looked surprised. "So your religion is so strong," I said, "that you are prepared to give a hundred francs more for a donkey with the Sign of the Cross on it?"

"Not exactly that," he admitted; "the grey donkeys are much better workers and are hardier than the brown ones, and are cheap at a hundred francs difference in price."

The inn at Asco was no grand hotel, but its hospitality was profound. The host was the mayor, a lineal and spiritual descendant of the *Savio* of Asco. He remembered me from my visit years ago, and sent for all the local worthies to join me after dinner.

I went upstairs to brush my hair; not that this is a failing of mine—a morning tidy generally suffices for the day—but a keen wind had been blowing, and my hair was a tousled mop. The difficulty in Corsica is to find a mirror in the proper place; as often as not there is no mirror at all in the bedroom: you are expected to wash, dress and shave from memory. Where there is a mirror, it is placed in some inaccessible position; furthermore, it is not just hung lightly on a nail so that you can take it down, but it is firmly fixed. In one place I found it battened to the roof, and in several others it was so high above my head that I had to stand on a chair or the bed to shave. At Asco I discovered it suspended at such an acute angle from the wall that in no standing posture was

it possible to see more than a small portion of my anatomy.
Only by half leaning and half lying over a bed was I able
to catch a comprehensive glimpse of myself.

I descended to the living-room by a rough ladder. The
mayor had produced his visitors' book: he had had quite a
lot of English visitors to his inn, he said. Well known
people—why, only a few years before there had visited
Asco the two sons of Bishop Incher. What, did I not
know Bishop Incher? I admitted sadly that my acquaintance with the bench of bishops was not so intimate as it
perhaps ought to be. But, he said, this Bishop Incher
was a really well-known man—no ordinary bishop, but a
man who said things that made people think. He was
well known even outside England. Still I was in complete ignorance, until he produced the entry in the
register, and I found that the correct spelling of the name
was Inge, and I was able to tell my host that he had
unwittingly promoted a very worthy dean.

The living-room was also the mayor's office. Stacked
on one side were all the records of births, marriages and
deaths of the village. The filing system was elementary,
but like a lawyer the mayor seemed to be able to put his
hand on any required bunch of dirty papers at will. I
ate an omelette of enormous proportions, and then
savagely attacked a fat partridge. After that I was
entertained by the conversation of the family and
friends.

The Corsicans have always been tremendously interested
in European affairs, and in any outlying village you can
depend upon intelligent comment. Their opinions of
Hitler did not differ vastly from mine, but their views on
Mussolini were so violent that it would be impossible to
commit them to print.

My feet demanded exercise. George is good for leg
muscles, but not for toes. Before me was the vast mountain of Monte Cinto, clamouring for attention. Judged

by Alpine standards it is of no great height—nine thousand and three feet.   True, that is more than twice as high as anything we have in the British Isles, and the remarkable feature about the Corsican mountains is that they rise so abruptly—Monte Cinto is not more than twenty miles from the sea.

For some hours the path was easy.   One of the company of the inn had volunteered to come with me.   The previous evening he had amazed me with his deep knowledge of English literature—a knowledge subsequently explained by the fact that, although a native of Asco, he was actually a professor of literature at the Sorbonne, enjoying a holiday in his old home.   For a while the path was well marked along the mountainside, high above the river valley below, passing a Genoese bridge of dreamy loveliness.   The beauty of the valley became more intense at every promontory.   It was wild and undefiled.   Here was no hand-made road, with its attendant string of telegraph poles, but a natural path, picked out only by the foot of man and beast, and indistinguishable at a hundred yards' range.   After two hours we crossed a stream by a rough bridge; then came a more rapid ascent as the path continued, rugged but clear, through a great forest.

The great forests of Corsica are of beech, oak and pine—especially pine, growing from the sloping mountainside to a great height of incredible straightness.   There are considerable plantings of olive trees, but it appears that the Corsicans do not husband their olives well.   I do not profess to be an expert on olive culture myself, but it was explained to me that although the scanty soil of Corsica is admirably suited for these hardy trees, the Corsicans make a poor job of it.   They do not guard their trees against insect pests, and don't even gather the fruit properly.   Olives, I was told, should be picked carefully and on no account bruised.   The Corsicans adopt a lazier method—merely banging the trees with sticks until the fruit falls off. There it is left lying about until somebody can collect it, and by that time, and on account of the bruising, the oil within the fruit goes rancid. Whether the criticism is entirely justified I do not know, but about the rancidity of the oil I can bear ample witness, for it is commonly used for cooking purposes.

We lounged by the side of the mountain stream; for an hour I experienced the greatest peace this earth knows, a contented mind in beautiful surroundings. Then a discordant noise shattered my dreams—the voice of a bird. I turned abruptly to my companion.

"The nightingale," he announced, answering my unspoken query.

I was scarcely in the mood for levity, and told him so.

"It was not a joke," he explained, perturbed. "Nor was the noise. Nevertheless, such as it is, that is the voice of the Corsican nightingale."

He was right. I confirmed it later. The Corsican nightingale in full song resembles a nutmeg-grater with a loudspeaker attachment. I have a friend who manages a theatre in Toulouse. One week a touring opera company was to appear: my friend is keen on any unusual publicity, and learning that the prima donna was born in Ajaccio billed her as 'The Corsican Nightingale'. When the lady saw the advertisement, she hit my friend over the head with the score of an opera—a heavy opera, too: the entire 'Ring', I believe.

Overhead the professor pointed out two great stretches of wire supported by occasional pylons: this was the only sign of the hand of man—a telpherway, constructed to carry down timber from a virgin forest to the road. It is a strange sight in this primitive place, miles away from the ordinary haunts of man.

Soon we reached the lumber camp, where about a

hundred men live for a week at a time.   They were mostly
men of Asco who came up to the camp on Monday morning and went home again on Saturday night.   As one
may guess, there are hectic scenes in the village when they
return.   It is always interesting to see lumber men at
work, but the professor had seen them before.

He was rather hesitant about the path—confessed that
it was twenty years since he had come this way.   Now we
were climbing steadily, and after five hours' hard work
reached the *bergerie* of Manita.   The peak now looked
ridiculously near, but the path had disappeared.   We
followed a stream until it flung us clear of the forest, then
the summit was so plain that it was only a question of
finding the easiest way.   Despite the fact that we were
in the height of summer, during the previous night Monte
Cinto had received a powdering of snow, and we slipped
and stumbled precariously over the rock, for we were
not appropriately shod.

The view from the summit was grand, enlivened by
the keen air and the fresh breeze.   I gazed about in
silence, while the professor quoted appropriate extracts
from the literature of three nations.   But when we had
been descending for an hour, sliding hazardously over
the snow-covered trail, we halted abruptly.

"We shall have to go back," he exclaimed.

"What's the matter?" I cried, dismayed, for I had
had quite enough climbing for one day.   "Have you left
something behind?"

"No, we have climbed the wrong peak."

"But that's absurd—we were on top."

"Yes, but there is a kind of pimple sticking away
from the summit.   I can see now where I made my
mistake: we have stood on the pimple, not on Cinto."

"But it looks the highest point."

"Yes, but in mountains looks are deceptive.   No, we
shall have to go back."

For once I was firm. I was getting tired—and hungry.

Asco was at its best in the cool of the evening. The goat herds, with their flocks of innumerable goats, were hurrying home. Their life is not as energetic as it might seem, for they spend hours doing nothing, while the goats find their own pasture on the mountainside. The women were at the springs, filling pitchers with water—and naturally indulging in pleasant gossip as they waited their turn. The pigs which had lain about the streets throughout the heat of the day were now vociferously exploring well-known corners of the village in search of illicit provender. The donkeys, their day's work over, took the places of the pigs in the road. It was difficult to walk a hundred yards without disturbing some animal or other.

"You will want to go on our telpherway to-morrow morning," the mayor suggested.

"Not on your life!" I exploded, for on my previous visit I had been persuaded to enter a crazy timber construction, and to suspend myself hundreds of feet above the valley in the company of logs coming down from the forest. This would have been no more than an exhilarating experience, but unfortunately the mechanism operating the telpher broke down and left me stranded in mid-air. I can be moderately courageous on my feet, but I have never forgotten my sensation of apprehension as I gazed down on the blank space, terrifying in its vastness, which separated me from the green trees below; and, as we had waited for the thing to get started again, the mayor with deplorable tact had begun to whistle Chopin's "March Funebre."

XV

So I declined my host's invitation for a second aerial journey, and got on George. At least there I knew where I was. Nor was he likely to remain stationary for a period of hours. In the freshness of the morning we rode happily along the lovely gorge of the Asco river. Then struck towards the east, through Ponte Nuovo.

It is but a tiny hamlet grouped about an ancient bridge. Yet Ponte Nuovo helped to make history. In 1768 the Corsicans fought a great battle here against their Genoese masters—and lost. The situation was critical. The Genoese had sold Corsica to the French—who insisted, however, on vacant possession. The Corsicans in despair offered their island to Britain. But we in our turn wanted to be quite certain of a secure occupation. Everything depended, therefore, on the result of the battle. If the Corsicans won, the island would have become British, not French. That would have been important, but yet trifling as compared with the consequences. For, three months after the battle, a male child was born in Ajaccio—a boy named Napoleon Bonaparte, who was thus born French and not British.

A railwayman joined me as I leaned over the bridge. For a while we discussed the inevitable subjects—Hitler and Mussolini. Then I began to talk about the Corsican railways, gently pulling his leg. When I told him my story of how I had caught the train before, he did not appear to regard this feat as anything out of the ordinary. He told me that on one occasion the 11.53 at Bocognano arrived and departed so promptly to time that *all* the intending passengers missed it—including the station-master, who was going into Ajaccio, and was shaving

when the train came and went. There was great in-
dignation, said my friend, when the passengers discovered
that the train had gone. Ugly scenes developed on the
platform, and a riot was imminent—when the station-
master discovered that the train that had gone was
really the one before, nearly four hours late, instead of
the usual one; so the crowd, immediately pacified, walked
contentedly up and down the platform for another
five hours.

I turned away from the main road to go to Vescovato,
one of the most interesting hill villages of Corsica. Once
a Roman town, later it was the seat of a bishopric, and
its narrow streets still exhibit spacious buildings which
have descended from nobler times. Murat lived here
after the loss of his kingdom. Most of the streets are
completely impassable to wheeled traffic—a shady alley
or picturesque stair. On occasions a road tunnels right
through the rock of the mountainside to find a convenient
exit to the road to the valley. On neighbouring spurs of
the mountain are twin villages, picturesquely sited facing
over the narrow plain.

The road to Bastia was almost flat and quite
monotonous after the glories of central Corsica. Bastia
is the largest town of Corsica—considerably bigger than
Ajaccio, and easily the most important commercial centre
of the island. It has now two harbours, the new wherein
the steamers from France and Italy call, and where one
or two small naval vessels are usually riding; and an old,
which houses a strange medley of small fishing vessels
against a background of tall narrow houses, a striking
and picturesque scene. If only Bastia were not so dirty,
it would be a pleasant place: yet maybe its odours are
part of its character.

The attitude of the Corsicans to hygiene is difficult
to understand. So far as the person and house are
concerned, the Corsican is almost a model. I do not even

recollect encountering a piece of uncleanliness which would give offence to the most careful housewife, and I never had nocturnal visitors. But in the disposal of refuse the Corsican standard is even lower than that of Spain. Some of the courtyards of the houses are a disgrace—piled with refuse of all shapes, sizes and smells, to a depth of two or three feet.

It was very hot, and as I strolled about Bastia my costume was as abbreviated as may be—shirt, shorts, stockings and shoes. Suddenly two urchins stopped dead in front of me. Then they broke away excitedly, and I heard one of them cry: "*C'est lui! C'est lui!*" But within a few minutes the cry seemed to have collected the whole of the juvenile population of Bastia. They trailed behind me, and it was easy to see that they were indulging in a bad attack of hero-worship. I might have accepted it more gracefully if I knew what I had done. I could hear their murmurs: "Look at his arms! And his legs!"

Their attention became rather embarrassing: the numbers were increasing and people were staring at me from all directions. I saw a policeman striding towards me. A café offered a suitable retreat—and the ordeal had been so unnerving that I was ready for refreshment. To my horror, when I emerged the crowd of small boys was still there. Now, to my surprise, they took no notice of me whatsoever; their concentrated gaze was staring on a man who stood upright on the seat of a rickety motor car: he wore nothing but a leopard skin, and in his powerful hands he held a thin rod of iron which he twisted into fantastic shapes. Plastered on to the car was a poster proclaiming the wonders of the renowned M. Tarzan, the strongest man in the world, who would appear in a local circus that night. So ended my brief morsel of glory: still, it was something to be mistaken for Tarzan, even for half an hour.

The newsagents of Bastia did a roaring trade that evening. Dr. Gayda had made another reference to Italy's claim to Corsica. (Dr. Gayda is supposed to be Mussolini's mouthpiece; he must always have a dirty taste on his tongue.) The people at my little hotel could scarcely eat their dinner for their fury. Before the meal was over there was a torrent of noise in the street below. Hundreds of men and women were marching along. I did not capture the words of the slogans they shouted, but understood nevertheless. I left my dinner and joined the throng. They proceeded to the seashore, where the head of the procession revealed a dummy figure alleged to represent Mussolini. Actually it was black, but not nearly fat enough. A pole was erected on the foreshore, and amid cheers and boos Mussolini was ceremonially hanged. I wish Dr. Gayda could have witnessed this scene! Then maybe he would not have written so airily about Corsicans clamouring for Italian 'protection' against French oppression.

XVI

One of the loveliest runs in Corsica is the tour of Cap Corse, the pointing finger to the north of the island. In grandeur of scene it cannot compare with the mountains of the centre, but in continuous pleasantness it is unrivalled.

In the early morning light the Islands of the Tuscan Archipelago away to the east shone through the haze as if phosphorescent. Capraja, the nearest, was naturally the most distinct, with Elba and Monte Cristo faintly discernible against the horizon.

The road lay between the sea and the pleasant hills of Cap Corse—vastly different from the wild and savage parts of central Corsica. This was the charm of the

L

miniature, not merely refreshing after the massive grandeur of the southern mountains; littleness has a charm of its own, as Cowley confessed.

There was interest on every hand. Here a grotto, next a picturesque village; every few miles was one of the old watch-towers which once guarded the Corsican villagers against predatory invaders. The road wound in gentle curves, almost on the edge of the delicate slopes of the hills. It was not flat, but after the variations of the interior its convolutions were hardly noticeable.

To one convent I turned in some curiosity. I am not normally interested in relics, but this convent housed a particularly remarkable stock, according to local reports. Actually, no two verbal lists given to me were alike, but I gathered from an assortment of villagers that the relics included the following antiquities: the rod with which Moses divided the Red Sea: a piece of cloth spun by the Virgin Mary: Aaron's rod that blossomed: a piece of manna from the desert: a piece of John the Baptist's garment; and—pricelessly unique—a piece of the clay from which Adam was made. Unfortunately the relics were not on view; nor on exhaustive enquiry was I able to discover anybody who had ever seen them. This was a pity. I would like to have seen a portion of the original Adam.

At the little *marine* of Macinaggio, we were almost at the northern extremity of Cap Corse. This actually is the nearest port to the Continent, though its isolation from centres of population and commerce has forbidden its exploitation. It was from this little port, I was told with pride, that Paoli, at the height of his power, launched the expedition against the Italian island of Capraja, which was actually captured by the Corsicans. It was here, too, that Paoli landed after his exile in London. Jumping from the ship, he knelt and kissed the ground of his beloved Corsica, his eyes gleaming with emotional tears.

The Cap Corse peninsula is more intensely cultivated than the mountainous country in the south. Maybe its comparative freedom from the ravages of the vendetta had something to do with this, but a better explanation is that it is a favourite district for the resettlement of emigrants who have spent most of their working life in France or even in South America. As they have usually prospered abroad and bring with them some small capital, they have been able to develop the land to some small advantage, despite its natural paucity. There is, at any rate, evidence of endeavour in the banked-up terraces on the mountainside, and the vineyards were in an admirable state of culture. Cap Corse is famous for its wines, which are stronger than those in other districts in Corsica. I noticed pleasant groves of olives, orange and lemon trees.

There was an air of prosperity about many of the villages, with their clean streets and substantial houses. The countryside was neat and tidy as we climbed the little pass over the northern divide, commanding a magnificent landscape on either side. The rough mountain road wound a rapid descent towards Centuri—the place where Boswell landed on his famous visit to Corsica.

Nonza is the most picturesque village of Cap Corse. It is very small, built haphazardly on a rough rocky promontory. The stone houses top the vertical rocks with such lengthy precision that both blend into one. Each block of buildings is of irregular shape, to suit the haphazard configuration of its foundation. Dominating the seaward side is a Genoese watch-tower which has a great history. It was in the year 1768 that the Genoese sold Corsica to France over the heads of bitterly disappointed patriots. Nevertheless, France had to fight for its newly acquired purchase. The war was largely guerrilla in form, and soon a host of minor sieges were joined. Among them was that of Nonza, where an officer named Casella garrisoned the tower with the assistance of a few dozen local men. He was armed with ancient muskets and unreliable ammunition; and the garrison, realizing the hopelessness of the prospect, tried to persuade their captain to surrender. He refused, whereupon they abandoned him during the night. Not at all disturbed, the old man fixed his antique muskets in appropriate apertures and ran from window to window firing in turn.

The French officer commanding the attackers, impressed by the fury of the resistance, sent a messenger under a flag of truce, pointing out that the remainder of the garrisons of Cap Corse had now surrendered and that it was useless to hold out any longer. Casella, with rare cunning, asked time to hold a council of war: eventually he agreed to surrender provided that the garrison might march out with the usual honours of war and its artillery and baggage. This was agreed, and the besiegers drew up before the tower to await the march-out of the garrison. At last Casella appeared, bending under the weight of a huge pile of muskets.

"But where is the garrison?" demanded the French officer.

"I am the garrison!" said Casella proudly.

The descendants of Casella still live in the district. Mussolini has to conquer them, even if he should force Corsica from the unwilling arms of France.

St. Florent is rather a sad town, living on its memories of greatness, in a district now unhealthy. There was hardly any sign of life as we rode into the little square. The town is not dead, but it is very, very moribund. The ruins of spacious buildings of ancient days only emphasize its present insignificance.

Away to the west the road stretched through bleak

and desolate country, the Desert des Agriates. The only indication of life in this desolate and picturesque place came from the smoke of charcoal-burners' pyres. I pedalled for miles without encountering a human habitation. Then at last I saw a man who was squatting by a box-shaped stone hut—a temporary dwelling for the summer, when a few francs could be made by burning wood into charcoal. In the winter he would return to a neighbouring village.

The scene was grand but savage; imposing but unfriendly; bleak mountains on every hand, their slopes sometimes utterly bare, sometimes covered with *maquis*, which by its precarious hold on the shallow soil had wilted beneath the summer sun. Yet it was a fine and magnificent finale to a grand ride round Corsica, and George and I were highly content as we dropped into Ile Rousse. Here is one of Corsica's most pleasant little towns. It is not ancient like the rest—it was founded by Paoli in 1768 to rival Calvi, which remained faithful to the Genoese. It takes its name from the islands of red rocks in the bay.

There was time for a final dip on the grand sandy beach before the hoot of the steamer warned us to the jetty. From the deck I turned for a final glimpse at Corsica. It is the loveliest island in Europe, far too magnificent to deserve to be a place of strife.

When I arrived that night in Marseilles, I found another telegram from Marie Therese, warning me to be careful, as the girls of Marseilles had a certain reputation, and were not at all bashful!

XVII

Mussolini alleges that his claims to Corsica are backed by history. Let us therefore glance at the story of this delectable island—with a casual side glance at one of its 'romantic' productions, the vendetta.

According to early writers, including the younger Seneca (who was banished to Corsica for eight years from A.D. 41), the first inhabitants of the island were Ligurians, that strange tribe which pushed out its human tentacles from the Gulf of Genoa towards France, Switzerland and Spain. Nevertheless, their hold on Corsica was no more than spasmodic. They were followed by a mixed motley of races. First the Phœnicians from the eastern Mediterranean. Then the Etruscans, who in turn were driven off by the Carthagians. The all-conquering Romans were the island's next masters, and in their day Corsica was regarded as a derelict place, used as a suitable place of banishment for political opponents—maybe this is its attraction in Mussolini's eyes.

The procession continued after the fall of Rome. Vandals and Goths fought for the island—which by this time was considered of great value because of its unlimited supply of tall trees, so admirably suited for shipbuilding purposes. More Goths and Lombards followed, with the Byzantines as easy winners in the popular game of squeezing taxes out of the wretched inhabitants. It was in A.D. 713 that the Moors from northern Africa began to join in the scramble, until their settlers were ruthlessly exterminated by Charlemagne. Eventually the Tuscan count Boniface became feudal overlord of the island.

If the population now hoped for better and settled times it was bitterly disappointed. The Moors came back, followed by sections of all the evanescent races of the Mediterranean, then almost nomadic in their voluntary and involuntary flittings. Added to the resultant disorders was the confusion of feudal anarchy, when baron fought against baron, and both ravaged the land. Gradually a rough division reformed the island: in the south feudalism still held its sway, with the Counts of Cinaca as predominant overlords: in the north a crude kind of communal republic was formed, with an elected 'council of twelve' as its rulers: the exception was found in the Cap Corse peninsula, which continued under the sway of a series of petty feudal squires.

In their misery, wearied by continuous attack from without and internecine strife within, the Corsicans appealed in 1077 to the Pope. Gregory VII accordingly proclaimed the island a Papal fief, and handed its administration over to the Bishops of Pisa. Their clerical brothers of Genoa were jealous of the gift: intrigue at Rome was followed by open war in Corsica. The Aragonese joined in the fun, and Barbary pirates raided indiscriminately. Eventually, after three hundred years of indescribable anarchy, the Genoese came out on top, and in 1347 granted a rough sort of constitution to the island.

This is but a superficial chronicle of a tragic pageant of history: of a beautiful island continuously ravaged by a succession of callous invaders. The effects of this continual freebooting will be immediately apparent. Not one of Corsica's conquerors cared two hoots about the place except as a supply of timber and taxes. The Genoese hold, in fact, was only substantive in the coastal area. It was almost as much as a foreigner's life was worth to venture into the interior. Genoese tax-collectors in Corsica could only go about with overwhelming and powerful armed escorts. The wretched inhabitants of the island, who were of a weird medley of blood, lived but little above starvation level, while brutal and sudden death was their most merciful lot. From the seaboard towns thousands of miserable men and women were periodically pirated, condemned to unspeakable lives in galleys and brothels. Small wonder that Corsican thought even to-day is suspicious of governments.

Corsican ideas are founded on the family; any other unit was too big to be trusted—a village, of course, was generally one large family. Above all, rulers were people to be hated, not revered. Law was oppression, never justice. In this hereditary mentality, born of the wrongs of centuries, is to be found the first birth-pang of the self-made justice, the vendetta.

Despairing after a long series of rapacious overlords, the next mistake of the Corsican people was to offer the sovereignty of their island to—of all things in the world —a bank! This was the Bank of San Giorgio in Genoa, which gaily seized upon a speculation which promised unlimited riches. Its rule was ferocious: the slight traces of law established by the Genoese republic were at once swept away. Even local patriarchal squires fell beneath its treacherous hands: the basis of everything was force.

It was at this time that the vendetta was born. Just as the rest of Europe was ending a period of petty feudal wars and looking forward to a new civilization, Corsica went back a thousand years. The vendetta was the direct result of the absence of justice. It was the essence of that rough-and-ready personal justice based on revenge. Men made their own laws, crude and primitive; the blood feud began.

It would not have been so devilish had it not been promptly encouraged by the agents of the bank. Perceiving that the vendetta favoured its methods of ensuring the weakness of Corsica, the family feuds were encouraged and stimulated. How could dogs rise against their masters while they were busy eating dogs? The story of these dark days is too terrible almost to relate. The bank was the most rapacious of all the successive overlords of Corsica. Defence was neglected, and the island was purged by pirate raids. Pestilences followed famine—and all these at a time when the vendetta was man's idea of justice. When I consider the defects of the Corsican character to-day—its uncommunal disbelief in government, its contempt for law, its distrust of high motives or ideals—then I blame not the Corsicans, but the Bank of San Giorgio.

After this miserable period, Corsica reverted to control by the Genoese republic. This was the age of Sampiero da Bastelica, the Corsican national hero, who led the courageous islanders against overwhelming odds and won victory after victory. The revolt was crushed, not by the Genoese, but by that ancient scourge of Corsica, petty local strife. Sampiero was murdered, the victim of a vendetta. This was one of the deadliest blows which the blood feud dealt to Corsica.

The vendetta, of course, is not peculiar to Corsica; it has flourished freely at different times in Kentucky and Tennessee, in Ireland, and in several districts of southern Europe. But in Corsica it survived with startling force until our own times.

XVIII

The simple vendetta was not so serious. A man killed his enemy, or someone who had wronged him, and then took to the *maquis* to escape the vengeance of the other's family. But far more terrible was the *vendetta transversale*. In this the whole families of the disputants were concerned—their dependants, their hired servants, and any friends who proclaimed loyalty to either. Each family killed indiscriminately among the members of the other, little private wars in which no method of slaughter was too mean or despicable. After heavy casualties on both sides—and sometimes after the feud had continued for generations—a treaty of peace would be drawn up, formally and legally. Then assassinations would cease until a new vendetta began.

A great deal of sentimental nonsense has been written about the vendetta. It has been represented as the romantic and chivalrous method of settling disputes in a lawless age—something akin to the duel. This is ridiculous. Here was no fair fight under recognized rules, punctiliously observed, and marked frequently with outbursts of chivalry and generosity. In a vendetta the very last thing you did was to meet your adversary face to face; you stabbed him in the back or shot him from behind a rock. There is nothing very romantic in that.

Attempts have been made to calculate the evil effect of the vendetta on Corsican life. One historian, who claims to be moderate, estimates that no fewer than a million casualties have resulted from these personal wars. Even more serious was the effect on the land, for farms were abandoned and fields became sterile as the blood stream poured. Small wonder that Paoli, before he declared war on Genoa, first declared war on the vendetta.

The idea of the vendetta having taken firm root, the course of events in Corsica fostered its rapid growth. Only the miserable plight of the islanders could have made possible the next episode in Corsican history. A German adventurer, Baron Theodore von Neuhof, landed in Corsica with a shipload of arms and ammunition, and with great stories of further assistance to come from continental powers. He wore a kingly costume of the comic-opera kind: a Moorish cloak, Turkish trousers, a Spanish hat with curled feather and a belt which supported a huge Moslem scimitar. But the Corsicans had never seen a king before, and for all they knew this might be the real thing. In any case, his shipload of arms was practical talk which they could well understand, and he had little difficulty in proclaiming himself as King Theodore I of Corsica. A generous constitution was immediately granted. Orders of nobility were created and gravely bestowed upon unsophisticated peasant

ASCO AND MONTE CINTO

MAIN STREET IN A CORSICAN VILLAGE

CORSICANS HANG MUSSOLINI—IN EFFIGY

WARNING NOTICE OF THE BANDIT CAVIGLIOLI

squires. A new coinage was struck. It seemed as if Corsica were on the verge of a new era.

But the intervention of Theodore redoubled the repressive efforts of Genoa, and the war continued with greater fury. Soon the Corsicans began to ask for the further supplies that Theodore had promised. He left the island and made a weary tour of the courts of Europe, vainly seeking help. He found it at last in Holland, and once more landed in Corsica. But by that time France had taken a hand in the game. Eventually Theodore obtained British aid, but it was too late. The people were weary of his promises, and he had to retire to England—where he was flung as a debtor into the King's Bench prison. He died in 1756, and was buried in the graveyard adjoining St. Ann's, Soho. Inside the church is a memorial tablet recording the end of this Ruritanian king.

This was the first interest of England in Corsican affairs, but our rivalry with France kept the island on the political map. Unfortunately, England was slow in seizing her chances. Genoa, a decadent republic, sold Corsica to France, and at the end of Paoli's gallant war of independence Corsica became French. Twice during the revolutionary wars the island was occupied by the British, but in 1815 it was restored to France.

In early days there was certainly no love for the new overlord. The outlook was altered by the emergence of Napoleon Bonaparte. At first he was regarded with suspicion by his fellow countrymen, but there is nothing so rousing as success. A liberal sprinkling of Corsicans followed Napoleon on his campaigns; many of them attained high rank, and even after he met his Waterloo the Corsicans looked in affection towards the country to which they had supplied a great emperor. According to Mussolini's reckoning, Napoleon was an Italian. He certainly conquered Italy!

It would have been thought that under the French rule the vendetta would have disappeared. But for nearly a century France merely existed from one crisis to another, and administrators in Paris were too busy to concern themselves with the internal evils of Corsica. So the vendetta survived, though diminishing gradually with the influx of modern thought and the introduction of French courts of law. When at last Corsica was seriously considered, the French wisely realized that any premature attempts to suppress the vendetta would be regarded as an attack on the ancient rights of the islanders. They chose to repress it gradually, therefore, linking it with a respect for law and justice.

The policy paid. In our own times the number of bandits at large in the *maquis* was reduced from about a thousand to forty. In another couple of generations the change would have been completed. That its end had to be hastened by force was perhaps the fault of Chicago, or Edgar Wallace.

Banditry, of course, was the direct result of the vendetta. A man took to the wilds of the mountains and the *maquis* to escape the consequences of his murder. He was not avoiding the law, but the relatives of his victim; he lived a precarious life, supported surreptitiously by his relatives and the game of the island. The bandit of Corsica bears little comparison with the plundering brigand of neighbouring Sardinia and Sicily. Until he was contaminated by modern 'civilization' the Corsican bandit was never a robber. To this day murder is classed in Corsica more lightly than theft.

The gangster methods were introduced by some of the more desperate spirits—Romanetti among them. They had heard strange tales from Chicago, maybe, and jumped at the chance of money for nothing. Some adopted the methods of the old robber barons of the Rhine, and exacted a tribute on every sack of charcoal

exported from their 'territory'. But most turned their
eyes to the new method of mail delivery by motor van
then being introduced into the island. It was an easy
adventure to hold up these cars—or, better still, to force
the man who held the postal concession to pay a fee for
'protection' while his vehicle plied the road of the bandit's
'territory'.

The first attempts at organized extortion were not very
successful, as the bandits unfortunately could not agree
to the division of territory among themselves and merci-
lessly bumped one another off. Then André Spada came
on the scene. He had every qualification. He was the
son of a Corsican mother and a Sardinian father—a cross
of related blood which has frequently produced surprising
results. It certainly did in Spada's case.

Taking to the *maquis* after a vendetta killing, he became
lieutenant to Romanetti. On his death, Spada took over
his equipment, his headquarters, his ideas and his mistress
—Antoinette Leca. Spada, however, was a full-blooded
man—he admitted to me when I met him in 1931 that he
had a dozen women scattered up and down Corsica. It
was impossible for a bandit to have one fixed home, he
explained. One of his liaisons was destined to have
dramatic results, for he took as his mistress the sister
of another bandit named Caviglioli. I remember this
gentleman very well.

In 1931 I was tramping along the road between Sagone
and Cargese. I was rather disgusted with myself. A
well-known newspaper had received a hint that the
French Government was about to take stern action against
the gangster bandits of Corsica who played such havoc
with its mail service. I had been sent out to establish
contact with these bandits before they were shot down.
To date I had met only two or three of the most harmless
of them. But as I passed along this lovely road skirting
the coast I encountered a rough post to which a piece of

boxwood had been nailed. Scrawled on the wood in illiterate fashion were the startling words: '*Chasse defendu. Sous peine du mort. Bandit. F. Cav.*'

Apparently playing at bandits was a favourite game of the local boys. Yet two miles further on another notice caught my eye. Then another: '*Chasse defendu, du Pont Stagnoli au Pont Liamone, 25 juillet.*' And again the signature in varied founts: '*Bandit. F. Cav.*'

I halted for refreshment a few hundred yards away. As I sat, I noticed a man approach the notice board, strewing thorns about its base. By this time I had deciphered the meaning of the inscription. '*Bandit. F. Cav.*' must be Caviglioli, and the board must mark one of the extremities of his 'territory'. So I walked towards the board. It needed no Big Five to guess who the man might be. But he left his task and disappeared into the scrub. I took a photograph, then waited. I had no doubt that he would return.

Nevertheless, I had some apprehension. I was about to interview a man I believed to be a notorious bandit—yet how to begin? If I said: "Are you Caviglioli, the man who murdered somebody at Guagno last month?"—well, I saw that he carried a gun and a dagger. It is much easier to interview statesmen than bandits.

Fortunately the first question came from him. Why had I taken a photograph of his notice? I was happy to find that he was not in the least annoyed: indeed, he seemed rather proud that England should be so interested in him.

We sat together on a rough stone bridge: there was a drop of twenty feet below, but I was at least four stone heavier if it came to a rough and tumble. I looked at him casually but closely. His face was covered with a black stubby beard; his chin was narrow and his forehead broad. Only one feature marked him from a dozen of the peasants of the district—his lower jaw was mutilated;

his mouth was distorted in shape, and a dimple of un-natural size in his cheek betrayed a bullet hole.

When he found that I had a superficial idea of his activities he talked freely—there is a streak of exhibition-ism in all gangsters. He claimed that he performed valuable services—he gave real protection to those who paid him for it. He swore that he had never killed any-body—except, of course, those who had opposed him!

Delicately I led the talk round to the subject of his mutilated face.

"Ah, Spada did that," he explained.

"A vendetta?" I asked.

"It is now," he said. "One day one of us will die by the hand of the other—but it will not be me. Oh, if I had but killed him the first time! I would, but for my sister. This man, Spada, is as amorous as a butcher's dog. He has mistresses scattered all over Corsica. My sister was one. The fool says that she loved him. He kept his women easily, the ugly devil; so I went to him one day. I offered him the choice, marriage or death. He is a cool devil. 'Death if you like,' he said, 'but marriage never.' So I shot him; I could have killed him, but for my sister. Then his turn came; he caught me unawares as I sat in a café. He shot me through the head, and left me there for dead. But I was not dead. This is the place—I have a pretty mouth? But I am not dead. Spada's territory is near mine—just away to the south—and he wanders along it. One day he will wander too far!"

An awkward moment followed. I bent down for some reason, and a little dagger fell out of my pocket. It is a small thing, but solid; I took it from a German officer on the Somme, judging that it would be safer for me in my possession than his. Caviglioli picked it up. It was a hectic moment—I was unarmed.

"This is not a good tool," he complained. I asked why, and he produced his own to show me. "Because there is no purchase in the handle; it is not long enough: yours is a mere jabber, mine is to kill. How do you use yours?"

I did not like to confess that its sole use for thirteen years had been the opening of refractory sardine tins, so I said: "Oh, just jab."

"But that's all wrong! You jab at the body—you may strike a bone, and not have time to strike again. No, get a real dagger, and always aim at the throat. This is the spot." And he placed his own dagger at my throat, while I made a mental will. "What is more, do not spend all your force on the inward stroke; save half of it for a turn sideways, and then you cut the windpipe of your man, and he dies quite painlessly."

I am always ready for useful hints. I now count myself as a fully-trained daggerman.

XIX

For years a dozen bandits and their gangs ravaged Corsica, holding up traffic, setting postal lorries on fire, and murdering freely. Such a menace to a civilized state could not be tolerated. The armament of the gangs included machine-guns and bombs. *Concessionaries* who failed to meet their demands had a bad time; their motors were burned and their drivers murdered. For several months dozens of villages about Ajaccio had no mail service at all, because André Spada, the master bandit, would not permit it. It was estimated that at this time he was receiving an income of three thousand pounds a year in 'tribute' from his victims.

In November, 1931, the French Government took stern action. The garrison on the island was mobilized for duty, and was reinforced by six hundred gendarmes, accompanied by sharp-shooters, imported from France.

Even tanks were pressed into service. Already Caviglioli had been killed; another dangerous man, Bartoli, whom I had unsuccessfully sought at Palneca, but had run to earth in the vicinity a few days later, had also been killed in private vengeance. He was a very nasty piece of work: I confess that I got on very well with Caviglioli, and Spada was particularly good company; but I did not like Bartoli at all. He was the commonest type of gangster. His nerve was certainly consummate. It was reported that when an operation on his leg was necessary, he lay on the table in the hospital at Ajaccio; he refused an anæsthetic, not trusting the doctor, and lay on the operating table with a pistol in his hand. The operation was successful!

His outstanding exploit was the murder of two gendarmes at Palneca, shot in cold blood. It is a queer tribute to the power of the vendetta that no one in the village would touch the bodies, which lay unattended for twelve hours. When more gendarmes eventually did arrive, no one knew anything about the murder. The mayor himself, who lived two doors away, declared: "I saw nothing, I heard nothing." Of course, practically everybody in the village, as I have said, was a relative of the murderer.

At last, however, Bartoli met a man of his own temper. This was a young timber merchant named Simonetti, who had fallen under the bandit's ban by refusing to pay the necessary protection money. At first he seemed to lose by it, for he was obliged to close down his sawmills—local labourers were afraid to work for him. At last he asked Bartoli to meet him, ostensibly to arrange suitable terms of surrender. Simonetti soon tired of talk; he drew a revolver and shot the gangster dead.

The French expedition was partially successful. Tanks and armoured cars were early discarded, if only because they gave such warning of their coming. They found,

M

too, that trained mountaineers could easily slip through cordons of uniformed gendarmes. Only by cunning could the bandits be cornered. First Bartoli's commune of Palneca was completely isolated, and most of his associates were roped in. Caviglioli's territory was then occupied, with more than a hundred further arrests. Balogna, the scene of Caviglioli's death, added a comic relief to the war of attrition which now developed. The mayor of the village was arrested and jailed in Ajaccio. From prison he issued notices convening a meeting of his parish council—and as all its members were also in prison, he was able to hold it!

As I saw the work of the expedition, I wondered whether I was witnessing a tragedy or a comedy. Micaelli, the bandit occupying the eastern front, wrote direct to the French Minister for War.

"I must respectfully beg to bring to your notice the attitude of our local Colonel of Gendarmes. By dressing his soldiers in civilian clothes, he is neither acting in accord with rules of warfare nor playing the game. A soldier should never fight but in uniform.

"Also you must realize the danger that such an action brings upon the peaceful inhabitants of Corsica and the tourist public. It is obvious that my fellow bandits will be obliged to take all civilians who approach them as gendarmes in plain clothes. In this way regrettable errors, which I myself would be the first to deplore, are almost certain to occur, while quite rightly all blame would fall directly on the colonel."

And, believe it or not, the colonel was ordered that his gendarmes should henceforward fight only in uniform! By doing so the one real chance of capturing the principal quarries disappeared.

The gaoler at Ajaccio saw another intriguing scene. By accident or design, two of Spada's mistresses, Antoinette Leca and Marie Caviglioli, were locked in the same cell.

Their mutual concern was soon drowned in a revival of jealousy, and three men were needed to drag them apart —each grasping a bunch of the other's hair as a relic of the fray.

Eventually some of the principal bandits and most of their gangs were rounded up. The prisoners were removed to France for trial, for almost certainly they would have been acquitted by Corsican juries. Even then it was difficult to produce sufficient evidence, so fierce is tradition—and intimidation. When some of the Bartoli gang were tried at Lyons in January, 1932, an interpreter was required, as some of the prisoners and witnesses only spoke the Corsican dialect. The judge directed that a Corsican police inspector in the court should act as interpreter. He, however, begged to be excused. "If I do this," he said, "and then return to Ajaccio, guns may go off by themselves." And another man was found for the job.

The cases of some of the old 'bandits of honour' who had not turned gangster were even more fantastic. One gentleman I met in the south, named Eddoii, actually negotiated his punishment before his surrender! He agreed to accept a nominal sentence of five years' imprisonment, to be reduced later, and on the official pledge, he promised to give himself up within forty-eight hours. He kept his word. The whole countryside turned out to greet him with a mixture of cheers and sobs. At least he had done them one good turn—he had kept other bandits off his territory. When a couple of years later he was released, the local people petitioned the authorities for the return of the bandit's gun, and when this was refused, promptly subscribed to buy him another!

Yet, although more than two hundred arrests had been made, Spada escaped the vast net spread over Corsica. For more than a year he defied the authorities, but the final scene was the most fantastic of all in this strange drama.

One Sunday morning the people of a mountain village in central Corsica were startled as strange cries echoed down the mountainside. A man approached, unshaven and unkempt. He was singing hymns lustily. The men nudged one another in concern, whispering: "André Spada!" Women pulled their children indoors: yet Spada harmed no one, instead he halted in front of the church, ceased his singing and began to lead the assembled company in prayer! Of all things, this bandit, gangster, murderer, had been smitten with religious mania.

It soon wore off under the cold douche of a prison cell. At his trial at Marseilles, it was argued in his defence that he was mad. French justice was determined to make a dramatic and precautionary end to the whole vendetta system, however. Spada's crimes were recited and proved: murder after murder. A veritable arsenal of weapons was produced. He was condemned to death and guillotined. As he sat in his chains, for the prison officers took no chances, he slipped back into that religious frenzy which had caused him to submit himself to the judgment of man.

XX

It used to be argued that the Corsicans did not like Napoleon because he left Corsica. The numerous statues to his memory discredit that legend. Further, if emigration were a cause of unpopularity, three out of every four Corsicans must be unpopular. There are nearly nine hundred thousand Corsicans in the world, but only two hundred and eighty thousand of them live in Corsica. The resources of the island are hopelessly insufficient to provide for more. Since urban industries are almost impossible, emigration is imperative. Further, the Corsicans have an extraordinary aptitude for the fulfilment of executive official positions. You will find Corsicans among the permanent staff of officers and particularly non-commissioned officers of every regiment in the French army. You will find them holding high positions in the police forces of the large provincial towns.

Their aptitude for the military life forces one to the conclusion that Napoleon was no fluke. Some of the most doughty fighters of France since his time have been Corsicans. It is significant that over forty thousand Corsicans were killed during the last war—a number out of all proportion to the total population of the tribe.

The Corsicans are a hardy people. They could scarcely be described as hard workers, but they have at least one compensating virtue in that they admit it and do not pretend to be otherwise. They agree that they only do enough work to make a living, and do not see the sense of doing more. One of the attractions of the life of the professional soldier was that after a period of service he could retire on a small pension. It is amazing what small quantity of francs a week are necessary to support a Corsican in retirement.

The Corsicans have many of the virtues which are generally found in peasant Europe. They are kindly, easy going, courteous and hospitable almost to a fault. Most of the minor vices seem to have escaped them; although a vendetta murder would be passed over without comment, the theft of a penny would raise a storm of abuse. Like almost every other mountain people, too, the Corsicans are proudly independent and courageous. Their greatest fault is to be found in that hot and uncontrollable temper which has been the cause of the greatest misfortunes of the island.

The women of Corsica have no pretensions to beauty;

their homeliness is rather surprising when their ancestry
is considered, with its Italian and Greek background.
Yet even if the Corsican girl had beauty, it would be
strange if she retained it. It is a hard life; physical
energy is the greatest gift which nature can give, and the
Corsican woman usually works harder than her man.
Large families are the invariable rule—this again is
probably a relic of older days, when constant possibility
of a vendetta made innumerable offspring essential if
the family and race were to be carried on. The family is
a vital link in Corsica; the authority of its head is very
real. Corsicans will come or send from the ends of the
earth to the aid of relatives in distress. Family love can
even transcend sex in Corsica, and when a husband calls
his wife 'sister' he is paying her the highest compliment.

Considering the educational difficulties of mountain
country, it is remarkable that Corsican children turn out
so well intellectually. Almost invariably they are in
excellent physical condition; this is to be expected, for
only a sturdy stock could survive the rigours of a mountain life. Those who go abroad make good almost without exception. Artistically Corsica is a back number,
despite the advantages of its situation. The people
themselves have a poor sense of beauty; they are too
shrewdly practical even to dream. In its thirty centuries
of history Corsica has produced many soldiers, but not a
single artist.

Folk-lore is scanty, particularly when compared with
other and equivalent peasant people. Where are the
ballads of yesterday? Alas, Corsica had no yesterday;
their stories are no more than bloodthirsty tales of the
vendetta. Ancient and pleasing manners and customs
have been stifled by the mental restraint of feuds, suspicion
and murder.

Each time I stumbled across folk-lore it was concerned
with death. In Corsica the professional mourner still

flourishes, probably a relic of a fashion introduced from northern Africa. From southern Europe comes the *vocera*, the dirge which is chanted at a funeral. At first I thought I was on the track of a real artistic tradition, like the impromptu chanting which is a feature of a Transylvanian funeral. Soon I doubted its spontaneity: it was but a conventional meandering round set and recognized themes, and lacked inspiration.

For all these disabilities Corsica can blame its history. The Corsicans have always been a subject race; they have taken the view of a disgruntled tenant with a rapacious landlord—why should they try to improve their property when only others would benefit? So they have lived only for the day. If a man felt a greater urge, he went abroad, for the atmosphere of his own land would soon stifle him. Thus follows the paradox that Corsica, endowed by nature with advantages which might be envied, has done nothing for the world because she would do nothing for herself.

A historian wrote seventy years ago: "These sister islands (Corsica and Sardinia), lying in the very centre of the Mediterranean, at almost equal distances from the centres of Latin and Neo-Latin civilization, within easy reach of the Phœnician, the Greek and the Saracen, endowed with obvious and tempting advantages, have nevertheless remained unknown, unheeded, and certainly uncared for during the thirty centuries of European history. . . . These islands have dialects, but no language; records of battles, but no history. They have customs, but no laws; the vendetta, but no justice. They have legends, but no poetry; beauty but no art. . . . Near the forces of European civilization, in the very spot which an *a priori* geographer would point out as the most favourable place for material and intellectual, political and commercial development, these strange sister islands have slept their secular sleep, like *nodes* on the sounding board of history."

All this is substantially true to-day, yet the virile qualities of the Corsicans compensate for many failings. To-day, fearless and determined, they make no secret of their animosity towards the Italian despot who would become their master.   I do not envy him his task, should he attempt to impose his will on Corsica, where they know more about guerrilla warfare than Mussolini will ever learn.   In the dark days of the subjection of France, fierce hearts still beat in Corsica, and in its lovely mountains the voice of freedom is not stilled.

CHAPTER FIVE

TUNIS

I

SOME towns are dreaded by travellers because of their hopelessly inadequate hotel accommodation. Birmingham is the prize example in England, Marseilles in France. Any hotel proprietor in Marseilles who does not hang out his 'L'Hotel est Complet' board every night immediately contemplates bankruptcy.

I wandered about for an hour, vainly seeking accommodation. Then a benevolent hall porter produced a kind of cell, with a couch but no window. I was weary with much voyaging, and accepted it. Yet the atmosphere was intolerable. Even when lying in the nude on top of the bedclothes the heat was stifling. Eventually I got up, dressed, and slept on a bench in the Canebière. It was much more successful than the cell, except that suspicious policemen woke me up every hour or so.

It is amazing what countries will do to attract visitors and then what steps they take to make travel difficult. The docks at Marseilles were a confused snare, and it was just as well that I allowed a couple of hours to get on the boat. The police would not stamp my passport until I had a ticket, and the clerk would not give me a ticket until I had my passport stamped. And George—by the formalities one would have got the impression that I was taking a tank to Tunis.

I was somewhat annoyed with the shipping company, too. They had sent me details of sailings, and the leaflets

said that the boats had first and second class. After I
had bought a second class ticket, I discovered that they
had third and fourth class as well! In the third class you
got a berth but no food, while in the fourth you had
to camp out on deck beside a corral of cows. Most
of the fourth class passengers were soldiers returning
from leave: France never did treat her warriors over-
generously.

It was a pleasant voyage: the sea was smooth and the
company good. The soldiers inevitably produced a
weird collection of musical instruments, and even the
cows joined in periodically. My cabin was insufferable
from the moist heat, and at night I slept fourth class,
on deck with the soldiers and the cows.

I made at least one friend on the boat. He was a very
intelligent man, a schoolmaster. I took him for a
Frenchman, but he was an Arab. He accepted this as
an unprecedented compliment; soon I was to visit him at
his village. He had been spending his first holiday in
France, but as we approached the shores of Tunis, his
excitement was intense.

"Look, there is my village—Sidi-Bou-Said, on the
headland! It is the loveliest village in all Tunis. And
look, just round the corner—that is Carthage!"

There was little to see from the distance, but the name
was enough. Who cannot thrill to Carthage? I promised to come out on the morrow. I proposed to give but
cursory attention to the town of Tunis itself, for the
moment. It is always a mistake to see the capital of a
country first.

Yet in the cool of the evening I succumbed to tempta-
tion. The boat had threaded its way through a long
channel, for the port of Tunis lies on a lake, miles inland
from the sea. There was a spot of bother about George:
the authorities could find no precedent for an English
bicycle, and in the end I had to fill up the same form as

if he were a motor car! Then I found a modest hotel
in the French quarter of the town.

Resolutely I promenaded the main avenue, determined
to keep to the European quarter. On every hand were
men clothed in the flowing *burnous*, or women with veils.
I decided not to look at them. The markets of Tunis
were the best in the country—it would spoil all the others
if I saw them first. Then, sandwiched between a motor
car and a tram, I saw a camel. This was too much, I
succumbed, and passed through the ancient gateway
into the Arab town.

Wisely, the French have left the native quarters un-
touched throughout their African empire: any modern
developments, such as the introduction of electric light,
have been accomplished by the Arabs themselves, even
if the suggestion and the materials were French. Each
town in Tunis is two towns, Arab and French side by
side: sometimes three, for there is often a quarter
where modern Arabs have settled beside French
neighbours.

French Tunis is a city of white buildings and wide
boulevards: Arab Tunis is a city of small hovels and
narrow streets, mostly enclosed within the ancient walls.
Centre of the place is a maze of irregular streets occupied
by tradesmen and craftsmen: these are the *souks*, the
markets. To a European they are the most remarkable
thing in Tunis.

The shops are little more than large boxes; a bearded
Arab squats with fine dignity on the floor, surrounded by
his wares. If you show an interest, he will deign to
name a price: should you think it unattractive, he will
relapse into his aloof contemplation. In the next box will
be another man, rather fatter, dressed in the same sort
of loose clothes, surrounded by exactly the same wares.
Yet at your approach he will jump up excitedly, forcing
his goods on your attention. Unless you are firm, he

won't let you get away without a purchase. He *looks* like an Arab, but he is a Jew.

Some of the shopkeepers are artisans, bending over tiny benches making fantastic bracelets and ear-rings. A street generally houses one trade or profession only. There will be a dozen or twenty shops in a row, all occupied by men making heelless slippers in bright red or yellow leather. It was a mystery to me how purchasers chose one shop from another: another mystery how some men ever did any business at all, for they reclined for hours at a stretch without making a sale.

I wandered entranced: that the crossing of a narrow sea should bring me into another world. A dozen times I was lost, but one street was as intriguing as another. At my hotel they had given me a street map, but it would have spoiled all to have consulted it. Soon I had been overpowered by the atmosphere, and found myself squatting on the ground amid a hundred Arab *burnous*, listening to a professional story-teller. The fact that I did not understand a word of his story did not lessen my interest in his tale.

II

I paid my formal call at the Residency next morning. I was courteously offered letters of introduction to local governors, but conveniently forgot to take them away. Yet I was to find in Tunis that there was another power almost as powerful as that of the Resident as an opener of doors. I was introduced to a very intelligent young man, who asked a lot of questions and who was particularly interested when he heard that I proposed to ride about Tunis on a bicycle. Probably a keen cyclist himself, I hazarded.

It was time to give George a trial spin; the schoolmaster

of Sidi-Bou-Said had invited me to visit him. First I
must pass by Carthage.

Yet who could pass by Carthage? My classical history
is weak, but here was a place which once ranked with
Rome. Yet first impressions were disappointing: a saus-
age-shaped piece of water alleged to be the ancient harbour of Carthage. Was this the place where the galleys
rowed to their anchorage? It seemed too small and
warped, scarcely exciting enough for a sailing place for
model yachts.

Fortunately the land remains are slightly more impressive. Not of *the* Carthage, the Phœnician city, for
on its site the Romans built freely, and their stones have
more stoutly resisted the march of time.

You need imagination at Carthage, and when I had
shaken off the persistent Arab guides and souvenir-
sellers, I relapsed into the atmosphere of the place.
There was a great amphitheatre, almost as large as the
one at Rome, but very badly preserved. The barrier
round the arena has been reconstructed in concrete, and
is an eyesore. Nor do the monuments blend with the
scene—though their site is appropriate enough, for they
are erected to the memory of Christian martyrs eaten by
lions. There are other memorials down below, in the
vast caverns where prisoners and lions were stabled.
All the memorials were to the martyrs, by the way: the
lions were not even mentioned.

Close by were enormous cisterns—again Roman, not
Phœnician. They were once fed by a great aqueduct,
but have now been dry for 1,500 years. To-day they
are occupied by human inhabitants—nomads, induced
to settle down by the unique opportunity of a rent-free
home.

I was glad to find the Punic cemetery, for everywhere
else the influence of Rome was predominant. There has
been much excavation, and a theatre and many streets

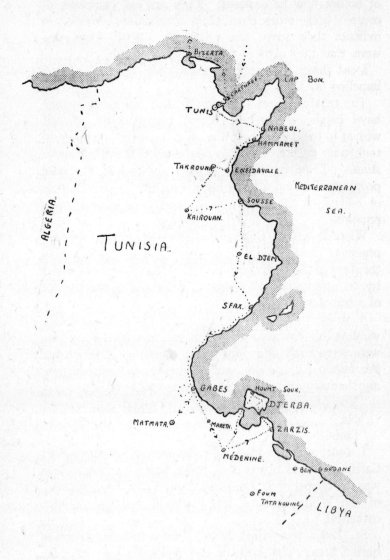

of houses now lie exposed. They are not complete, of course: little more than their foundations remain, to indicate their scope and character. What fools men were, that they allowed these things to perish.

I sat down to think: or maybe the oppressive heat impelled brief relaxation.

The trouble about Carthage is that too many people have helped themselves. Until recent years, if you wished to build a house in the neighbourhood, you merely took your cart to Carthage and loaded it with Roman stones. There was no one to stop you: indeed, the local people would lend a hand for a few pence. In hundreds of houses of the district it is possible to find Roman remains.

What is left of Carthage is interesting, but not impressive: there is no real suggestion of the grandeur of the days of the city's glory. Its martial glory is replaced by an atmosphere of peace: a dead peace, reminiscent of a cemetery.

A priest halted before me: save for a snake lazily winding his tortuous path through the thin grass, we were apparently the only living creatures in Carthage. We talked for a while, while I endeavoured to disguise my shadowy acquaintance with classical history.

"You have seen our museum?" he asked.

"No."

"Come!"

I went, and was glad. On the summit of the hill of Carthage I had observed a great white building. This was the chapel of St. Louis, surrounded by the monastery of the White Fathers, and overshadowed by a great cathedral.

St. Louis was killed before Tunis, and his heart is buried here. The work of the White Fathers goes far beyond the custody of his heart. They have rescued what they could from the wrecks of Carthage.

In the green garden are pillars and statuary, both Phœnician and Roman: indeed, I saw more Punic relics here than in Carthage itself. The museum is a revelation of the standard of the civilization of the ancient city. I knew that the Carthaginians were good fighters and clever artists, but I did not know that their women used lipstick and rouge. I ought to have remembered that this has been a feature of femininity throughout the ages —even the early civilizations. I recalled later that the Biblical prophets were continuously exclaiming in wrath against such immoralities. Some of the jewellery looked so new that it might have been lying on the shelves of Woolworth's.

It was all very interesting. Yet the best museum in the world cannot compare in atmosphere with an historical site. Were it not for the wholesale looting, Carthage would be the show-place of the world, instead of a pathetic and incomplete reminder of greatness.

I thanked my White Father and returned to my reverie.

I mused long over the sad fate of this strange republic of merchant princes. Founded long ago by Phœnicians from the eastern Mediterranean, it became 'mistress of the seas'. It established colonies and trading stations far and wide; it sent exploring and colonizing expeditions far down the coast of Africa; it traded with the inhabitants of the British Isles. It was the proud boast of its rulers that no man could so much as wash his hands in the sea without their permission.

It ruled unchallenged until, over a disputed colony, it came into conflict with the growing power of Rome. At first the Carthaginans were jubilant and confident of victory, feeling that no mere country of land-lubbers— for such at that time the Romans were—could ever invade or overcome the fleets of the city that ruled the waves.

But the Romans had a 'secret weapon'. On the prows of their triremes—which they had only learned to build by copying the wreck of a Carthaginian ship—they mounted 'crows' as they called them, a sort of maritime drawbridge. These they dropped on to the decks of the enemy ships—then over the bridge went the boarders, and what had been a sea battle of manœuvre became a hand-to-hand fight. In this work the Romans were unexcelled, and from the conflict the ships of Carthage returned homeward, the prows of their ships covered with skins in token of defeat.

This, the first 'Punic' (Carthaginian) war ended in a treaty and a cession of territory, but it was only the prelude to more ruthless struggles. The second war was noteworthy for an astonishing military feat. While the rival armies were struggling for the mastery far from Rome, the mighty warrior Hannibal led an expeditionary force—without the consent of his government, who thought he was merely taking it into the colonies—right across Spain and down into Italy from the north! He marched about the peninsula, raiding and laying waste the countryside and besieging the smaller towns. He even attempted to besiege and overcome mighty Rome itself.

But the power of Rome, that nation of warriors—was sufficient both to wage a desperate war overseas and to overcome any invasion of their own land. New armies rallied to defend the city, the equivalent of our Home Guards, and defend it they did. Repulsed, Hannibal was still undefeated, and again his army marched about Italy, looting and ravaging the land. So strong was he that he could not be overcome, at least not by the forces then available in Italy, in open fight.

Instead, the Roman general Fabius began a very successful 'war of attrition'. His forces shadowed the Carthaginians wherever they went, avoiding pitched

N

battle but harassing them, cutting off stragglers, severing lines of communication, and impeding them from obtaining supplies. So successful was this method that at last, deprived as they were of the possibility of reinforcement, the armies of Carthage were weakened enough to be attacked—by another less cautious general—and defeated.

This Second Punic War left Carthage at the mercy of the conquerors, stripped completely of her empire, and with no possibility of again becoming a menace to Rome. But she still retained her trading supremacy and her merchant fleets, and there were rulers in Rome who grudged her even these. The 'censor' Cato, one of the most unpleasant figures in history, maintained in season and out of season a compaign summed up in the slogan which he introduced into every debate in the Senate of Rome: "Carthage must be Destroyed!"

He had his way, and destroyed Carthage was, after a heroic seven years' resistance and one of the most dreadful sieges in history. Its people mostly died of starvation during the siege or in the street-fighting, or were slain out of hand by the victors. The survivors, save for a devoted few who sooner than submit to its rigours plunged into the fire which burned before the city's idol Moloch, were sold into slavery—and Roman slavery might have been run by the Gestapo itself. Finally the city was destroyed and buried, and its site was ploughed with salt with the idea of rendering it a barren waste; a solemn curse was invoked upon whoever would try to rebuild it. The desire of Cato was fulfilled, and Carthage had been destroyed.

Yet the malice of Cato recoiled upon his own land, for it was from the Punic wars that there set in the gradual degradation of Rome. The soldiers who had won the war found themselves, as peasant proprietors, unable to cope with the mass-production factory methods of the financiers who had enslaved the survivors of Carthage and turned their colonies into serf-run estates. Rome fell first into the hand of gangster politicians and then into those of emperors some of whom were no more than gangsters themselves; she was unable to oppose the growing might of the savage barbarians of Europe and collapsed into a welter of warring states.

H. G. Wells suggests that the old enmity between Carthaginian and Roman lived on under another name as the struggle between Romanized Christianity and Muhammadanism, between the North of the Mediterranean and the South. Nowadays the South has been itself dominated by France, and the struggle has taken a new form in the rivalry between France and Italy. Had it not been for the collapse of the French homeland we might have seen some far-reaching results here—and in spite of this collapse I would not like to say that the struggle is over yet. Not easily will the people who inherit something of the tradition of Carthage submit easily to the domination of Rome.

My reverie was interrupted by a further horde of those jackals who frequent famous places. They offered me Roman coins, Roman lamps, and even Phœnician lamps. They had so many that I suspected that they were fakes. At this the vendors got excited, and for a few moments the conversation took a heated turn. Then, anxious to do them no injustice, I offered to pay double the prices demanded if they would dig up some coins and lamps especially for me. To my surprise, they immediately accepted the challenge. I was led to a spot half a mile away where there had been a lot of digging— careless, haphazard excavation of the type which would pain an archæologist. It was pleasant to sit in the heat and watch other people work.

Yet they were right and I was wrong. Within half an

hour I found myself the possessor of two lamps and seven coins. When I paid up, the youths jumped in the air in high excitement.

"What's wrong?" I asked.

"Nothing—everything's right!"

"Then why the antics?"

"We are glad to get the money—we did not expect to be paid double."

"But I told you I would."

"Yes, but we thought it was only a boast."

Evidently I had not yet plumbed the depths of Arab mentality. I rode on to meet my schoolmaster friend: maybe he could give me useful advice.

The village of Sidi-Bou-Said is a show-place of Tunis, and worthily so. Nevertheless, visitors who picture it as a typical Arab village are grievously mistaken —there is none other like it in Tunis. Its site is imposing, perched on top of the red cliffs which form the nose of Cape Carthage: its streets are paved and clean, its flat-topped houses of an incredible whiteness. There is an ordered leisureliness about its atmosphere which is very attractive.

The schoolmaster awaited me impatiently: he had shed his European clothes, and wore a splendid *burnous* and fez. I halted at the door of his house while he warned his wife of my coming: she was not veiled, but otherwise my reception was very Moslem—she greeted me humbly, then immediately retired. Even in enlightened homes women have no exaggerated ideas about their importance.

The house was substantial. Outside it was a white box, almost windowless. Now I found myself in a central court, lined with gay tiles, a small pool of water flanked by palms giving a suggestion of coolness to the sultry air. The sleeping- and living-rooms, with a kitchen, gave off the court. The living-room was Arab, with

low couches and carpets—even the wall decorations consisted of carpets. In the bedroom, however, a large bed
of Tottenham Court Road design had incongruously
intruded.

We halted only for ceremonial coffee, accompanied by
small pancakes, fried in oil, in shape like a ring of sausages.
Then we must climb to a house above the village, to take
more refreshment with its owner, to gaze over the smooth
sea, the flat roofs of the adjacent houses. There below
was a place of size: a palace of the Erlanger family: in
its park I saw graceful gazelle of the desert. It was
whispered to me in awed tones that this palace was
remarkable—it was not only heated in winter, but cooled
in summer. And to the north I saw uglier things:
barbed-wire entanglements on the beaches, and guns on
the cliffs.

III

Before plunging into the heart of Tunis—or Tunisia,
as the country itself is more properly called—a superficial
survey of its character is essential.

The Phœnician settlements in Tunis scarcely affected
the inhabitants except in the coastal areas. The Berbers
who inhabited the interior were only concerned to a
minor degree, and the Punic yoke was of the lightest.
After the Roman conquest the country was more
thoroughly organized. There was considerable settlement, blocks of land being allocated to legionaries.
The vast remains testify to the wealth and power of
the Roman centres. At this time Tunis was exceedingly
fertile, yielding rich crops of corn: its herds were famous,
and its mines an essential supply source for the Roman
war machine.

It was in Tunis that Latin Christianity made its most

vital rise: here Christian literature was nurtured: from
Roman Tunis Christian culture flowed to Europe—to
Tunis belonged such scholars as Tertullian, Cyprian and
Augustine. For a century the country was overrun by
the Vandals, then recovered for a further century by
Rome; but in the middle of the seventh century it was
conquered by Arab invaders from the east. The city of
Kairouan was founded as its capital, and a new phase
of its life began.

Christian civilization disappeared in a generation.
Roman settlers were massacred or fled. The Berbers
were easily converted to the Moslem faith—their Christianity had been no more than superficial, and they
retained many of their polytheistic beliefs. These they
carried into their new religion, and to this day they
worship dead marabouts as fervently as Allah: sometimes
living holy men too, for that matter.

Tunis suffered the successive scourges of North Africa:
waves of invaders of many nationalities and creeds.
Bedouin from Upper Egypt ravaged the country in the
eleventh century. They were nomads, quite incapable
of organizing an empire. Their own lawless and predatory habits have left their stamp in Tunis to this day:
the first task of the French administration was the
stamping out of the effects of Bedouin rule eight hundred
years previously.

There was a brief interlude under the Normans of
Sicily, but Moslem predominance was restored by the
Almohade invasion. Then a succession of native princes
ruled Tunis, with loose allegiance from local tribes—by
this time of very mixed blood. The Bedouins, as the
more warlike of the peoples of Tunis, had to be placated
by land and riches, to the discomfiture of the native
Berbers: there were continuous wars and insurrections.
In spite of these, Tunis waxed rich and powerful—until
the advance of the Turks.

George and the Camels

A Street in Tunis

Camels Hauling Water

Market by the Coliseum, El Djem

Fearful of the might of her new neighbours, who had now conquered Algiers, the Bey of Tunis appealed to Spain for help. The Spanish did actually occupy some of the coastal towns, but the interior was utterly beyond control, a desert of anarchy. By the end of the sixteenth century the Turkish conquest was complete, and Tunis entered on a new era.

Tunis was virtually independent of outside authority, though torn with dissension within. It became a pirate state: its harbours were choked with loot: its markets were filled with Europeans to be sold as slaves. A dozen times the Christian powers of Europe addressed themselves to the menace, but not until 1819 was the power of piracy broken—and with it the prosperity of Tunis. The finances of the state had depended largely on the sale of loot: the loose administrative system fell into chaos. In a single generation three-quarters of the cultivable land went out of cultivation.

By this time great tracts of Africa had passed under European suzerainty. Hopelessly bankrupt, the Bey of Tunis sought a protector. His first choice was Britain: for a moment British influence was supreme: many of the public works of Tunis are of British origin. Then in 1878, at the Congress of Berlin, Britain agreed to give France a free hand in Tunis in exchange for a like concession in Cyprus.

The French occupation was not effected without opposition, for the fanatic Moslems refused to accept Christian overlords. Gradually the country was subdued, a 'protectorate' established, and the government reorganized. The Bey remained the titular authority, but a French Resident supplied official advice! Local councils were retained, and the *caids* or tribal chiefs acted as provincial magistrates. On the whole the French administration has been most beneficial. While retaining full control of national finance and defence,

the French have freely delegated power to local chiefs
and councils: the Arabs are now represented on the
national council and there is a growing demand for
further responsibility.

The French occupation of Tunis was a severe blow to
Italy. Late in her national development, Italy was inevitably late in the colonial field. Nevertheless she had
looked on Tunis as an Italian sphere of influence because
of its proximity to Sicily. There were more Italian
settlers in Tunis than of all other European nationalities
put together. But Italy, as usual, was too late in staking
her claim, and sat in sullen fury as France did what she
had intended to do herself.

Her next move concerned the status of the Italians in
Tunis. By a convention of 1896, the French guaranteed
their Italian citizenship to them. The same privilege
was granted to the British—an important point, because
of the number of Maltese in the country. The status of
the Italians continued to be a source of quarrel, but in
1935 M. Laval made a pact with Mussolini: for the next
twenty years the present form should be maintained, but
children born after that time should be French citizens.
It is interesting to note that, as compensation to Mussolini, M. Laval agreed to the extension of Italian economic
influence in Abyssinia.

Mussolini translated this into a tacit approval of
aggression by arms. Nor did he ever ratify his pact
with Laval.

In December, 1938, he formally denounced the pact.
The previous month the cry of 'Savoy! Corsica! Tunis!'
had been raised in the Italian Chamber, and it had
become obvious that the question at issue was not the
status of Italian colonists, but the possession of Tunis
by Italy.

In the meantime Fascist policy had itself weakened
the Italian position in Tunis when it introduced its

anti-Semitic laws. A proportion of the Italians in Tunis
were Jews: others, of native Italian stock, did not
appreciate the new policy. They were generally the
wealthiest supporters of the Italian cause, and the loss
of their sympathy was serious. Further, many of them
in disgust applied for French citizenship. The Italians
furiously accused the French of a deliberate campaign
of assimilation, but it was totally untrue. The French,
indeed, slowed up naturalization processes so as to rob
the Italian complaint of its background. I can bear
witness that in 1939 there were thousands of Italian
Tunisians clamouring for French nationality; a dozen
times I was entreated to 'use my influence' on somebody's
behalf.

It is not difficult to make contact with the Italians,
for they occupy comparatively limited districts—about
Tunis, the Cape Bon peninsula, Bizerta, and other coastal
towns. They are scarcely encountered at all in the
interior. One feature I remarked was that they had
retained that regionalism which Mussolini has tried
so hard to stamp out. Meeting a European, I would
ask his nation. "A Sicilian!" he would reply: not an
Italian.

The population figures for Tunis (by the last census
of 1936) are very interesting:

French	108,068
Italians	94,289
Other Europeans	10,848
(Mostly Maltese, with some Spaniards and Greeks.)	
Jews	59,222
Tunisians	2,265,750
Other Moslems (Algerians and Tripolitans) .	64,623

In view of our glimpse at Corsica, it is interesting to
note that over 6,000 of the French are Corsicans. The

Italian figure includes over 5,000 Jews of Italian origin.
They form the bourgeoisie of the Italian population—
include most of the professional classes. Most of the
Italians proper are labourers or peasants—over 80 per
cent of the working population.

In this simple fact is to be found the basis of the Arab
antipathy for the Italian. The Frenchman comes into
Tunis as an administrator or trader: very often, after
his period of service, he returns to France. The Italian
comes in as a competitor, and is hated accordingly. The
problem is complicated when the Italian has a little money.
He will buy a small olive grove from an Arab. The
improvident Arab spends the money, and then hates
the man who has 'taken' his inheritance.

Economically the Regency is overwhelmingly under
French influence. When the Italian does attain the
proud dignity of being *patron*, it is almost invariably of
a small local works or farms. Of the agricultural produce
of Tunis, 41 per cent is French-produced, 12 per cent
Italian, the remainder Arab. In the industrial life of
the country, French interests outweigh Italian by nearly
five to one: the same proportions mark the transactions
of French and Italian banks.

There are separate Italian schools in the principal
towns. Not all Italian children attend Italian schools,
however: some attend none, because their parents think
education is a waste of time: others prefer the French
schools—indeed, while 15,000 Italian children go to
Italian schools, 8,000 go to French.

When Mussolini denounced his pact with Laval, France
could legitimately have returned to the agreement of
1896, much less favourable to the Italians. In pursuance
of the policy of appeasement, however, the French began
to apply the 1935 pact. They had the disadvantage of
facing an opponent who did not understand appeasement.

A battle without arms began. A vast propaganda

campaign was launched, with the wildest exaggerations. The campaign was more successful in Italy than in Tunis: so far was it carried that in many Italian towns a street was named after Tunis—and after Corsica and Savoy too.   A dictator does not merely count his chickens before they are hatched: he gets ready to cook them.

Many times I found myself listening to the echoes of the propaganda campaign.   I was assured that Italians were shot for listening-in to Italian broadcasts—it was, of course, an absolute lie.   More than once I tuned in a radio in an Italian home to an Italian station, and called in a French officer to listen.   It exposed the lie, but did not kill the propaganda.

On every hand I heard complaints about Italian 'rights', but no one ever gave me the same description of those 'rights'.   It was useless to point out that, but for the duplicity of Mussolini, the Italians in Tunis could enjoy all their legitimate rights without question.   It was too plainly obvious that the Italians did not want their 'rights'.   They wanted grounds for disaffection which would serve as a basis for a demand for the cession of Tunis—or its conquest by force.

Two things should be explained: (*a*) not all the Italians of Tunis rally to Mussolini; (*b*) the Arabs prefer the French to the Italians—in fact, they don't like the Italians at all.   My own impression was that, if Italians had made war in September, 1939, the French would have had to restrain the Arabs from wholesale massacre of the Italians, so bitter was the feeling against them in many parts of the country.

In the meantime, the French administration has been troubled by the political demands of the native population.   A patriotic party, the Destouriens, was founded, declaring uncompromising hostility to European rule.   In the fashion of such organizations, however, its leaders

quarrelled among themselves, and of late years it has
made little headway, for the Italian threat has rallied
thousands of Tunisians to France.   The collapse of France
and the prospect of Italian rule may have important
effects on native agitation.

Nor has Tunis been free from labour troubles.   The
difficulties of the Popular Front regime in France were
reflected in Africa.   In some districts there was a swing
to communism; in others a great strengthening of native
trade union organization—under men of a national
character which does not understand the word com-
promise.   There were many strikes and incidents: in
April, 1938, scenes of violence in the streets of Tunis,
riots resulting in many casualties.   The French suspected
Italian prompting of the disturbances, but they were
probably no more than symptomatic of the growing pains
of Arab nationalism.   At any rate, it is worth while
pointing out that Tunis rallied loyally to France at the
outbreak of the war—doubly affirming that loyalty,
despite the difficulties of the days, when Italy entered the
fray.   Even the Destouriens, with all their distaste for
French rule, have only one idea about Italy and Fascism.
The vicious Italian methods of colonization in Libya, and
their ferocious massacre and torture of opponents in
Abyssinia, have united the native parties of North Africa
against them.

Tunisia comprises nearly 50,000 square miles—about
the size of England; of this, nearly one-half is desert
country.   Considering its irregular rainfall, the northern
half is surprisingly fertile: the rains are dependent on
variable winds, and change from district to district and
from season to season.   One zone gets 600 mm. per
annum; another only 136 mm.   In the south, cultivation
is only possible in the occasional oases and near the sea,
where in spite of low rainfall and sandy soil, the heavy
dews favour the cultivation of the olive.

The corn crops vary considerably from year to year, according to the rains—some soil will only yield one crop every two years! Native cultivation is neither scientific nor regular; and large tracts of land have been allowed to revert to semi-desert. Since the French occupation this problem has been tackled; grants of land have been made to suitable peasants, and public companies formed to exploit neglected areas. These have achieved remarkable success.

The cornfields are found in the north: along the east coast are the olive plantations, of great economic importance. The orange trade is small, but date palms are plentiful in the oases. Cattle-rearing flourishes: its more leisurely procedure suits Arab mentality better than intense cultivation. There are still traces of the ancient and usual feud between cattle-rearers and cultivators—to us a farmer is both, but in more primitive states the old distinctions still survive. There are huge flocks of sheep and goats, and considerable herds of cattle. The animals are often driven from district to district in search of provender, according to the season.

The greatest wealth of Tunis lies in its deposits of phosphates, the largest in the world. The possession of these merchantable supplies is probably one of Mussolini's prevailing ideas in his claims on the country. A second consideration may be the abundant supplies of iron ore, essential to a bellicose personality.

We have seen that the country is but sparsely populated, numbering slightly over 2,000,000 inhabitants. This is reasonable enough considering the enormous desert or semi-desert tracts which are not populated at all. Nearly ninety per cent of the population lives in the towns and villages along the coastal belt: the interior is almost empty. There are great expanses visited only by occasional families of wandering Bedouin.

The original Berber stock is now well mixed with

that of successive waves of Arab invaders. There are many interesting survivals of ancient tribes, particularly in the isolated mountain areas and on the island of Djerba.

Legally, Tunis is a French protectorate. The Bey still occupies his palace, but a French Resident-General is at his side to 'advise'. There are native ministers for justice and home affairs, Europeans being excluded from their jurisdiction, and local tribal custom has been amended to accommodate French control: considerable executive power still rests in the hands of local *caids* or *sheiks*, the headmen of the villages or settlements. Though French civil controllers have the final word, most details of native administration are in the hands of the *caids* and their advisory councils.

The climate of Tunis varies. Naturally, it is a hot country, but in the coastal areas the temperature is lowered by the sea breezes: these, however, can, on occasion, be like enervating blasts of steam. The interior suffers the climatic variations of the desert, even in the highlands, which are bare and desolate. The rainfall is of the utmost importance to life. In the extreme north-east it is seasonal but regular, of adequate strength. In the interior it is scanty and irregular. The land responds amazingly: but also declines, so that a cornfield in a rainy season may be a desert in a dry summer.

Only in the north-eastern corner has Tunis recovered its ancient prosperity. Further south gallant adventures in reclamation have been essayed by the French, often with amazing results. I was surprised to find that trees could be made to grow in sand. The contact with European ideas has been good for the placid, over-easy, fatalistic Arab temperament, and given freedom from strife Tunis ought to be able to look forward to a long period of progressive development.

Although the people are commonly referred to as Arabs,

they are properly Berbers, who have generally assimilated successive waves of invaders. Occasionally I met white-skinned Arabs, with the long and aquiline nose and clear features so typical of the race. Generally, however, blood is so mixed that it is difficult to distinguish between the Berberized Arab and the Arabized Berber. The people of the interior are almost without exception Berbers, themselves of mixed origin in antiquity.

The firmest binder of the peoples of Tunis is their religion. Islam is more than a creed, it is a mode of life, a civilization in itself. The law rests upon the Koran: it can scarcely be claimed that our law rests on the Bible!

In Tunis Mohammedanism has seen interesting developments in the cult of local marabouts, or saints, who are much venerated. Their *koubbas*, or tombs, are places of pilgrimages. Many of them were simple men of great piety—for the Moslem religion knows no priests: some were mystics, others prophets. Their sayings are still quoted, and their exhortations obeyed.

Family life is an important feature of Moslem culture. In Tunisia considerable authority rests with the head of the family: local organization, indeed, is almost tribal. Marriage is, of course, almost an obligation: a Moslem bachelor is rare and despised. A childless marriage is considered a tragedy: a barren woman runs a serious risk of divorce.

The position of women is not so lowly as is generally imagined. They work far harder than the men, it is true, and there is never any question about the master. Yet they have their specified rights—and even in conservative Moslem circles it is realized that the scope of these rights must soon be extended.

The Arab house is simple: it is spaced about a courtyard: the rooms are long and narrow. The living-room is sparsely furnished, by our standards, though even in

modest homes there are often carpets and mats of quality.
A carpeted bench usually runs round the sides of the
room, but it is just as comfortable to squat on the floor.
Often there are no windows at all—the door provides the
only light: if there are windows, they give on the courtyard—the outer wall presents an uncompromising façade
of whitewashed plaster.

For reasons of security the population always clustered
in towns or villages—the isolated farmhouse or cottage of
the English countryside is completely missing. The
town houses are somewhat more substantial and often
run to a second storey; yet in plan they are often the
same, built about a courtyard, often with a vine or palm
in the centre: if the family is affluent, a tiny fountain of
water. Often they house rare examples of beautiful
carved plasterwork, delicately tinted. Occasionally hand-
baked bricks replace the plaster, with striking effect. The
poorer quarters are not so artistic: the foulest East-End
slum is clean and pleasant by comparison.

Tens of thousands of Tunisian families do not live in
houses at all. Many have but a simple hut, called *gourbis*; they are made of dried earth or matted rushes, according to the materials available: they can be erected in
a few hours—and abandoned without regret if the call
comes to move. It does, frequently, for the family's
fortunes often follow the rains: the few precious sheep or
goats must emigrate to fresh pastures. The stench
of the *gourbis* is often appalling, and vermin find a
happy home in the interstices of the rough walls and
thatch.

The *gourbis* are usually considered a social step above
the tent of the nomads. Actually, the family tent is far
more spacious and hygienic than the miserable *gourbis*.
I saw some which had remained on the same site for many
years. Others change a dozen times a year, as its occu-
pants follow the seasons. On a lower grade are the casual

shacks of nomad shepherds or labourers, merely a couple of camel-hair blankets to give shelter from the sun and to keep out drifting sand.

The Jews of Tunisia are largely town dwellers. Many of them are descendants of the Israelites who fled from Palestine in the first century, to escape the terrors of the Emperor Titus: we shall meet one Jewish tribe which settled in Tunis long before that distant date. Others came from Spain with the Moors. Another important group came from northern Italy in more recent times. Others are actually the descendants of Berbers converted to the Jewish faith! This is indeed remarkable, for in Tunis the Jews are not generally liked by the Arab population. Only in 1859 were the severe laws imposed upon them finally abrogated. Except for the educated and professional classes, they are not a good advertisement for their race.

Tunisia is not a French possession, but a protectorate. So far as external relations are concerned, the difference in status is more apparent than real, but the internal administration demands the exercise of much tact on the part of the French officials: they do not direct policy, they 'advise'. The Bey is nominally the sovereign of Tunis, and he does possess some real powers of government over the Arabs, the administration being deputed to *caids*, or prefects: these men have a force of *spahis*, or police, to maintain order: they act as magistrates—and as assessors and collectors of taxes. They are supervised by French Civil Controllers. Europeans are, of course, tried before French Courts: Jews take their civil cases before their own rabbi. On the whole the system of administration works remarkably well.

The railways are not yet fully developed. There is an adequate service in the north, but a single line serves the south, with a long branch to the phosphate districts. The roads generally follow the railways: or, it would be

o

more correct to say, the railways followed the roads. The surface of the first-class roads is good; that of the second-class roads varies from indifferent to very bad. All others are simply indescribable—mere camel tracks over the desert. There are far more tracks than roads, especially in the south.

The problem of Tunis, as of most African countries, is that of the poor and landless peasant. Thousands of them are bound by an iniquitous contract called a *kham-messat*. By this a landed proprietor, usually a native sheik, allots a peasant a piece of land, and even advances seeds for sowing and money for tools: for his services he takes four-fifths of the subsequent crops. The unhappy *khammé* cannot possibly support a family on one-fifth of a crop, so he gets even further into debt with his master. This is a native system, but one day the French will have to prohibit its use.

A better arrangement is that called the *mgharsi*, commonly used on the vast estates of olives. The developing company, usually French, allots a plot of land to the *mgharsi*: he plants olive trees in it, but the company supports him until the trees begin production. Then they take one-half of the crop. Further, the *mgharsi* is allowed to use the ground between the olives for the cultivation of his own vegetables and corn. This form of contract has achieved very successful results.

There are interesting examples of collective cultivation among the Bedouins of the south. To-day considerable areas of ground are reckoned as the collective property of a tribe. They are usually meagre pastureland at the best, but occasionally corn and palms are grown at an oasis.

Corn and olive oil are the principal agricultural products of Tunis. Fruits, especially dates, are also exported, and orange blossom, geranium and roses produce famous perfumes. The principal animals are the sheep—the

of Jerusalem. Yet I suppose the peep-show was the Arab equivalent of our magic lantern.

George, in the meantime, was not so happy. I had left him in the charge of the guardian of a *fonduk*, and I returned to find him surrounded by grumpy and suspicious camels. Accidentally I caused a riot. A nearby camel made a vicious bite at my hand; I dodged in time, and the camel bit George's bell instead. It rang, and it was worth the fright to see the amazed alarm in that camel's eyes. The beast hurriedly retired a couple of paces, in its haste trampling on a somnolent neighbour. The neighbour began to kick, and that's how the row started. Half an hour later yelling Arabs were still trying to sort out the mess of incensed camels, and I was still awaiting an opportunity to dart in and rescue George, helpless in the midst of the storm.

The *fonduk*, or inn, was dirty and gloomy: a series of shelters about an irregular yard. At the height of the day it was almost impossible to move for camels and donkeys, while tethered poultry and goats littered every free space. The stench was indescribable. And this was of the same pattern as the inn at Bethlehem.

I never saw so many camels. Nor did I know that they had so many uses. Some carried great bundles, slung over their backs in traditional fashion: others were harnessed in great wooden carts, looking singularly awkward and ungraceful. Earlier in the day I had seen them pulling ploughs, their great bulk towering absurdly over the simple appliance they towed.

Nabœul is famous for its pottery. There are one or two factories of moderate size, but most of the work is a family industry. It was like a flash-back to Biblical days to see the potter at his wheel, or his wife at the oven. Nor has the character of the wares changed in two thousand years. In shape, at least, the vessels of Nabœul are identical with those of Roman days.

Altogether an interesting day, I mused as I rode on, wondering where I would stay the night. My problem was settled by accident, as I like it to be. On the sand track beside the road was a European on a mule: he hailed me, and I halted to talk. He was Italian, owner of a small orange grove. Visitors seldom came his way, it appeared: half an hour later I was installed in his timber and plaster cottage, arguing about Italian rights in Tunis.

v

There was still green country about me as I rode on next morning: green in Tunis is the colour of wealth. Orange groves contrasted with the darker olives. There were even flower gardens: for it is in this district that the pungent but pleasing scents of Tunis are distilled.

Soon I was in Hammamet, picturesquely situated on the seashore. The native town is entirely enclosed within brown castellated walls, flanked on two sides by the sea. On a third side was the cemetery, strangely unkempt. These people do not bury their dead deeply enough: dogs and jackals scratch up the sand and exhume the corpses. Human bones were scattered on every hand. It was all very surprising, considering the Moslem insistence on proper burial.

They call Hammamet the City of Pigeons, so I kept my hat securely in place. Some Arabs were preparing to bathe, and I joined them. Then I found that I had unconsciously joined a fishing expedition. The bay is full of fish, even in its shallow waters, and our nets reaped a rich harvest.

Hammamet is a resort for the Europeans of Tunis, but has a small resident European population. I was amazed to find it unpopular with the Arab inhabitants. When I sought for reasons, I heard stories of loose living, of a character which shocked Arab morals but which might have been accepted in Nazi Germany.

In spite of the heat, I discovered an appetite for lunch. An hotel on the sea front offered me a warm welcome, the host disclosing that he was once *chef du cuisine* at the Midland Hotel, Manchester.

The road to the south was good and flat: for miles we had it to ourselves; then we would meet a nomad family moving north. The man usually rode on the camel, padding along the sand track by the roadside: the women tramped behind, carrying babies or other family property. In one stretch of twenty miles the only house was an ancient caravanserai, guarded by an old Algerian with startling military reminiscences.

I lost count of the oddments of Roman remains I passed: a ruined bridge, a broken aqueduct, a temple, a triumphal arch—now quite devoid of any atmosphere of rejoicing: sometimes outlines of houses and streets revealed by desultory excavation. In the heat, with miles of uncultivated land, it was difficult to picture this as a thriving, populated colony.

Yet at Enfidaville the French have shown what can be done with semi-desert country. A vast scheme of reclamation has been consummated, artificially irrigated. Two generations ago this was a district of thin scrub and sand: now it is a vast olive plantation, covering hundreds of square miles. The village is a curiosity, for it is primarily European, with only a few Arab inhabitants.

I had thought to halt there, but to the west beckoned a curiosity, an Arab hill village. After the flatness of the coastal plain, the sudden hills were surprising. Rugged brown rocks had weathered into fantastic shapes, crowned by the brown protecting walls of the village, and dominated by a little white mosque. I pushed George wearily up the rough road towards Takrouna.

Women stared curiously at me. They were carrying
water to the village: it all had to be carried from a well
in the valley, laboriously drawn and then carried in great
pitchers. The women ran a rope through the handles
and placed this over their brows: their skulls must be
tough, for the strain is tremendous—I tried it, and had
a headache in a few minutes. Nor did it seem that the
water was worth so much trouble, for it was lukewarm
and insipid.

A remarkably handsome and fair-skinned Arab greeted
me as I gained the rough streets of the village. He
might have been expecting me, for he led the way to his
own house with great assurance. There I was presented
to his brother: both spoke excellent French. First we
walked round Takrouna, which has scarcely changed a
stone in seven centuries. There was something attractive
in the rugged defiance of its site, so striking after the
monotony of the plain. For generations Takrouna has
lived its isolated life; I could readily understand its
atmosphere of the past.

Yet when we settled down to talk, there was no
suggestion of ancient platitudes. The two brothers were
keen politicians, and very modern. The men of the
village squatted around, though few of them could have
understood a word of our conversation. I was highly
interested, for here was a new viewpoint. These Arabs
were nationalists. They had no serious complaints
against France, but wanted independence. They did not
belong to the Pan-Arab school of thought—they wanted
an independent Tunis. Any suggestion of Italian
domination they denounced bitterly: better a continuance
of the French regime than that. Yet the French task
was almost complete: they had done much useful work
in Tunis, but now the regeneration of the country could
only be completed by the Arabs themselves. Their
arguments were indeed exactly equivalent to those of

the Indian nationalists: and their difficulties were similar
—an extraordinary wide range of population, ranging
from educated and highly intelligent people to nomads
utterly devoid of political sense and responsibility.
Successful freedom is a matter of careful or inspired
timing.

As we talked animatedly, a remarkable thing happened:
it began to rain! No one moved to go indoors, so I sat
on, and got wet. The women were smiling—this would
mean less water to carry. They had my sympathy: I
could almost feel those ropes around my brow. Arabs
use their heads very extensively for transport purposes:
on the average they are not nearly so strong in the arm
as Europeans.

"And now," said one of the tall fair-skinned, blue-eyed
Arabs, "tell us the latest news of the world."

Immediately the congregation of listeners increased.
Soon all the men were gathered about, the women in the
background at a respectful distance. My news items
were translated one by one, to be greeted by wagging
heads and occasional exclamations.

The rain ceased, and the flies returned. We adjourned
indoors for a meal; it was difficult to eat the *kous-kous*
without swallowing a fly, which clung on grimly to its
succulent dish until the last fraction of a second. It
seemed to be assumed at once that I would stay the
night as the guest of the house, and I was led in
ceremonial fashion to the guest chamber: it housed no
bed, but had a mattress—a good one, too—and coarse
blankets.

The two brothers led the way between an avenue of
women. At the door one of them halted.

"I do not know the custom of your country," he said,
"but I have heard that it is sometimes the custom in
Europe to place a woman at the disposal of a guest. If
you would care to choose——"

"It is *not* the custom of my country," I hastened to interject.

"Ah! Then sleep, for in sleep is refreshment as great as that of water."

He was right.

VI

I was making for Kairouan, the Holy City of Tunis. There were two roads—a cut direct across the desert from Enfidaville, or a roundabout route via Sousse, on the coast. I put my poser.

"The coastal road is the safer, but much longer," said my Arab friends.

"How do you mean, safe?"

"Well, the direct road is safe in that you will not be attacked by man or beast. But it is sixty kilometres to Kairouan, and you will not meet a man or a house on the journey. That is, if this machine of yours breaks down, you might be stranded on the road for days, for but few people pass."

If such was their fear, there was nothing in it. George was not likely to 'break down' at this stage.

For that matter, we passed one tiny village in the course of the ride; and a few wandering nomad families as well. But I admit that it was a desolate ride. The country about was semi-desert: hard sand, producing but an occasional rough scrub. I was told that from time to time it can be persuaded to produce a crop, but this seemed almost incredible. For long stretches the country was utterly deserted. On my left hand was a shallow lake, miserably brackish. The only living creatures in view were camels and snakes.

Yet the surface of the road was quite fair, and almost flat, so that it was still early morning when the flat dome-topped roofs of Kairouan appeared on the horizon. Here even I could surely draw virtue, for to a Moslem seven pilgrimages to Kairouan count as one to Mecca.

My reception was unexpected. Infidels are allowed to visit three of Kairouan's famous mosques, under proper safeguards, and application has to be made to the French Civil Controller. As soon as I appeared in his outer office, the young lady on duty took one startled glance at me, then dashed through an inner door. I thought her conduct unreasonable: while it was true that I carried a quantity of the sands of the desert, distributed about the visible portions of my person and my clothing in a reasonably even layer, I was scarcely so grotesque as to deserve such a hurried departure.

The inner door reopened, and a pleasant smiling Frenchman in tropical dress approached.

"Mr. Bernard Newman, I believe?" he said, grasping my hand. "Please come in."

Thoroughly mystified, I went in. Immediately he began to talk about Kairouan—thoroughly interesting talk too; eventually he placed his good offices at my disposal. Yet there was a mystery which required solution.

"Your intelligence service is pretty good," I commented.

"Why do you say that?"

"Well, you appeared to be well warned of my coming—and your girl recognized me at once."

"That isn't secret service," he grinned, broadly. "Didn't you see yesterday's *Dépêche Tunisienne*?"

"No."

He passed it over. Now I began to see things. The intelligent young man who had asked so many questions when I called at the Residency in Tunis was, I discovered, chief reporter on the local paper. He had published a long interview with me, giving my impressions of the

European situation, with especial reference to the claims of Mussolini. Further, he had commented on my frame and personality, mentioning admiringly my massive and uncovered knees. I had to admit that the girl clerk had exhibited no especial detective skill in recognizing me.

Now the visit to the mosques was easily arranged: or to anywhere else I cared to go. A guardian was, of course, essential, and I drove off in the Controller's car accompanied by a bearded Arab.

The city of Kairouan is not particularly impressive, but it is 100 per cent Arab—the small French settlement is well outside the city. The name is derived from the word caravan, and there is a curiously temporary atmosphere about the untidy and dusty streets, despite their ancient whitewashed houses. The city dates from the Musselman conquest in A.D. 671: it was founded by the doughty chief Okba ben Nafi, because of its central position in Tunis, and its first function was that of a fortress. Generations later, under the rule of the Aghlabides, holiness mingled with martial glory, and the fame of the mosques of Kairouan became a legend in the land.

Most famous of all is that of Sidi Sahab, outside the city walls, and close by ancient cisterns still in use—and small boys were defying local regulations by bathing in them: my Arab driver turned out to be a policeman, and his action was swift and peremptory—he confiscated all the clothes, bundling them in the car: no need to take names and addresses—the culprits must now come to the police station in their birthday suits to recover their more mature garments.

If you asked a Frenchman of Kairouan for the Mosque of Sidi Sahab he would probably fail to understand, but if you asked for the Mosque of the Barber he would direct you at once. For Sidi Sahab was one of the companions of Mohammed, and was entrusted with the special duty of cutting the prophet's hair. Here, in his tomb, are three hairs from Mohammed's beard, and these alone would make the mosque a place of pilgrimage. Yet the tomb is the least imposing feature of the place. There is a colonnaded court of charm and beautiful proportions, a graceful minaret, and delicate stucco and tiles which recall the best features of Moorish Spain. The tomb of Sidi Sahab, however, is surrounded by votive offerings from thousands of pilgrims: some are simple, but most are tawdry, apparently purchased at Woolworth's for the occasion.

The Grand Mosque of Kairouan is in the old Arab city; it takes its name from Sidi Okba, another holy man of great renown. It is a tremendous place: a vast quadrilateral of walls encloses a great courtyard. Dotted about are wells, whence water may be drawn for washing the feet or other holy offices. The ancient ropes have cut deep ruts into the protecting stones. One side of the courtyard is dominated by a minaret, solid and imposing rather than elegant. From its platform I commanded a marvellous view of Kairouan. Far below me was a white desert of flat roofs, relieved only by the little dome of some obscure mosque. Beyond the walls, in violent contrast, was the brown-red semi-desert country, with its occasional relief of rough scrub or coarse roots of grass. The feature most readily missed in the African scene by the European eye is trees.

Opposite the minaret is the great mosque itself, a grandiose structure which will house many thousands of worshippers. Hundreds of pillars support the tremendous roof: most of them are far older than the mosque itself —they were freely removed from Roman and even Phœnician ruins; a good section of Carthage could be found at Kairouan. They have not been intelligently used, however, by the native architects. Some of the pillars and their inscriptions are upside down!

The columns are borrowed, but the plaster-work is pure Arab, as delicate as lace, carved from mud with ordinary knives. Equally fine is the pulpit, a thousand-year-old masterpiece of carved wood. Yet no infidel can really appreciate the atmosphere of the mosque. A place of worship only becomes alive when it is thronged with worshippers, and at such times visitors may not intrude here. The attendant hurriedly gathered up the rush mats as I passed along, so that they should not be defiled by unbelieving feet.

Kairouan is famous for its carpets. Their manufacture is a home industry, and in dozens of squalid hovels I saw girls at work. The whole process depends upon hand-work. Two girls, working ten hours a day, will weave one square metre of carpet in twenty days. I do not know what wages they are paid, but the average price of a square metre is 150 francs. Even if the girls got the lot, it would only work out at sixpence a day!

The patterns of the carpets are traditional and famous, based on those of the holy mosques. Mohammed, the guide, took me into a shop to buy one: if I chose a small one, it would not be too expensive to send it home by post—assuredly I did not propose to carry it on George!

"Six hundred francs, this very fine mat," declared the shopkeeper.

"The Englishman is the guest of the Civil Controller," said Mohammed.

"Five hundred francs," exclaimed the shopkeeper, thus avoiding a lengthy bargaining process.

Later I made another purchase. When a rug or carpet is completed, the man of the house hoists it over his shoulder and wanders the streets, looking for a purchaser. Such a man I encountered in one of the *souks*. Mohammed had left me, but the bargaining was amusing, and I was very satisfied. My first purchase had been of the standard wool pattern: this was of camel hair, and my feet repose on it as I write.

The *souks* of Kairouan are not nearly so extensive as those of Tunis; nor are they so picturesque, but I found them far more interesting. The French have been wise in their administration, and have never sought to penetrate the native quarters. In Kairouan they have kept right outside, and I wandered for hours without meeting a European.

Over dinner the Civil Controller introduced me to a local *caid* whose French was better than mine. He took me home: behind a blank whitewashed wall lay a house which was a treasure of Arab art. The tiles lining the lower walls were extraordinarily good, and the carved plaster above magnificent; from an alcove a little band of Arab instrumentalists showered strange music.

"Is there anything I can do for you?" he asked, at the moment of parting.

"Nothing, thank you. Yes, there is—you can advise me. In Tunis there was a fair, and I saw an old man who stuck nails into himself without hurting. He told me that he came from Kairouan, and that his mosque was here."

"Ah, he would be one of the Aissaoua," said the *caid*.

"The Aissaoua?"

"Yes. They are a sect of our religion—you too, I believe, have your different divisions. They have two *Zauoia* in Kairouan. These people are of intense faith, and they show their devotion to the Prophet by inflicting pain upon themselves."

"There were similar sects in early Christian days."

"Yes. But the Aissaoua are remarkable—I will say that, though I do not belong to their sect. Their faith is so strong that they cut themselves, but blood does not flow."

"That is what I would like to see."

"Ah! It is difficult. There are some men who exhibit themselves, like the man you saw at Tunis, but generally their ceremonies are private. Even I have been but two or three times, by invitation—and you are not a Moslem."

"The last thing I want to do is to hurt anybody's feelings," I said. "But it is in the spirit of the investigator of truth that I suggested this."

"I understand perfectly. There are some things which cannot be believed until a man has seen them for himself. Well, of such are the rites of the Aissaoua. Well, let me try. I have a friend among their company. You can wait until to-morrow evening? That is the time of their weekly meeting. But I may fail."

Yet late in the following afternoon, as I sipped refreshment in an Arab café, a man approached me.

"You are the Englishman?" he asked.

"Yes."

"Then come."

I followed him through the winding streets: into a house. To my surprise, he slipped a white *burnous* over my shoulders, its bonnet over my head.

"You had better take off your glasses—they are so European," he suggested. "Now you will come with me; I warn you that you may see nothing—sometimes the spirit does not move. But whatever you see, you must say no word. And when I say come, you must come— there are parts of their service that you must not see. That is understood?"

"Perfectly," I said, gratefully.

We walked to a little mosque near one of the city gates. The *burnous* fell awkwardly about my knees. I entered the mosque with misgivings. My bare feet seemed unduly prominent, for they are of some size. Yet in the mosque no one took any notice of me.

"Many of these men would be friendly enough even if they knew," said my unknown Arab before we entered. "But others are fanatical. Therefore we must be careful. If anyone speaks to you, do not reply. I shall say that you are dumb; then they will respect you because you have been afflicted by Allah."

We squatted down by a pillar at the back of the mosque. There would be seventy or eighty men present: elders predominated—though whiskers and *burnous* make it difficult to estimate the age of an Arab. First a *caid* said a prayer: the congregation responded by high-pitched sounds akin to moans. More prayers: then men, squatting on the floor, began to play with their fingers on drums. At first the tapping was sedate: then the tempo increased. Agile fingers produced rolls from the parchment-covered drums. Now they worked in unison: I felt myself responding to their thrill, and was not surprised when a man got up and began to prance about in an ecstasy.

Others followed, till a dozen of them were dancing to the music of the drums. They tore off their hampering *burnous*: one boy leaped about stark naked. They were chanting as they danced: a weird refrain in strange rhythm. I was more interested in their faces. Their eyes revealed men whose minds had passed out of the mosque. Their shouts became uncontrolled: my neighbour nudged me hard.

Two men held up a broad sword: a third ripped off his loose shirt, and dashed himself against its edge. I do not know how far it penetrated, but a line of blood appeared across his stomach. It must have hurt, but he showed no signs: instead, rushed on the sword again.

Another man held spikes in both hands—spikes like a four-inch nail, not very clean. With a great cry he plunged them into the flesh of his naked thighs. This at

P

least was easier to watch: there was no fake—the spikes penetrated the flesh for a good two inches: yet only a thin film of blood appeared about the wounds.

By this time the mosque was overwhelmed by an atmosphere of religious fervour and emotion. More squatting figures rose and joined in the dance. So furious was the swirl of cloaks that I could no longer see what was happening. But my neighbour nudged me again, and I followed the direction of his eyes. I had to rub my own to believe the evidence they offered. A youth of fourteen or fifteen years was climbing a pillar. When about eight feet from the ground he turned himself upside down and let go; his skull struck the tiled floor with a terrific crash. Almost I forgot my part and cried in alarm. Yet the youth, so far from being hurt, appeared to like it, and did it again and again. I gazed in amazed fascination as he dropped hard on his head, to rise immediately and join in the religious dance and chant.

Maybe I was showing signs of my rising excitement, for my neighbour grabbed me by the arm and pulled me away. Perhaps he was right: had I seen more, I must have imagined myself a victim of hallucination. I can attempt no explanation. Nor can I blame anyone who does not believe what I have written: I would not have believed it myself had not my own eyes seen it— although the phenomenon is fully vouched by many competent observers.

Because of my obvious interest in all things Arab, my friend took me to a *fonduk*—and I promptly decided to stay the night. This surprised everybody: later, I was surprised myself. I had been attracted by the company without looking at the accommodation, which is a very proper outlook. Yet the charges were reasonable. The *fonduk*, or caravanserai, consisted of two adjacent courtyards. The first was lined with shallow

arches: here I might shelter with the camels and donkeys
for half a franc. The second on three sides was fringed
with stables: the prices ranged from one franc to three
francs for the night—but, as the caretaker pointed out,
a man could accommodate his entire family as well as
his cattle in the larger sheds. The fourth side was
occupied by a dark lodging-house, very smelly: most of
the rooms had no windows, but only a small grating
giving on the courtyard. The one allocated to me contained a decrepit iron bedstead, a filthy mattress, and
a camel-hair blanket. The grating was small, but it let
in more than its share of the assorted scents from the
animals parked in the courtyard. With so many camels
at close quarters, a few flies were inevitable, but I would
never have believed that one mattress and four mud walls
could have housed so many bugs.

VII

It was a desolate road from Kairouan to the sea, over
a series of low ridges, covering country striving desperately hard not to deserve the appellation of desert.
Yet its character can be estimated by the fact that in
the first thirty miles I passed but one house, a wayside
café. Twice, however, I halted by the water-holes,
where Bedouin were filling goatskins with water. They
gave me to drink: the first pool yielded a pale blue liquid,
like weak ink: the second a brown muddy fluid. Neither
was attractive, but I was thirsty. If the Arabs could
drink it, so could I.

I struggled along against a fierce head-wind, which
blew the cruel particles of sand without mercy into my
ears, eyes and nostrils. At times I could scarcely see the
road for the clouds of sand about me. The Arabs used
the wind: it is part of their agricultural system.

Such land as will yield crops of corn is laboriously
ploughed by an ancient implement of wood, scarcely
scratching the surface. A camel, donkey, or pony—or a
combination of two of the three—pulls the plough. If
Allah is kind and sends rain, then there is a crop to be
gathered. It is reaped laboriously by hand, and the
threshing process has not changed in a thousand years.
Sometimes the corn is beaten by a wooden flail. More
often the sheaves are broken about a threshing-floor,
and a small chariot makes a circular journey about it,
drawn by camels or horses, weighted down by a driver.
Often I saw a small boy seated in the chariot behind his
father, to his great delight. Round and round in irregular
loops the chariot moves, the driver shouting and cracking
his whip like a circus master. The low wheels batter
the corn out of the ears, and the women gather up the
straw.

Then the family must await a wind. With wooden
shovels men and women fling the corn and husks into the
air. The corn falls abruptly on to the threshing-floor,
the light husks are carried away by the wind. It was
easy to know when I approached a scene of harvest, for
the husks mingled with the sand, to my discomfiture.

VIII

Sousse is not so interesting as the other towns of Tunis.
I did not discover this immediately, for its beach and sea
offered relief from the torment of driving sand. It has
a considerable European population, mostly French,
Italians and Maltese: the native city is still enclosed
within its ancient walls, but its *souks* did not grip the
imagination: they were too sophisticated. Even the
musicians in the Arab café chantant had been replaced
by wireless—an appalling din, discordant sounds which

were merely a great noise. Arab music is seldom
soothing at its best, but when transmitted through a
raucous and ill-adjusted loudspeaker, it is something of
an ordeal.

Sousse ought not to be sophisticated, for it is an
ancient place, built on the site of the classical Hadrumetum, a Phœnician city built ten centuries before Christ.
In Hannibal's days it was an important naval and military
base. Nor did it share the fate of Carthage, for during
the Roman occupation the old city prospered. Its
hinterland was fertile—it is strange to read to-day the
glowing accounts of ancient chroniclers, and to reconcile
them with the driving sand which greeted me! Yet there
are many traces of its ancient glories, even of its great
port: hundreds of statues and other architectural remains
have been unearthed, to testify to the bygone wealth of
the merchants and warriors of Sousse.

The most interesting survival of ancient Hadrumetum
is to be found outside the present town. As in other
parts of the Roman Empire, Christians were persecuted,
and could only worship by stealth. Their meeting-
place became their sepulchre, and in the course of centuries
great catacombs were hacked out of the cliff face.
Many of the galleries have been lost, but even now it is
possible to wander through many miles of underground
passages, housing over 15,000 tombs. Some of them are
remarkably ornate, with fine sculpture in their monuments. Close by is a Roman cemetery of conventional
type, great stone coffins still lining the road after nearly
two thousand years of exposure.

There is a famous building in the Arab quarter of
Sousse called the Ksar El Ribat, which dates from the
ninth century. It is a splendid example of an Arab
castle and mosque combined, its dignified courtyard
flanked by heavy pillars, with great staircases leading
to the prayer-room above. Its walls command a fine

view of the old town: I noticed especially some delicate minarets completely lined with tiles of pottery.

And yet, in spite of all its historical interest, my most pleasant recollection of Sousse is of basking in its delicious sea.

It is rather strange. All these Tunisian towns seem alike at a first glance, but on closer acquaintance prove to be very different. The street life is always fascinating: the cubby-holes of the merchants and artisans belong to an earlier age: '*burra! burra!*' cry the donkey drivers, urging on their laden beasts: camels pad along noiselessly, rounding the abrupt corners with gaunt awkwardness. The Arab woman knows no perambulator, but straps the baby on her back: the duty is in fact often relegated to small girls. The colourful robes, with white as a background, give the appearance of a stage scene to the street.

Pastry-cooks parade with trays of their wares on their heads; at least at this height the customer is unable to see the swarms of flies about the pastries. The meat stalls are offensive to the eye and nauseous to the nose. In spite of all the movement, it is amazing how few people are actually working: only the artisans, hammering interminably at copper, or stitching slippers in highly coloured crimson or yellow leather.

The men generally do the shopping—sometimes allowing the women to carry the purchases home. Some of the town women are veiled, but the Berber women from the countryside are not: copper-hued faces of clear features, with a liberal glimpse of brown flesh through the long slits in the loose rough robe.

I passed by a house whence came wails and sobs. This was a house of death: professional mourners had been summoned, and were earning their money, sobbing vigorously and scratching their faces, loudly proclaiming the virtues of the dead. I was told that the inventiveness

The Chameleon Does a Tight-rope Act on George

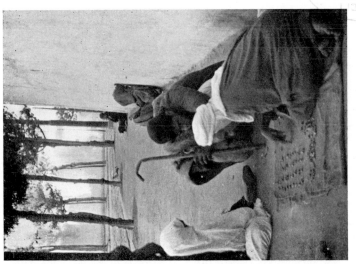

The Fortune Teller

CAMELS AT A *KOUBBA*

THE DESERT OF SOUTHERN TUNIS

of the professional mourners is remarkable. Often they
do not even know the dead person, but by clever general-
isms, supplemented by shrewd observation, their laments
give the impression that they were the bosom friends of
the deceased.

Women did the weeping: men squatted stolidly on the
doorstep. From a neighbouring house came sounds of
music of another kind: to the thin accompaniment of a
flute men were singing. Their voices were high-pitched
and wavering: the air had an irregular rhythm and little
tune.

I suffered an awkward moment as the sultry evening
air drove me into a café for refreshment. An Arab band
was playing—flute, drum and a native guitar. Abruptly
girls appeared and began to dance: they were young but
plump, and they soon discarded their cumbrous robes.
Here was my old friend the belly dance, which is intriguing but not graceful: the girl stands with feet apart, and
so manipulates her muscles that her stomach seems to
chase itself round in a circle.

Of course I contributed to the inevitable collection,
and apparently I was a fraction too generous, for one of
the girls came and sat beside me: very close. Under her
paint I saw signs of prettiness, and her eyes were certainly
attractive. Her French was elementary, but sufficient.
I had not realized that I was in the street of the *Ouled
Naïls*, the courtesans of the town. They are a feature
of every Arab place. While the virginity of the bride is
a matter of the utmost importance, I doubt if you could
find an Arab youth of sixteen who could claim such
distinction.

It was a matter of tact to put off the young lady without hurting her feelings and lowering my dignity—for
grave eyes stared at me from all corners of the café, where
men squatted on the carpet on the bench by the wall.
Eventually, placated by a small present, she continued

the dance—giving me full opportunities for technical examination by doing the belly-wriggling at a range of eighteen inches.

IX

We plodded south over monotonous country, relieved only by anæmic olive plantations and an occasional Arab village. Suddenly, from a slight eminence, a great sweep of country was exposed. Dominating it was an enormous structure of stone, visible twenty miles away. This was the amphitheatre of El Djem, second only in size to that of Rome.

It was difficult to believe that in the third century El Djem—then known as Thysdrus—was one of the greatest cities of North Africa, for to-day it is but an insignificant Arab village of squat houses: yet not so difficult, for if the coliseum were typical of the city, then indeed it must have been magnificent. El Djem is completely dominated by the vast structure, rising in great arcades of columns. Its proportions are grand, and its seating arrangements could scarcely be bettered by the designer of a modern stadium. Sixty thousand people could watch every detail of the games in the great arena.

They were stern games. Below the surface are dens which once housed lions, hungry for prey. The swords of gladiators clashed above in preparatory combat for the great event, when the lions were loosed. Such stories could be told of El Djem as would make the romantic novels seem tame.

Until two hundred years ago the amphitheatre remained intact, in all its glory. Then a group of rebels took refuge within its mighty walls, and the governing *bey* made a breach in them to get at his refractory subjects.

Recently some restoration has been attempted—rather badly, for it is too obvious.

Yes, the ancient Thysdrus must have been a great place. As if one coliseum were not enough, there are remains of an older one a mile away. This has been ruthlessly pillaged throughout the centuries for building stone, and you need imagination to picture it in its old glory. In the other direction are the scanty remains of a circus, once of great size. As the city was reputed to be prosperous, the entertainment of its citizens was evidently a matter of importance.

By some ancient cisterns I saw a man digging in the shallow earth. He rushed up to me and offered me a Roman lamp which he had just found. I suspected that he had just planted it, and made him go on digging. Soon he found another. Fired with archæological enthusiasm, I borrowed his wooden spade and began to dig myself. I wish my neighbours could have seen me: they call me lazy with the spade, and the condition of my garden justifies this criticism. But now I worked furiously in a desert sun: the temperature must have approached treble figures. Soon I dug up a lamp for myself; close by were some coins. Eventually I excavated a stone pillar, with carved reliefs on its sides. With regret I had to leave it behind. There are limits to George's carrying capacity and my energy.

It was impossible to lose my way as I wandered haphazard about the countryside. Even if a group of olive trees temporarily hid the amphitheatre from my view, I could always regain the El Djem by following the smell. For it was market day, and there were many camels.

By the rich brown stone walls of the coliseum peasants gathered for their barter: the markets of rural France were dwarfed by the length and excitement of the bargaining processes. At least an hour was essential for the

selling of a sheep.   A considerable crowd gathered about
two men who haggled over the price of a camel.   When at
long last a bargain was about to be struck, the camel
spoiled it all by making a vicious bite at the seat of the
purchaser's pantaloons, and the argument had to begin
all over again.   I was highly amused, until the indignant
camel made a grab at me: in my alarm I dropped George,
who fortunately eased his fall by descending on the
camel's capacious toes.   He bit George then, but retired
abruptly with toothache.

X

The road to the south was again a picture of desolation
as we moved on.   The road for many miles was bordered
by brown earth, like sand held together by some unifying
agent: it disintegrated at a touch.

Then after hours of monotony, with no other company
than an occasional family of roving Bedouin, we entered
a huge olive grove.   For miles its avenues stretched
about us: it was easy to distinguish the French farms
from the native—the French trees in beautiful straight
lines, well cared for.   Soon there were indications that
we approached a considerable town: here was an Arab
suburb.   Each whitewashed house had a little garden,
enclosed by a bank of dried mud crowned with a hedge of
cactus.   A cooler breeze swept from the sea: the temperature could scarcely have been above 80° when we swept
into Sfax.

The place looked interesting, but a swim was the first
essential.   This was disappointing: there was a beach,
but it was so shallow that swimming was almost impossible.   I waded out so far that I half expected to find
myself in Malta.

There must be deep water somewhere off Sfax, for boats

were floating on the water: enormous red sails dipped over at crazy angles, till it seemed that the boats must capsize. Men worked great oars—the wrong way, by our standards: yet half a mile from shore the shallow sand persisted, and poles replaced oars.

I dressed and wandered round to the harbour—of some considerable size. Some of the boats brought in fish, others sponges. The fish were much more attractive than the sponges: indeed, I don't think my lady would cuddle the sponge in the bath if she saw it in the raw state.

Larger ships were loading phosphates, the great material wealth of Tunis. They have made of Sfax the second city of the protectorate, and a grateful monument to the discoverer of the vast deposits was no more than a just due. The European quarter is extensive and modern: and the Arab town is fascinating. Like all the others, it is enclosed within its ancient walls, red and castellated.

There is almost as much to see as in Kairouan. Arab quarters seldom give any impression of age, for they carry a fresh coat of whitewash, but some of the houses of Sfax have maintained themselves for a thousand years. Presumably their walls are now thicker by at least a thousand coats of whitewash.

The walls and some of the guardian towers date from the eighth century, the great mosque from the tenth. Unbelievers may not enter, of course, but I could believe the stories of its magnificence, for its exterior is most promising. Its seven-sided minaret is particularly interesting, and an illicit peep revealed rows of pillars reminiscent of Kairouan. Incidentally, they had the same origin, for the Roman ruins of Sfax were freely used by the Arab builders.

The *souks* were a fascinating study. These narrow streets are a torment to a photographer. The white walls tend to give a flat picture, and the one desire of the inhabitants is to envelop the street in shade. Many of them are completely covered over, so that at the height of the sun artisans work below in a dim gloom: others slept unashamedly. In an Arab town there are always twice as many people resting as working. Many a time I have lounged in a *souk* and wondered how on earth the shopkeepers got a living at all.

XI

The road skirted the sea for a hundred miles. The olive plantations continued to line its course, occasionally varied by almond trees. Gradually the soil degenerated into sheer sand. It was just as if the trees were growing on a tideless beach. To this day I do not understand how they survive, even allowing for artificial irrigation. This did not seem to be organized on the vast scale one would have considered essential.

At times the fine light sand invaded the road, driven by the welcome breeze from the sea. I halted at Mahares, an Arab fishing village—sponges again supplying the modest wealth of the place. The local lighthouse was primitive enough—an iron cage, hoisted on a pole, in which a fire is lighted when boats are at sea by night.

The country got worse. Even the hardy olive trees, spoon-fed by men, could scarcely survive, and at last gave up the attempt. I crossed a stretch of barren desert, relieved only by an occasional oasis of sickly date-palms. Even the survival of these was a mystery, for as often as not the water-hole was dry: otherwise it produced mud.

I found the oases as depressing as the desert. When they were inhabited, the Arabs seemed to be resigned to the unequal struggle with Nature, and gazed indifferently as the sands invaded the plantations of palms. The native houses were of the crudest type, mere shacks of matting: the standard of life was obviously appallingly low.

But one French-speaking Arab expressed the local philosophy admirably, when I commiserated with him. "Well, if we don't like it, we can always get up and go!" he said. He was right. The entire riches of his household could have been piled on the back of a single donkey.

My greatest torments in Tunis were the flies. They must number more to the square mile than in any part of Africa. They hung about me like bees about to swarm. Often I fought them fiercely, slaughtering hundreds, but thousands remained. One day I made a disgusting discovery, after vain swishing at a fly with distinctive markings. I was not entertaining the local flies, which had perhaps some claim on my hospitality. The same gang of flies was following me about all over Tunis! This was grossly unsporting.

The Arabs ignore the flies. I saw one old man asleep, mouth wide open: flies crawled amiably about his skin, and even explored the insides of his lips. Less amusing were the children, with masses of flies about their eyes: or the animals, unendurably tortured.

The sun beat furiously on the red sand, and on my back. The tarred road reflected the intense heat. Nor did the eyes offer relief, for all about was sheer desolation. Sometimes a burst of scrub or prickly grass would force through the sand: sometimes even an isolated tree, usually in the last stages of exhaustion. My mouth was parched as I plodded on. Even my coarse palate had revolted at the liquid alleged to be water produced at the last well, and I was now well set towards the agony of intense thirst.

You do not appreciate water until you have ridden over a desert.

Abruptly I reached a new oasis. There was a sign of real life about it. The trees were green, and the sand was sparse. Rapidly the prospect eased—here was even a stretch of coarse grass. Then I nearly fell off George, as a bridge carried the road over a running stream! It was a very ordinary little brook, but I stood and gazed at it as a real curiosity. So I knew I had reached the great oasis of Gabès.

Yet I did not appreciate the marvel of it all until I had wandered from the road. At last I realized what an oasis was. It seemed incredible, after the miles of sandy desolation. The area is not large—about seven miles by four—but is astonishingly fertile, especially in comparison with the desert by its borders. There are two hundred thousand palms alone at Gabès, and many thousands of olives, vines, apricots and other sub-tropical fruits.

I parked George, and fell into conversation with a dark-skinned Arab. He talked very intelligently of the affairs of the day, and I was very surprised when he revealed himself as a guide. Rather hesitantly he offered his services. If I had no money—and as I came by bicycle he assumed that I was of small means—he would gladly accompany me if I would pay for the hire of donkeys. There were no visitors at Gabès, and he wanted exercise: besides, he liked my conversation. I liked his, so we went to get a couple of donkeys.

He was the only guide I ever knew who earned his keep. Four hours later we returned to the hotel—four energetic hours, especially for an Arab. By this time we were on very friendly terms, but I hesitantly enquired what his terms would have been if I had been an ordinary tourist. Forty francs—including the hire of the donkeys!

We pursued a tortuous path through the maze of palms. The very shade was a delight, and the eternal green a solace to the eyes. We passed one or two amazing villages. Some of the streets were arcades, houses built above the low arches, against which I bumped my head frequently. The stones of the houses bore Roman inscriptions—as further north, the remains of antiquity have been freely plundered.

Mohammed talked to his friends in a high-pitched wail as we passed, conversations beginning and ending a couple of hundred yards apart. We halted to pass the time of day with friends in some of the solid stone houses, dark and dingy. I sat on a stump of a pillar which had probably once graced a Roman temple.

My donkey had the natural abhorrence of its race to speed, but I was content to laze on its capacious back; both of us ignored Mohammed's insistent calls to action. The time came when he himself was constrained to halt, for the sun was hot once we emerged from the sheltering palms. Here in a primitive hut of matting and palm branches was an old man who lay sick: he had been bitten by a snake. His women were carrying water: they were handsome, as Berber women often are. Their loose robes had the traditional long slits, inviting glances at their lithe brown bodies. Moslem Africa is strange: in some corners the women veil their faces, in others they bare their breasts.

The scene near the source of the little brook which brings green wealth to Gabès would be classed as pleasant anywhere. In Africa it is sheer loveliness. A great green pool of clear water, reflecting the dignified palms —and its extremity flanked by a dam constructed by the Romans two thousand years ago. Low ridges of dried red sand flank the scene, commanding a rare panorama over the green sea of Gabès. The power of water is forcibly illustrated: immediately above the source the oasis abruptly ceases, and the land becomes desert again.

The brook was lined by tall weeds, and graceful palms: their reflections in the evening light made a picture of real beauty. At first I thought it had overpowered Mohammed, till I realized that it was the time for evening prayer. First he washed his feet, then turned to the east, kneeling in prayer, his forehead bent to the ground.

Tortoises gambolled playfully in the tepid stream; they had an uncanny resemblance to Walt Disney's creation. Water snakes glided smoothly in the shallows, and a myriad insects buzzed overhead. A crazy path followed the stream, rough and irregular, but my donkey negotiated it with ease. There was interest on every hand—here the *koubba* of a dead marabout, there another village of palm-leaf shacks or Roman stone cottages; next, cave dwellings in the cliffs of hard red sand.

The atmosphere of the oasis was reflected in the character of the people. In the morning I had passed disconsolate Arabs, squatting in despair at the sight of the invading sand. At Gabès everybody had something to do, and was doing it. The Arabs are not naturally a cheerful race, from our point of view, but here at least was comparative content.

The French town of Gabès is insignificant, but the native quarters are extensive, forming three distinct towns. One has an arcaded market place which is remarkable—and again the pillars have been plundered from antique constructions. I wish it could be said that the place is as sanitary as it is picturesque. Yet it doesn't seem to matter: the smells didn't harm me, and the Arabs didn't seem to notice them.

I lounged with Mohammed outside the hotel in great content. These four hours in the oasis had refreshed my mind and eyes. I would wander its paths again and

again, for they offered peace.   Then I happened to glance
upwards.   On the roof of the hotel was a look-out post,
manned by soldiers.   It was the tallest building in Gabès,
and commanded a wide view, especially to the south.
There had been a spot of bother a few months earlier,
Mohammed whispered: some of the local Arabs had been
roused by nationalist propaganda.   Now the look-out
post had been maintained—lest the Italians should invade
from the south.

There was a beach at Gabès—of a kind.   The port is
undeveloped but houses many fishing-boats.   Mohammed
did not consider it very interesting, and led me off to a
military encampment further south.   Here I was warmly
welcomed, and spent a convivial evening.

XII

Thirty miles south of Gabès are the Matmata Mountains.   Mohammed said that I would find them interesting: not as scenery—his intuition was keen enough to
discover that I was more interested in people than things.
Unfortunately he did not know how to ride a bicycle, he
added regretfully, otherwise he would certainly have
come with me.

He might at least have given me a warning about the
road.   It was excruciating, the worst I had struck in all
Tunis.   (There were still worse to come.   The few main
roads of the country are very good, but once off them
the descent in quality is very rapid.)   I passed by the
koubba of Sidi Boul Baba, the patron saint of Gabès:
through a miserable village in a depressing oasis: then
plunged into desolation.

Such depressing country I never saw.   The sand was
baked hard: every few miles a dozen weakly palms would
make a ghastly attempt to survive.   Great stones littered

Q

the roadway, and even the gentle friction of George's tyres raised a trail of dust behind us.

The morning sun was powerful: soon I was thirsty, but dared not exhaust the small flask I carried. The map promised a stream and a village, but the *oued* was a bed of sand, and the village did not exist: so far as I could trace, it never had existed. At the moment when thirst became really painful, I sighted the tents of a military encampment.

Already I had begun to climb. Now the rough road swung into the heart of the mountains. The gradient was not severe, but the appalling surface entailed much pushing. The rising scene commanded a fine view, but it was a picture of desolation. In twenty miles I met but one man, riding a camel. I was to wish that I hadn't.

He halted abruptly at my approach, staring at me curiously and at George in great interest. Probably he had never seen a bicycle before, for he dismounted to make a closer inspection. As I displayed George's charms to him, unfortunately I caught my sleeve in the bell, which clanged loudly. The startled camel promptly ran away.

The Arab chased after it, shouting violently. I did not understand anything he said, but I doubt if any of the names he called that camel would be found in the Koran.

I am a very tender-hearted man. I was responsible for the camel's flight, however inadvertently, and I ought to catch it. Fortunately the beast was keeping to the road, and was running downhill. The Arab was hopelessly outpaced. I gave George his head, but the rocky road so hindered fast movement that two miles had passed before I caught up the camel. I had just pushed up those two miles, and now had to do it again. I joined in heartily with the Arab's remarks when he arrived: I remembered several words I hadn't used since 1918.

Now the weary climb began again. It was beyond human comprehension why men should choose such inhospitable mountains as a home. Yet they did, for I passed two habitations, hacked out of the mountainside: there was no one at home, and though the doors were open, inviting entry, I could find no water.

The road now rose steeply, and I made a hot climb to the pass, on the shoulder of a gaunt mountain. Now before me lay an upland valley, entirely enclosed within desolate hills. At last there were signs of life: I saw a small group of whitewashed houses, and about them tiny groves of palms.

The houses were the market place of the valley: close by was a primitive inn. The *caid*, headman of the valley, called upon me as I inspected the stock of liquid refreshment offered. It would be necessary for me to report to the French military controller, he said—the Officer of Native Affairs. I promised urgent attention as soon as my tongue had come unstuck from the roof of my mouth.

I found the French officer a mile further on, in a small barracks pleasantly—but strongly—situated on the mountain above the valley. In the northern two-thirds of Tunis the administration is in the hands of Civil Controllers, but in the extreme south military officers have supreme charge. Both are assisted by native *caids*, who are in general charge of local native affairs. The officers who run the *Bureaux des Affaires Indigènes* are of a fine type, well chosen. The one at Matmata made me welcome, and gave me the free run of his district. This was nice of him—if only there had been roads fit to run on!

When I came out of the office, I found some of the soldiers of the little garrison gathered round George, shouting with laughter. I joined them, then opened my eyes wide in amazement. I had read of chameleons, of course, and have accepted their peculiarities with the usual discount for travellers' tales. Yet here they were, changing colour before my eyes.

They were smaller than I thought—eight or ten inches long, not unlike a lizard in shape, but with much longer legs. One was perched on the white doorstep of the house: a soldier picked him up and put him on George's saddle: immediately he began to turn black, and in a few seconds the process was complete, almost eerie to watch. Fascinated, I carried chameleons from one point to another, dumping them against backgrounds of different hues. I could have played this fascinating game for hours.

But what amused the soldiers was not the colour-changing, which was no novelty to them. Apparently the chameleon is the acrobat of the lizard family, and is as full of tricks as a monkey. Two or three chameleons had discovered George, parked against a wall, and had decided that he was a gymnasium sent by providence. One had clambered among his spokes, using them as a trapeze, swinging gaily as his fore-paws clutched a horizontal spoke. Another, a real comedian, even bolder, had climbed down from the saddle, and was using George's cross-bar as a tight-rope! Despite the opportunities for skidding, he negotiated the precarious passage with careful ease: then, unable to make head or tail of the front bracket, made the return journey backwards, to the applause of the troops.

The garrison to-day is not large, but this was one of the last districts of Tunis to accept French rule: even so late as 1914 there was an insurrection on a considerable scale. I could distinguish forts on the crests of the neighbouring mountains. From one of them ran a great alley-way, guarded on either side by a solid stone wall.

This had protected soldiers descending to the valley against Arab snipers. Fortunately, most of the Arab weapons were antique. But one of the veteran French soldiers remarked: "It was not a pleasant campaign. I was never frightened, but always thirsty." I could sympathize!

I have seen troglodite dwellings in many parts of Europe, but the caves of Matmata are a thing apart. When a man of Matmata wishes to build a house, he begins to dig. First he excavates a great circular hole, twenty feet deep and forty feet across. The dried sandstone works easily, and yet is remarkably firm.

The hole completed, he burrows a tunnel by its side to reach its lower section: this is his main entrance. Then he digs a cave in the side of the cliffs of the hole: this is his house. As his family increases, he will dig another cave on the opposite side of the hole, or even an upstairs cave as a bedroom, connecting to ground by an outside staircase carved from the red earth.

He lives in a primitive pit not because he is poverty-stricken but because he gains coolness in summer and warmth in winter. The Matmata folk are not classed as poor in Tunis. Their fields are often six or seven hours away from their homes: the poor man is he who has no camel or donkey to carry him to his work. The principal part of his labour consists of irrigation. High in the hearts of the mountains are great cisterns, which the winter rains fill. They must be of colossal capacity, for their waters support twenty thousand people throughout the summer. At morning and night you may see the women at work, carrying the precious fluid on their backs in great pitchers, supported from their foreheads by rough ropes.

Never did I see such a village. The main street consists of an irregular series of holes in the ground—there is not so much as a brick showing above the surface.

Except for occasional wifts of smoke from the caverns below, these might be ancient dene holes.

I wandered into several of the holes, to receive a welcome mingled with great curiosity. The furnishings were not elaborate. The living-room contained a bed, some rush mats on the floor, and a number of bottles. On the other side of the hole was a primitive kitchen. The room above was just a cubby-hole for the children.

The Arab inn at Matmata did not profess to be an hotel, but was a grade better than a *fonduk*. It consisted of one room, made of dried mud; the room also served as the general shop for the village and some of its wares were pungent. However, there was a great pitcher of water, almost colourless, and not more than lukewarm. For a bed they gave me a rush mat on a dried mud shelf; no blanket was necessary, for the night was sultry. Yet I was a sensation when I undressed—the Arabs who shared my lodging merely removed their *burnous*, and lay down in their shirts and pantaloons. Pyjamas were a real novelty to them, and each garment was handed round for minute inspection. My host was so intrigued that he called in his wife. I was in no conventional state to receive a lady, but no one seemed to mind. It may be improper for a man to look on a woman, but it doesn't appear to matter how much a woman sees of a man.

XIII

I ought to have returned to Gabès in the cool of the morning, but the *caid* had invited me to attend his morning court. Although I did not understand a word said, it was all intensely interesting. There was little ceremony: the *caid* sat on a carpeted shelf behind a simple table in a plain room, but his own personality, grave and experienced, gave a suitable atmosphere of solemnity to the proceedings. There were but two cases: the first, a man charged with stealing a basket of dates. The charge was easily proved: the sentence was a fine of fifty francs—a lot of money to an Arab—and the repayment of *two* baskets of dates to the aggrieved neighbour. Before the culprit was allowed to depart, the *caid* delivered a long and effective homily, apparently pointing out to the man how he had reduced his chances of entering paradise.

The second was a dispute between two Arab farmers about water—the most desperate cause of quarrel. They gave their evidence at great length, frequently contradicting each other; at times I thought they were going to fight. For two hours the wrangle dragged on; then the *caid* adjourned the case. He told me that he would look into it on the spot—four hours' journey away.

"I see. You think one of the men is lying," I suggested.

"No. I *know* that *both* of them are lying," he replied.

He insisted that I should rest after lunch, and it was mid-afternoon before I took the road. Yet I was quite happy—it was downhill all the way. Yet I had forgotten the appalling surface of the road. Despite the descent which should have provided a comfortable coast, the rocks and stones were so abominable that often I had to dismount and push. The air was more than usually sultry; when I reached the valley the atmosphere was oppressive; I was glad to see the round tents of the military camp.

It seemed that everyone was asleep: even the sentry was somnolent. When I demanded refreshment he vaguely indicated a bell tent which seemed to be a canteen. I stepped inside, to find that the tent was pitched about a great hole: evidently the troops had borrowed the cooling ideas of the Matmatas. Ten feet below the earth men were asleep, and declined to be roused: but I espied bottles, so descended and helped myself.

I sensed something strange in the atmosphere as the rough road carried me clear of the mountains. I thought I had already shed all surplus perspiration, but it rolled from my face. Winding by the side of the mountains came a gentle southern breeze. It struck me like a fire. I gasped for breath. The road was flat, but I could scarcely raise the energy to drive George along.

It seemed that the intense heat drove the air upwards, leaving behind a semi-void of heat. It was painful to touch George's steelwork, and I glanced anxiously at his tyres. If they failed, then I was hopelessly lost: assuredly I had not the energy to march in this astonishing atmosphere.

Wearily I plodded on a few miles: I doubt if I moved at five miles an hour. I was really distressed: never have I felt so helplessly weak. By the end of the afternoon I was scarcely conscious: my feet were moving slowly and mechanically. My brain was not functioning at all: George must have steered himself.

I can recall nothing of the last hour of the journey. I remember a thrill of joy as I rounded a spur of a hill and saw the palms of Gabès below me, listless and wilting in the burning breeze. I rode through the town without encountering a soul in the streets; I had scarcely the strength to lift George up the steps of the hotel. I staggered across the hall, then fell hopelessly over Mohammed, sleeping heavily on its tiles.

Yet he roused himself; I sat on the floor, unable to rise.

"But why—*why* do you ride this afternoon?" he whispered.

"It is too hot," I agreed.

"Too hot! You must be mad! To ride when the sirocco is blowing!"

"So that's what it is!" The desert wind, direct from the sun-deadened vastnesses of the Sahara.

"Yes. I looked at the thermometer in the porch two hours ago. It stood at 51° C."

I made rapid calculations. 51° C. would be 113° F.— in the shade. And I had known no shade for a moment of the ride!

I tried to rise, but my strength was already sapped to exhaustion. Mohammed was already asleep again: I stretched beside him on the tiles of the hall, and slept.

That evening, rummaging in my pack, I chanced on a piece of paper—the doctor's instructions to cure my tired heart. The first I have already quoted: "Don't walk uphill." The second direction was equally clear and direct: "Avoid sun."

XIV

In the evening a breeze from the sea countered the insufferable heat of the sirocco. Mohammed recovered before I did. I awakened to a lovely sense of cool, to find him pouring cold water through my hair.

Strangely enough, I was hungry. After a meal, in the short twilight, we wandered into Grande Djara, the native market. Gabès had staggered back to life: the women first, for water must be carried whether the temperature was in three figures or two.

A fortune-teller squatted by an ancient Roman pillar. As a client engaged him, he poured out a little bag of sand on to the floor, dividing it into mystic shapes before uttering his prophecies. A rival used beans, sorting them into strange patterns.

"He is very good, this man," said Mohammed. "Often I have consulted him. He even told me that my wife would have two girls before she had a boy. It was a nuisance, but quite true. You would like to consult him, perhaps?"

"Why?"

"Well, your wife——"

"Family matters seem too far away at the moment. But I would like to know if it will be cool enough to ride to-morrow."

"Ah, to him that is easy."

The fortune-teller looked at me with suspicion, evidently scenting a sceptic. But a skinny brown paw accepted my two francs and poured out the fine yellow sand.

"He says you will ride to-morrow," Mohammed announced.

"Good!"

"But you will not reach your journey's end."

"Well, I don't expect to! But what does he——"

"Or the next day, or the day after that, he says."

"My dear Mohammed, I never expected to get to the frontier in three days. Ask him——"

"He will say no more. He repeats that you will not reach your journey's end."

Mohammed was worried. He interpreted the message as unfavourable. It must mean that I would be killed or injured on the way. The thought preyed upon him, and soon he was begging me not to go.

"It is playing with fate, to defy such a warning," he insisted.

"But the fellow didn't know which way I was going. Whatever is to happen might come just as easily if I turned about and went north. Besides, if he says it's going to happen, by your reasoning it must happen, surely?"

"Yes. But why invite it?"

We entered into a long argument on predestination, and soon were both hopelessly out of our depth. We sat on a sandy hillock under a palm: suddenly Mohammed jumped to his feet, pulled me aside, and beat vigorously with a stick.

"A scorpion!" he cried, indicating the corpse.

I gazed at the venomous insect, an insipid creature six inches long, well camouflaged against its sandy background. Then I was silent at my own innocent temerity: during the last few days I had seen dozens of these things—had even sat down beside them, not knowing what they were!

XV

At least the old man was right in one of his prophecies, for I was on the road the following morning. It was not a picturesque road; the same desolate stretch of semi-desert which by this time was to me synonymous with the Tunisian countryside. To the west the dark mountains of the Matmatas appeared vaguely through the heat haze. Near at hand were reminders of the stern affairs of the day, for I passed many concrete forts and belts of barbed wire.

At Mareth I was at the place whence the defensive system of southern Tunis takes its name. It is a military encampment of some size—the native village is negligible. Here were troops of all arms, French and colonial. The principal problem is that of sustenance, for the palms and eucalyptus trees of the oasis make no more than half-hearted efforts at survival. There are water-holes, even a tiny stream, except when it is dried up—but the garrison depends on huge artificial systems which hold vast reserves of water. The transport of the camp included hundreds of tankers—some for petrol, others for water.

It was obvious that I was now in a military district. There were frequent barriers across the road: the police were courteous enough, but the lengthy enquiries about my purpose in making such an unusual journey wasted a lot of time. I was tempted to wish that I had accepted the offer of a general letter of introduction from the Residency. Then I had a brain-wave: from my pack I drew out a ragged piece of newspaper—my interview in the *Dépêche Tunisienne*. After that there were no more interrogations, but the hospitality was just as lengthy.

At the little town of Metameur I rubbed my eyes in wonder: then passed on to neighbouring Médinine, to confirm that I was not dreaming. Such strange places I never saw. The dwelling-places of Matmatas were unconventional enough: a street in Médinine is like a picture of a gnome's palace in an old fairy story-book.

When a man of Médinine decided to marry, he built himself a house. It was no elaborate structure: rather like a large barrel, with one side flattened out for a floor: or the Nissen hut, beloved of the Army, reduced to minute dimensions—say, eight feet high, eight feet across, and ten feet deep: or, if the bridegroom were particularly energetic, a few feet bigger. This was his *ghorfa*.

As his family grew, he built another one by the side of its first. Then, as he prospered, a storehouse was necessary, so he built a third *ghorfa* over and between the first two. By this time the houses of his neighbours were beginning to crowd in upon him: any further extension must be upwards. So long streets of *ghorfas* were formed, in irregular piles, the most extraordinary streets in the world; street upon street, back to back—they are called an *agglomeration*, which is a very descriptive word.

The best examples I found were within the ancient walls of the *kasba*: some, indeed, used the walls as their rear protection. I hung about long enough to be invited inside. Primitive they may be, crudely furnished they certainly are, but the people who live in them are not paupers. I climbed the precarious stairways to the granaries above: they were well filled: a man who could live simply would never starve.

Médinine is an important military centre, and a large camp adjoins the town. The medley of skins was remarkable. The Tunisian is not colour-conscious. Skins range from the almost pure white of the well-bred Arab to the jettest black of the negro. Yet all are esteemed as men.

At Médinine I was in the heart of the fortified area of Tunisia. Dictators can scarcely grumble if people take them at their word. Mussolini made no secret of his aspirations in Tunis, and France took the necessary precautions. The French system of defences in Tunis was founded on a sound principle of resistance, with mobile forces available for instant counter-attack.

Any Italian advance from Libya must of necessity depend upon roads. Light patrols can make desert forays, but the supplies for an army of any size can only be assured by road—there is no railway in the southern two hundred miles of Tunis. The passable roads of the district are scanty.

To the Libyan frontier there is only one, abutting the coast. Here is a spit of land only four miles wide, between the sea and Sebha el Bregat, a brackish lake. The isthmus is commanded by the fort of Alouet el Gounna, the first obstacle the Italians would have to face.

It is only an outpost, and unlikely to hold out indefinitely. The next line of resistance is twenty miles west—the oasis of Ben Gardane. The field-works skirt the oasis itself, with barbed-wire entanglements, trenches, pill-boxes, and anti-tank rails. The capture of Ben Gardane would be essential to any Italian expedition, if only to secure its water supplies.

The next obstacle is the desert: fifty miles of trackless country, with scarcely a spring: at the end of its exhausting passage, harassed from the air and flanks, are the Mareth Lines, the main defensive position. At first they were called the Daladier Lines, after the statesman who initiated them, but the local name has stuck.

The outposts are at Médinine, a considerable garrison town, the most important road junction of southern Tunis. Even in its Arab days its strength was famous. Now it is strongly fortified: and even if the passage were forced, there is worse to come.

The main Mareth Lines are yet another fifty miles to the north, with but a single road about which an invading army could move. Here is a perfect defensive position—another isthmus, less than twenty miles wide, between the Matmata mountains and the sea. The defensive system is intensely strong, approaching European standards. To an army that has necessarily travelled light over a hundred miles of desert Mareth would prove more than formidable.

The coastal plain, of dried sand with thin scrub, is strongly entrenched. Rails and deep pits form the principal obstacles to tanks, while infantry and cavalry are held up by barbed wire covered by loose surface sand—a devastating obstacle. There are frequent pill-boxes, and occasionally the contour of the ground is adaptable to the construction of a substantial fort on the Maginot pattern. I found that the desert lends itself to camouflage, and many of the brown forts are indistinguishable at a few hundred yards—or from the air!

Mareth is the centre of the defensive system, and apart from the garrison there is a strong field force for instant counter-attack. Yet just as important is Ain Tounine, on the edge of the Matmatas, gaunt desert mountains. Here is a great entrenched camp of overwhelming strength, the guns of its rock-hewn forts completely commanding the coastal plain. This is a defensive position which would be first-class in any land, for the Matmatas rise suddenly from the plain, a dark wall of forbidding strength. From Ain Tounine to Foum Tatahoiune in the south runs the defensive flank of the Mareth Lines. To the west is roadless desert country, only passable to small patrols.

I was impressed by the quality of the troops, both French and colonial. I believe that the Mareth Lines would have been impregnable except under two conditions, both unlikely to be realized.

If the native population favoured an invading army, then the French position would of course be serious. But I have emphasized the anti-Italian feeling among the Arab population. There is nothing but scorn for the Italian residents. They are as unpopular in Tunis as are the Jews with the Arabs of Palestine.

The second condition assumes that the Italians could gain command of the adjacent seas. The one main road of advance is never far from the coast, and no army could hope for success unless its fleet commanded the sea. This was unlikely, to say the least, while the French and British fleets commanded the Mediterranean. Command of the sea would be necessary for the transport of reinforcements—Italy would scarcely have expected to conquer Tunis with the forces at present in Libya!

There remained, of course, the 'Fifth Column' danger, among the Italians resident in Tunis. By no means all of these are friends of Mussolini, however: the French could be trusted to deal with any serious disaffection.

The French collapse is more than a tragedy. In Africa they held strong positions, and could have held them for years against any attacks the Italians were likely to develop. It is painful to consider that the Mareth Lines should be surrendered without a blow.

I made my duty call on the Military Controller at

Médinine. He lavished permission to travel wherever I willed. The country was free and quiet, he emphasized— but elementary precautions were necessary. As a traveller I had nothing to fear, he declared, except that I would be wise to avoid travel by night. The roving Bedouin are apt to be less restrained—and he made a pleasant gesture, indicative of cutting my throat. I assured him that I had no urge for nocturnal voyaging.

Nor, if the next stretch were indicative, had I any overwhelming desire for travel by day. The road moved lazily over low ridges, pitilessly exposed to the burning sun. Again I felt that hot wind from the south. The streams shown on the map had disappeared into their beds of sand. In the first three hours I passed but one water-hole, where a couple of Arabs were watering their camels. The liquid was so foul that even my hardened stomach rejected it.

I plodded wearily onward, wondering why on earth I had come to Tunis. What scenery! I had left the grandeur of the Alps and the charm of Corsica for a bare expanse of hard sand, sun-baked and lifeless. Suddenly the breeze changed its direction. It was now facing me, and gathering in strength. Yet I willingly granted the additional labour involved in facing a cool wind from the sea. Within ten minutes of my arrival at Zarzis I was sitting on a sandy beach, with little waves breaking over my head.

Zarzis was a very modest little place, but heavenly after the desert. There was running water there—you could bend down and scoop it up to drink. The Arab houses are neat and tidy. Practically all of them are modern, for Zarzis has been developed since the French occupation. The local tribe, called Accara, are hard-working, and the place now flourishes. True, agriculture is easy, for there are artesian wells giving a formidable flow. A giant cistern in the middle of the market place provides for bad seasons.

There were three Englishmen at Zarzis. I had heard of them all over Tunis, mentioned mysteriously, as if they were engaged on some secret mission. Actually I found that they were making a colour film of the French colonial army. I hope they got it completed and marketed while the subject was still topical, for they had gone to great trouble and expense to get the real thing—so many of these films are genial fakes.

The road turned abruptly to the north-west: eventually it ran into the sea. I pushed George on to a little ferry boat, which chugged across five miles of sea. The Arab captain pointed to ancient piles in the water alongside his course—the remains of a Roman causeway. The water was shallow: even our little boat had to make a detour to reach the further quay.

Yet there was a new atmosphere as we walked ashore: a gentle coolness we had not known for many days, a greenery restful to the eye, a people prosperous and unhurried. For this was Djerba, the Island of the Lotus Eaters.

XVI

Compared with the Isle of Wight, Djerba is not wildly exciting from the scenic point of view. Compared with the mainland of Tunis it is astounding. All over the country they rave of the beauty of Djerba's 'gardens' —which are not flower gardens, but colossal fields, green and fertile. Exotic trees flourish on every hand: mingled with them strangely are the hardier trees of the north. "You have but to stretch out your fist, and ripe fruit falls into it," declared a satisfied Arab.

The peoples of Djerba are tribes apart. The European

R

population is insignificant, but there are about forty-five thousand Arabs and five thousand Jews. The Arabs for centuries have lived detached from their fellows in Tunis. They follow one of the stricter Moslem creeds, the *ouahabites* or *ibadites*, a puritan sect akin to that of the Berbers of Mzab in Morocco. The Djerbans are hard workers, and their fertile island is intensely cultivated. There are one million two hundred thousand palms and five hundred thousand olive trees in the island—a mere twenty miles by twenty.

The houses were miniature, but neat and tidy. In the first village I halted: here was a strange procession. Men and boys were carrying women's clothes, proudly displayed: the most intimate garments were included, and two stalwart Arabs stalked along the road arraying between them a pair of knickers, flourished like a banner. I satisfied my curiosity: this was a bride's trousseau on exhibition—there was to be a wedding.

I followed the procession round to the house. The feast proper had not yet begun, but I was taken in to see the bride. Her feet and hands were bandaged; enclosed within the wrappings were preparations to make them soft and beautiful. Twice a day maids of honour sponged her body with sweet scents. The week preceding her wedding sees the grandest hours of an Arab girl's life—the only time she holds the centre of the stage. She is dressed up like a decorated doll. Married girls come to whisper to her details of the wonders in store. The bridegroom's friends come to admire and approve, and return to give her advice: if my informants were to be believed, of startling frankness. Great store was set on the opinion of men who had earned a suitable reputation, as a veterinary surgeon might have done. Their advice on the bridal hour was eagerly sought by the anxious bridegroom, even if he himself should be a man of experience in love.

"Come back in four days!" exclaimed the bride's

father. "That is the time of the marriage. We shall celebrate the Feast of the Entrance well. My daughter is a virgin, and her husband will be pleased, so everyone will be happy."

I promised to return if I were still in Djerba. The Feast of the Entrance sounded tempting, but in four days I ought to be well south, near the Libyan frontier. At last I decided to stay the night. Even the preliminary ceremonies were interesting. Local musicians came in, and played strange music. There was some dancing, and a wail which passed as singing. Then a *caid* addressed the girl: his discourse, I found when it was translated, was on the subject of her duty to bear children for her husband: men-children especially.

The *caid* was evidently much esteemed, for everybody listened attentively—his advice to the bride on the conception of children was by no means confidential. Later I talked with him: he spoke gravely even on the lightest subject, and quoted so freely from the Koran that I never knew whether I was listing to Mohammed's words or his own. In the course of ten minutes his conversation produced a whole string of maxims, intended for the benefit of the bride and bridegroom. I made a note of those I could remember later:

"A man with two tongues is like two men."

"Don't be too rigid or you may break yourself. Nor too supple, or you will be eaten (i.e. not esteemed)."

"The fear of God is the beginning of wisdom."

"Make a thousand friends, but never forget your first friend."

"Respect yourself and you will be respected."

"A true friend is only known in bad times."

"A married man already possesses the half of his religion." (The bride liked this one.)

"Listen to him who makes you cry, never to him who makes you laugh."

"The believer does good in weeping; the infidel does evil in laughing."

I had a long chat with the bridegroom, a man of thirty-five or so. He was very pleased with his prospective bride.

"Quite a bargain," he whispered. "Her father is an old friend of mine, and let me have her for three hundred francs!"

"She is—er—somewhat younger than you are," I suggested hesitantly.

"Of course. She is only sixteen."

"You like your wives to be young?"

"Naturally. Who doesn't? Besides, we lay great store on virginity. There is a much better chance of a girl being a virgin at sixteen than at twenty-six, is there not?"

I could not think of the answer to that one!

He took me outside to point out the marriage sign on the door of the house: a tree, crudely painted in white-wash, to symbolize life and fertility.

"It is a great pity that you cannot wait until the Feast of the Entrance," he reiterated.

"What happens?"

"Well, for a week my bride will have been prepared—many ceremonial bathings, and anointments with herbs and scents. On the evening of the seventh day, dressed in her bridal clothes, she is brought to my home. Women look after her while I and my friends go for the marriage service."

"She does not go?"

"Of course not! She may not enter the mosque. Her father answers for her. There is music in the procession, and more music in the home, and plenty to eat and drink. We shall be merry."

"I thought intoxicants were forbidden to the faithful?"

"So they are. But we shall still be merry. Then I

shall be seated on a throne, and my bride will be led to me, blindfold."

"Why?"

"So that the folds may be removed, and I may be smitten with her beauty."

"But you have seen her before?"

"Of course. I knew her when she was a baby. But now I shall see her in a new light. The guests will line the staircase, singing in joy, as I lead her to the nuptial couch. Then the music ceases; the guests sip coffee, and wait."

"How long?"

"Oh, I shall not keep them long! I am a man, and though my bride is young and a virgin, she is well grown, as you see—mark her shapely breasts, a sure sign. There is a great moment of rejoicing as I open the door and throw out the bride's shirt, for them all to see. They will wave it as a flag, glorying over its stains. Then the real Feast of the Entrance will begin—oh, I wish you could stay! I have only known it twice before—and I am much better off this time!"

XVII

In the morning I wandered on to Houmt Souk, the principal town of the island. I duly reported to the Military Governor, who invited me to dinner that evening. After I had lunched in the local hotel, I doubly appreciated his invitation. It was run by a Maltese woman who was friendly enough, but the world's worst cook.

There was ample time to explore the island. Houmt Souk has a harbour for fishing vessels, including spongers. Close by is a *kasbah*, a stone fortress, which was not Arab in origin, but Spanish: here, indeed, was one of the coastal settlements during the brief Spanish occupation.

The *souks* of Houmt Souk were fascinating: you would expect that from the name of the town, which is a corruption of Houmet Es Souk, the market place.   In the bigger towns I had seen artisans making saddles and shoes: here was more delicate work—the weaving of cotton cloths and fine silks, and the making of jewellery.

I bought a bracelet from a stout Arab who squatted in his box-like workshop.   There was no long argument as to price—he produced an antique balance and weighed the thing, and charged by the weight.   It was garish and very Eastern, intended as a present for a bride; yet it did not lack beauty.   I also bought a length of silk. In Houmt Souk its colour seemed moderate enough, but back in England its purple was so vivid that I had to search long for a lady bold enough to wear it.

Everything is miniature in Djerba.   The *souks* are a small edition of those of Tunis, but far more interesting and intimate: trades that have been pursued a thousand years in ancient narrow covered streets.   The mosques are small, sometimes so low that a neighbouring palm overshadows them: but they are dainty and picturesque.

Most interesting building on the island is the *ghriba*, 'the marvellous', near Hara Srira.   The Jews of Djerba are a remarkable tribe.   They are descended from a few families who escaped from Jerusalem at the time of the Babylonian captivity, and have scarcely changed their speech, costume, or habits.   There has been little intermixing with the local Arab population.   In Tunis the Jews are scattered, but in Djerba most of them live in three or four villages, plying ancient trades.   Centre of their area is the *ghriba*, the wonderful synagogue.

It is certainly a remarkable place.   On one side of the road is a great hostel for pilgrims, a giant caravanserai about a courtyard lined with delicate arcades.   Opposite is the synagogue: not imposing externally, but full of surprises within. Its woodwork is fine, and it has an atmosphere of dignity.

Sitting on its benches were a group of ancient Israelites who might have stepped straight out of the pages of the Old Testament. They were dutifully reading the Talmud, but willingly agreed to stay put for a time exposure, and then demanded financial compensation. I do not believe that the Talmud teaches this: it must be an instinct otherwise inherited.

Outside, a dozen men were squatting on the great stones. A debate was in progress: it moved spasmodially. Sometimes there would pass long moments of contemplation, followed by an intense babel of conflicting voices.

XVIII

Where did the lotus-eating come in? To judge by the countryside most of the people of Djerba worked. I decided at length that the ease of the water supply gave the island its legendary character of ease: no one who does not know the desert can appreciate water. There are ample water-holes, supplying sweet water. What is more, intense human labour is not necessary to gain the precious fluid. A camel is harnessed to the winding-gear of the well, and marches stolidly down a long runway. Bucket after bucket of fresh water comes hurtling to the surface, to trickle about the neighbouring 'gardens' or cultivated fields behind their walls of dried mud.

In one village there were potters at work. Their designs had scarcely changed in a thousand years. I would have bought some, but another hundred miles of desert had still to be traversed to the Libyan frontier. I could carry jewels and silk, but not pottery.

On every hand were huge enclosed cisterns, holding

large reserves of water in case the wells should dry. There may be something in this lotus-eating, I thought, as I lazed on the warm sand under the shade of a palm, refreshed after a cooling swim: by my side trickled a little stream of clear water. I never knew that I could get so excited about water!

When I returned to Houmt Souk, there were signs of great activity in the streets. Soldiers were rushing about, and native carts were concentrated with military lorries. I made my way to the commandant's quarters: I was ready for my dinner.

"I am afraid I shall have to ask you to put up with a rough snack," he said. "You have heard the news, of course?"

"No."

"Hitler has made a pact with Stalin!"

It hit me like a blow: the one thing in Europe I had feared.

My host was talking of his orders—he was moving at once to the Libyan frontier. I scarcely heard him.

"Well, at least we know where we are," he concluded.

"Yes, at least we know where we are. This means war, of course."

"Of course! It is just a question of the date. And as to Italy, well——"

"Colonel," I broke in. "I must get back to England at once. I have a job to do there."

"I thought you would say that! But I'm afraid you'll have to stay here for a couple of days. I've had to commandeer all the transport in the island. When I'm in position, I'll send back a car to take you to Gabès."

Two days lotus-eating, with the shadow of war over Europe! It was unthinkable.

"I have a bicycle," I said.

"But it would take you two or three days to ride to Gabès—you would gain nothing."

"Wait! There is only one train a day from Gabès to Tunis, I believe?"

"Yes—at six o'clock in the evening."

"I'm going to catch to-morrow night's train!"

"But that's impossible—you would have to ride all night!" he protested.

"I'm going to ride all night."

He thought for a moment. "Normally I would forbid it," he said. "The country is quiet, but if you met wandering Bedouin by night—well, they sometimes forget. You never know whether they will cut your throat or give you a meal. No, I ought not to let you go. Still, I suppose we shall all be taking risks within a few days, so I can scarcely forbid you from beginning now. Come to my office: I'll give you a pass."

He did more than that. He gave me a couple of motor cyclists to conduct me to the ferry at Ajim. They were more than useful, for the ferryman had gone to bed, and didn't want to get up. He grumbled that I would have to pay double fare. As this only amounted to one franc twenty centimes, I was happy to agree. I even added an extra franc, and his sleepy scowls turned rapidly into beams of friendship.

He landed me at a tiny hamlet, without sign of life; but there was a road; I climbed to the top of the cliff, and in the faint pre-moonlight surveyed its interminable length. I ran rapidly over George. By the map it was a good fifty miles to the next house; George must not let me down, in the desert by night.

We had put in a tolerably busy day, but his tyres swished easily over the surfaced road. There is a great charm in riding by night, but here it was eerie. About me was the vast desolation of the desert: such a silence I never knew. Even the noise of a corncrake would have been welcome in this deathly stillness.

At first I thought only of conservation of energy, driving

George forward at solid speed. But I could not keep my mind from the tragedy overhanging Europe. What kind of pact had Hitler made with Stalin? The commandant had no details—just a 'pact'. Surely not a military alliance! If so, we faced a stiff proposition. Yet how could people who had called each other liars and murderers suddenly become friends, even if they were dictators? Did Stalin want to plunge Europe into war, so as to spread his creed in the subsequent days of chaos and weakness? Was it really a clever plan for the ultimate downfall of Hitler and the raising of a communist Germany? Or was Stalin afraid of Hitler, anxious to turn his aggression into other directions? It was galling to be away from news at such a moment. So I pedalled harder: I must get to Gabès and Tunis; thence I could fly to France and England.

I skidded violently and fell abruptly. The wind had blown a loose layer of sand over the road. I felt my elbow bleeding, yet I would not halt—the urge would not let me.

The silence was oppressive: the time came when I must halt, for energy must be conserved. Yet I could not rest. I scarcely dared to sit down, for there were scorpions at large. I wandered from the road: here was a stone pillar, offering secure repose.

To the south a strange silhouette appeared against the clear night sky. Despite my haste, curiosity urged me towards it. Here were massive ruins of a Roman city. Maybe the night exaggerated their majesty, but it was eerie to walk in the dreadful silence by noble columns and mighty walls of masonry. Why did these cities die?

By the light of my lamp I wandered between the giant pillars of the forum of ancient Gighti. Then extinguished the light and stood alone with antiquity, watching the faint moonlight stream through a colonnade where once an emperor walked: nearby was the site of a coliseum where Christians were flung to the lions.

The silence was oppressive. More than once I halted, to strain my ears for the slightest sound. The miles passed with weary monotony: two incidents then crowded together. First I heard a flapping overhead: a great shape hovered, then descended to earth beside the road: a giant vulture, awaiting the moment when I would fall by the roadside.

A slight dip increased my speed, and this intensified my next spill. I hit something which grunted. On consideration I think it was unreasonable for a camel to go to sleep in the middle of the road.

Away to the left something flashed in the moonlight. It might be a lake of brackish water, impossible to drink, but refreshing to the skin. Yet I could not find it, though I wandered far. Maybe it was not there.

I returned to the road and recovered George. But I did not mount: a sound had disturbed the silence of the desert. Never have I listened so keenly. At last it distinguished itself—the padding of a camel's hooves on the sand. So still was the night that even this muffled sound was heard from afar; many minutes passed before the camel approached.

I confess that I nearly turned George about and rode hard. These approachers would be wandering Bedouin. Would they cut my throat or offer me a meal? An interesting conjecture in the abstract, but one which I would willingly avoid. In a moment I was surrounded: swarthy faces, half hidden by the hoods of grey-striped *burnous*: curious eyes twinkling in the darkness.

At least I would get in first. I asked for water. Now came the anxious second: if they gave me water, they would not kill me. A woman fumbled with the packages on the camel, and brought a goatskin gourd. As she bent to pour out the water, her breast slipped through the rift in her robe.   She did not halt to push it back.

("Of course they did not harm you," said my Arab schoolmaster later.   "Only a madman would ride a bicycle across the desert by night—and a madman is sacred in the sight of Allah!")

I sang aloud as I pressed on.   The Bedouin encounter, now survived, was exhilarating.   The night air of the desert was thrilling after the enervating heat of the day. The breeze freshened.   Unfortunately, it began to drive the sand before it: the fierce particles bit into my skin.

A few miles further on I met more Bedouin.   A considerable tribe this time, but now I was confident.   At first they were suspicious.   They lighted a lamp, and held it to my face, while each man in turn passed me under close inspection.   The grunts evidently decided in my favour.   They brought me water and amazingly sour bread: I had to eat it, though it nearly made me sick.

A man of the family spoke simple French, and we squatted by the side of the road.   He rained questions on me, translating my replies to his eager questions.

"Where is your gun?" he asked.

"I have no gun," I admitted.

"What—you travel alone, with no gun!   You have not even one of those little guns which fires several bullets at once?"

"No."

"This is not right."   He turned to talk to an older man.   The woman began to fumble with one of the rough packages loaded on the camel's back.   By the spitting light of the lamp I saw an ancient Arab musket, beautifully inlaid.

"It is old, but it will still fire.   We can give you powder and bullets."

Another man got up and snatched the gun, and a violent argument broke out.   I did not understand a word, yet

Ghorfas at Médenine

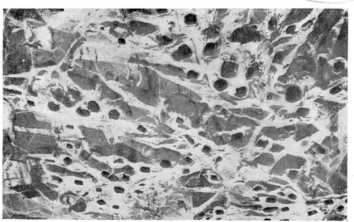

A Village in Matmata

JEWS OF DJERBA

A MOSQUE IN DJERBA

it was obvious what it was all about—a dispute as to the ownership of the gun. Now I had it in my hands, I coveted it: not as a lethal weapon, but as a wall ornament for my study. Evidently my first friend wanted to offer it as a gift, but I could scarcely accept it. If I bought it, that would presumably stop the row. But I had not the faintest idea how much it was worth. As I produced a hundred-franc note, however, the altercation immediately subsided into a hushed silence: a hundred francs is a lot of money to a nomad Bedouin. Gravely I handed it over: every man hastened to shake me by the hand.

The moment I left, the row began again—they now had to divide the hundred francs between them. Not until I was a mile down the road did I realize that I had come away without the promised powder and bullets. But I didn't go back: I didn't know how to load the musket anyhow, and it looked to me as dangerous from the back as the front.

I suppose the weight of the musket was about ten pounds. It seemed to double and treble as the long toiling hours passed.

Again a great silence as for another hour George plodded steadily forward. Why had I ever imagined that he would let me down? Despite the driving sand, his wheels moved with practised ease over the passable road. Only where the sand had blown over the road was he daunted: there followed more skids, cuts, and bruises.

A loud cry to halt startled the silence. Here was a military patrol of native soldiers. The commandant's pass satisfied them: I do not think they could read it, but the rubber stamp was reassuring. I was glad to see them. I must be approaching Médinine.

The rapid dawn was breaking as I passed by the town of *ghorfas*. I halted, and waited for a shop to open, for energy demands fuel. As I fed, I noticed streams of military transport pouring to the south. Evidently the

French were not merely going to sit back and let Mussolini attack the Mareth Lines.

Every few miles I was challenged as I passed to the north. Weariness developed as the sun gathered its cruel heat. Common sense suggested rest, but emotion urged me forward. When there is a threat abroad, instinct drives a man home.

I ascended the last desolate hill of red sand: the palmeries of Gabès were stretched at my feet. The sight was exhilarating. I was even prepared to thank Hitler and Stalin for prompting such a memorable ride. As I rode into the town I passed by the fortune-teller with his sand. I recollected with a shock that he was right—I had *not* reached my journey's end.

XIX

The daily train from Gabès to Tunis is an autorail. It covers four hundred and twenty-three kilometres in six hours, with twenty-eight stops, so it must move in between.

My partner in the little buffet—as the train consists of one large car, everything is miniature: the buffet seated only six people, but provided a good and inexpensive meal—was an Arab nationalist, a Destourien. An intelligent and educated man himself, he saw no reason why his people should be ruled by Europeans.

Yet a trivial incident as I boarded the train showed that his folk were not so advanced as he thought. I asked the railway clerk for a ticket for George. "Five francs, and something for me!" he replied.

From Djerba to Tunis in twenty-four hours was no mean feat. As it turned out, my energy was wasted. I had wired ahead to reserve a place in the daily aeroplane, only to find that it was now under military jurisdiction, and filled with officers returning on duty. It was galling to hang about for two days, waiting for a boat.

At least it gave me the opportunity to see Tunis. I could never tire of the *souks*, with their slow-moving vignettes of Arab commercial life. I wired to the school-master of Sidi-Bou-Said to come in and join me. Together we did some shopping, and with his expert help I got some bargains. It was Saturday, and the Jewish shops were closed.

The Great Mosque was of course forbidden to me: it is a place of size and age—founded in 732. Like many Moslem religious edifices, its services are also educational, and it houses a university of some importance.

The narrow streets flow out from the Great Mosque in all directions and in a confusing irregular pattern. I found that if you kept on going you were bound to strike one of the ancient gateways in the wall. Arab Tunis has now far outgrown the older limits, and there are consider-able suburbs outside the walls. I liked best the Hal-fouine, where a market flanked a picturesque mosque. The vegetables offered for sale were wholesome enough, but the meat was appalling.

Part of the little place was given up to amusement. Here was an old man plying one of the oldest trades in the world: story-telling. By the crowd about him, he knew his job. In another corner were acrobats—good acrobats, too: any circus proprietor knows that Arabs make good performers.

We wandered through the European quarter to the Belvedere Park, interesting in itself because of its variety of sub-tropical plants and trees, but commanding a fine view of Tunis, backed by blue mountains: between the city and the hills was an ancient Arab fort on a site of rare strength: it is still in use.

Yet the pride of Tunis is the Bardo Museum. The Bardo is the old residence of the Bey, and its sumptuous spacious halls show that he maintained a state equal to that of a European prince.   It is more than a palace; it is a fortified park with many edifices, some of dignity and beauty.   There are considerable barracks within the grounds.

The harem of the Bey's residence is now devoted to a famous museum, housing many of the treasures of Punic and Roman Tunis—especially of Carthage.   Many of the mosaics were remarkable: some of them came from ancient tombs, marvellously preserved.   So was the statuary.   A relief of Adam and Eve had weathered somewhat, but the serpent was still remarkably lifelike.   Particularly interesting, too, were specimens of the earliest Christian ideas of the Virgin and Child.   Other outstanding specimens —to my mind, that is: I have no expert knowledge and only a modestly developed taste—represented the sacrifice of Abraham, Jesus and the Samaritan woman at the well, and other religious subjects.   Even more artistic were the Phœnician remains, fewer in number, but revealing a high civilization.   And at least I was glad to confirm that my lamp and coins were not fakes.

I began to question the schoolmaster delicately on the subject of harems.   Yes, there were still plenty of men who had more than one wife, he said: it was all a question of cash.   Not many men could afford more than one. An hour later he nudged me violently.   Three veiled women passed in an ancient landau: on the driver's box was a very stout man with an elaborate black moustache. Here was a flash-back to older times—the eunuch taking his master's wives for an airing.

Generally, each wife of a harem has a separate household: as the husband of a plural marriage is generally wealthy, this is usually possible.   The women seldom squabble, but live happily together.   The senior wife holds a position of respect.   It is quite a common thing for a barren woman to urge her husband to take a young girl as his second wife. The first retains the prime position in the ménage. I recalled a wise and wealthy man I once met in Morocco: he had the maximum of four wives, but he not only maintained a separate household for each, but planted them in different towns. He claimed that the whole five were ideally happy!

XX

Tunis was fascinating, even after my glimpses of the cities of the south. Yet my atmosphere was heavy with apprehension, and in the cool of the evening I called on the editor of *Dépêche Tunisienne* to get the latest news. It was ominous: more 'incidents' on the Polish-German frontier, a quickening of tension everywhere. I gave him my superficial impressions of Tunis, and my ideas about Germany and Italy. In one respect at least I was right and he was wrong: I did not believe that Italy would enter the conflict until Mussolini was convinced that Germany was going to win.

There was an annoying incident as I left Tunis—a customs examination. What is more, I had to pay duty on all my purchases, although I was going to France. If I had to pay in England as well, my bargains were likely to prove very expensive! The climax was reached when they made me pay duty on my inlaid Arab musket. When I protested, the official declared that he was already doing me a favour in that he did not insist that I should take out a firearm licence for it! Maybe it was lucky that I did forget to bring my supply of powder and bullets.

The boat touched at Bizerta, the most European town in Tunis. Its naval port presented an animated scene, as French warships joyously prepared to give battle to

s

the Italians. The native town is small in interest compared with Tunis, but there is one unusual quarter, populated by descendants of Moors driven from Spain four hundred years ago. Nearby is the old Arab port, dirty and smelly: canals flank the native town, giving some picturesque corners. But ports are seldom places to stay at.

I had thought to make a leisurely voyage, to make up for long arrears of sleep. Yet the news forbade repose: and, as soon as I had planted myself in a deck chair, a strange thing happened. Two French officers sat beside me, addressed me by name and began to talk European affairs. Soon other people joined them; as one group dissolved, another formed. Everybody seemed to know me: I ought to have been flattered, but wanted a nap even more.

The mystery was soon solved. At Bizerta, after the night's voyage from Tunis, a boy had come aboard with newspapers, brought more rapidly by train. And another long interview with me appeared in the *Dépêche Tunisienne*. There was even a black smudge alleged to be a photograph, in which my bare knees were the only recognizable features.

The boat pursued a tortuous path, escorted by a destroyer: war was at hand. The direct crossing passes close by Sardinia: instead, we followed the coast to Algeria before striking across the Mediterranean.

Marseilles was a whirl of activity. French mobilization had been proclaimed—the third time in a year. Reservists thronged the railway station. Their spirit was dour. But I wondered as I saw a group of communists dragged off by the police, yelling defiance.

When I arrived in England, the atmosphere was calmer, but more determined. We are not a people to be easily rattled, and show at our best when facing a grim situation. Five days later we were at war.

In spite of this, for a brief moment at Marseilles I forgot the impending catastrophe. For as I walked from the boat, soft arms entwined themselves about my neck, and I gazed at close range into the eager eyes of Marie Therese.

"I am glad you sent me a postcard," she said. "I would not have liked you to have been alone in Marseilles. It has a certain reputation—the girls are not at all bashful. So I came to take care of you."

"And Emma."

"She is not here."

"Good. I could not bear to hear 'I told you so' just now."

Marie Therese was disappointed to hear that I must leave for Paris by the night train. We had a few brief hours in the southern sun, but the uncertainty in the air affected even the repose of Marie Therese. At the station, where some men cried excitedly in intoxicated patriotism, women wept as they said good-bye. Marie Therese wept in sympathy, thinking of those who would not come back.

XXI

This had not been one of our longest journeys, I pointed out to George—a mere two thousand five hundred kilometres on the road. He insisted legitimately that mountain and desert ought to count double: I would have agreed that those miles through the burning *sirocco* deserve a treble allowance.

As usual, George had borne me faithfully. Alpine snows and desert heat came alike to him, and my travelling expenses for the journey proper were precisely nil: we had not even had a puncture. Nor had the trip proved expensive. Calculations proved that on the average I was well within my allowance of five shillings a day.

Dutifully I reported to the doctor. He gravely examined my heart, pulse and blood-pressure, then beamed upon me.

"Wonderful!" he said. "I told you that if you took things very quietly for two or three months you would right that heart. It is remarkable—now you are as sound as a bell. You must have followed the treatment with admirable restraint. Now I could perhaps allow you to ride your bicycle again—short distances at first, mind, and walk uphill!"

I hadn't the heart to undeceive him: he meant so well. Yet when the day comes when I may not wander, I shall not need a heart.

Who would not travel, when you can see and feel so much for so little? Five fascinating phases of experience remained with me. The sturdy land of Alsace-Lorraine, so soon to know turmoil and tragedy. I shudder to think of Nazi heels stamping the enlightened pavements of Strasbourg. Or will Strasbourg overwhelm the Nazis? And the grand valleys of Savoy—how will they react to the raised hand of Fascism if defeated France is forced to sever her mountain provinces? I cannot believe that reaction could flourish in that stolid region. Mountains are the places of freedom: it is only in cities that men become slaves.

The blue skies of the Riviera are dulled by black clouds from the east, but the fighting spirit of Corsica is untamed. Here is a place where freedom shrieks to be heard. The proud Corsican spirit might tolerate a fierce discipline— but not from Italy. Why should free men be handed over like flocks of sheep?

Tunis comes under a different category, since France is there primarily for her own interests. Yet on the whole she has done well for the land—even the nationalists admit that, comparing her administration with the tyranny of Italian rule in Libya. The Destouriens are apprehensive to-day. From France they could in time hope for liberty: from Fascist Italy they know that they would be condemned to a new slavery.

We have witnessed one of the greatest tragedies in history: proud, spirited, courageous France collapsing after a single blow. If the people in high places had had the spirit of their men, then the blow would have been parried. France might have been overrun, but if the French fleet, air force, and a quarter of a million men had withdrawn to Tunis, Italy might have been knocked out of the war in two months.

Worst blow of all to those who love France is the spectacle as I write: of French deputies acquiescing weakly in the establishment of a Fascist state, in the vain hope of securing easier terms from their masters. Liberty, equality and brotherhood are to disappear from the official life of France; but they cannot be driven by decree from the souls of the people. To-day the mind of France is dazed and bruised, but a spirit cannot be killed.

In Britain our spirit survives, undaunted by reverses—indeed, heightened by adversity. Ours is a great mission: to bring liberty back to Europe: and then to save France from herself.

INDEX